UNITED
NATION

Frank Connolly is one of Ireland's most distinguished investigative journalists. His previous books include *NAMA-Land* (2017) and *Tom Gilmartin* (2014), both published by Gill Books. He has also published a novel, *A Conspiracy of Lies* (Mercier, 2019). He is Head of Communications at SIPTU and lives in Dublin.

Also by Frank Connolly

The Christy Moore Songbook (ed.)

*Tom Gilmartin: The man who brought down a Taoiseach and exposed
the greed and corruption at the heart of Irish politics today*

*NAMA-Land: The inside story of Ireland's property sell-off
and the creation of a new elite*

A Conspiracy of Lies

UNITED NATION

THE CASE FOR INTEGRATING IRELAND

FRANK CONNOLLY

Best wishe

Frank

Gill Books

Gill Books
Hume Avenue
Park West
Dublin 12
www.gillbooks.ie

Gill Books is an imprint of M.H. Gill and Co.

978 07171 9056 0

Design and print origination by O'K Graphic Design, Dublin
Edited by Michelle Griffin and Jane Rogers
Proofread by Ciara McNee
Indexed by Eileen O'Neill

Printed by CPI Group (UK) Ltd, Croydon CR0 4YY.
This book is typeset in 11/17 pt Minion.

A CIP catalogue record for this book is available from the British Library.

5 4 3 2 1

For my beautiful grandkids, Alannah, Rían, Fiadh, Van and Bodhi, whose generation can finally achieve our great hope of cherishing all the children of the nation equally.

ACKNOWLEDGEMENTS

It would take too long to thank all of those who contributed their time and energy to this work. I am especially grateful to those who participated in usually very lengthy interviews, sometimes more than once, and who are identified in the following pages. For others who are not included for various reasons – of space, relevance or because their words did not fit the narrative as it evolved during the writing – I am eternally thankful. Among many, I would like to mention Andree Murphy, Dr Bill Rolston, Robert Ballagh, Declan Kiberd, Gerry Adams, Rev. Gary Mason, Miriam Murphy, Frances Black, Brian Feeney, Trevor Birney, Peter Shirlow, Mike Tomlinson, Conor McGinn, Helga and Chuck Feeney, Jim O'Callaghan, Mark Daly, Brian Carty, Theo Dorgan, Ursula Barry, Paddy Cullivan, Seán Ó hUiginn, Peter Bunting, Tim Pat Coogan, Dr Illona Duffy, Mairéad Farrell, Rita O'Hare and Martin Mansergh.

There are many others who assisted with the preparation and production of this work and who deserve my thanks, including Deirdre Nolan, Rachel Thompson, Michelle Griffin, Seán Hayes, Claire O'Flynn and Teresa Daly of Gill Books.

My daughters, Síomha and Liadh, did invaluable work in transcribing the recorded interviews, and made insightful suggestions throughout the project. My partner, Mary, provided me with ideas and advice on numerous drafts, and the patience and love to sustain the long, and at times arduous, research, inquiry and writing that went into this book. My thanks also to my other children, Oisín, Saoirse and Caomhán Connolly, who assisted and encouraged me on this journey.

PREFACE

I n August 2020, in the early stages of this project, I met with the late poet, Thomas Kinsella, at his home in Booterstown, County Dublin. At 92 years of age, the translator of the Táin and the writer of 'Butcher's Dozen', his scathing response to the Widgery Report on Bloody Sunday in Derry in 1972, had much to say about the growing debate on a united Ireland. He was adamant that it would not happen.

'The Unionist people are different. Planted in Ulster for half a millennium; growing their roots still,' Kinsella said in an interview with me. He could imagine 'nothing more manageable than the present arrangement with the Good Friday Agreement. A documentary of their difference'. During two hours of discussion, which covered what he has described as the 'dual tradition' in Ireland, Kinsella spoke of the fundamental difference between the culture and poetry of the Gael and that of the planter.

'Ireland was the closest of England's colonies, and the most thoroughly civilized,' Kinsella wrote in his 1995 book *The Dual Tradition*. 'The mechanics of colonialism were tested in Ireland and the stages recorded in Irish literature, in both languages. It is one of the findings of Ireland's dual tradition that an empire is a passing thing, but that a colony is not.'

He was unmoved by the argument that demographic, political and economic change, and the decision of the UK to leave the EU in 2016, had altered the landscape. He was not convinced that the conditions were approaching when a majority of people in the North might choose to break the union and join a new and united Ireland through referendums, north and south, as envisaged in the Belfast or Good Friday Agreement (GFA). One of our greatest poets, Kinsella died 16 months after our discussion, in December 2021.

His arguments and analysis are important and will resonate with many readers. They help to explain why so many of the Protestant and unionist culture in the North remain steadfast in their deep hostility to constitutional change, even while their communities, their politics and their allegiances are under siege as never before. Now, many of those who previously supported unionist parties are drifting towards new ideas as the political and cultural winds of change across the island are sweeping away old certainties.

It is unsurprising that most unionist politicians, at least in public, do not wish to engage in the discussion about what a united Ireland might look like. By definition, they are part of the greater union and intend to remain so, even as that relationship is fraying at its edges, with an independent Scotland a real prospect in the coming years. For this book, I have engaged with influential figures in the unionist community who are open to discussion about Irish unity, but are also concerned that their identity, traditions and rights are respected in any such process, as guaranteed in the GFA. They have openly discussed the prospect and potential benefits of a united Ireland, and their views are widely shared among others whose traditional allegiance was to Britain but who are reluctant to declare their shifting position publicly. Many voted to 'remain' in the Brexit vote, and have since withdrawn their political support from the larger unionist parties.

These voters, along with many others who define themselves as neither unionist nor nationalist, and who are open to the idea of a new, inclusive and integrated Ireland, will be decisive in the forthcoming unity referendums. They wish to regain their citizenship of the EU – while retaining their British or Irish citizenships, or both.

In our discussion for this book in early January 2022, President

Michael D. Higgins said that it is now accepted that both societies that emerged from partition on the island were flawed and failed to deliver equality for all of their citizens. He argued that 'the oppression of the minority nationalist community in housing, employment and basic civil rights formed a different, but no less undemocratic and unequal, society in the North. Neither state had as its primary purpose providing for the wellbeing of all its citizens on an inclusive basis.'

Within the nationalist community[1] there is a growing momentum for constitutional change, intensified in recent years by the UK's exit from the EU and the possibility of a return to a hard border on the island. The nationalist community in the North is no longer a minority and is determined to exercise its right to self-determination, a promise delivered by the GFA. The Agreement provides for referendums, North and South, with the decision based on a 50 plus 1 majority in each. The economic, demographic and political changes that have occurred in both the North and the South since the GFA was endorsed in May 1998 – accelerated by the trauma of Brexit – have ensured that the decision will capture, if not dominate, the political agenda over the coming years.

In November 2018, along with 1,000 other journalists, artists, trade union and community activists, people in health, education, business and sports across the country, I signed an open letter to the Taoiseach, Leo Varadkar, asking him to ensure that the rights of nationalists in the North were protected as the prospect of a 'no deal' Brexit loomed. I subsequently participated in meetings and discussions of Ireland's Future in its growing campaign for a citizens' assembly and preparations for a unity referendum as it gained traction at home and abroad. Since then, the civic movement has extended from its nationalist roots to embrace people across society, North and South, including many from within the wider cultural, academic, professional, business and sporting life.

1   I use the word 'nationalist' in the text to include the republican community in the North.

When I first discussed this project with Deirdre Nolan of Gill Books in March 2020, I suggested that it would be useful if people knew what they were voting for when asked to make such a historic and transformative choice. This was a time of protracted and difficult negotiations between the EU and Britain over their separation. It was just before the world was struck by Covid-19 and the ensuing public health crisis.

In my written proposal for this book, I set out the parameters of the work that would have to embrace the questions of constitutional change. It would also examine the nature of the health, education and other public services in a new Ireland, the challenge of convincing a significant number of people from a culturally Protestant and unionist background to consider a future all-island economy and society within the EU and the extent of change that people on both sides of the border might expect.

The document made clear that the work was not about my views of what a united Ireland could look like, although I have supported the idea for as long as I can remember, but about how professionals, academics, artists, activists and politicians might imagine its future across a range of areas and interests. The vision of how Ireland can be integrated is gleaned through the perspectives of doctors, teachers, economists and historians, former police officers and soldiers, lawyers, academics, activists, artists, writers, actors, singers, poets and politicians; women and men whose views on what is possible are rooted in their life experience.

Some I know through my journalism, political campaigning and trade union activism over many decades, while others I encountered for the first time through this work. It has been a privilege to have access to their knowledge and personal stories, which are so central to making this an accessible and hopefully enjoyable exploration of our future, collective potential.

This work tracks the extended, turbulent negotiation of a withdrawal and trade agreement between the EU and the UK government, as well as the impact of Brexit on the island of Ireland. It also follows the course of the Covid-19 pandemic as it devastated the lives and livelihoods of people across the island, and examines the public health response of the two administrations as the crisis ebbed and surged between March 2020 and January 2022.

The interviews contained in the narrative began in June 2020 and continued until early January 2022, when the final manuscript was completed. Due to Covid restrictions, most of these were done over the telephone or on video calls.

United Nation does not seek to answer all the questions posed by the challenge of building a new and united island, and of integrating its parts after more than a century of partition. It does attempt to identify and outline in broad measure how fundamental constitutional, political, economic, social and cultural change can take place in a way that improves the quality of life and enhances the rights of all citizens on the island.

Much more detailed research and debate needs to be carried out to prepare the ground for a deep, radical and enduring transformation to emerge through a process of referendums in the transition to a new Ireland. I sincerely hope that this book makes a worthwhile contribution to the enormous and exciting task ahead.

Frank Connolly
Dublin
January 2022

CONTENTS

LIST OF ABBREVIATIONS

Afbi	Agri-food & Biosciences Institute
ANC	African National Congress
AP	Atlantic Philanthropies
ARINS	Analysing and Researching Ireland North and South
BIIGC	British–Irish Intergovernmental Conference
BMCA	Belfast Multi-Cultural Association
BMW	Border, Midlands and Western
CAP	Common Agricultural Programme
CCMS	Council for Catholic Maintained Schools
CIÉ	Córas Iompair Éireann
COP	Conference of the Parties
CSO	Central Statistics Office
DCU	Dublin City University
DEIS	Delivering Equality of Opportunity in Schools
DUP	Democratic Unionist Party
ECHR	European Convention on Human Rights
ECJ	European Court of Justice
ESB	Electricity Supply Board
ESRI	Economic and Social Research Institute
ETA	Electronic Travel Authorisation
EU	European Union
FDI	Foreign Direct Investment
FF	Fianna Fáil
FG	Fine Gael
ETA	Electronic Travel Authorisation
FICT	Commission on Flags, Identity, Culture and Tradition
FTTIS	Find, Test, Trace, Isolate and Support

GAA	Gaelic Athletic Association
GCSE	General Certificate of Secondary Education
GDP	gross domestic product
GFA	Good Friday Agreement
GPO	General Post Office
HPSC	Health Protection Surveillance Centre
HSC	Health and Social Care
HSE	Health Service Executive
Ibec	Irish Business and Employers Confederation
ICTU	Irish Congress of Trade Unions
ICU	Intensive Care Unit
IF	Ireland's Future
IMF	International Monetary Fund
IPCC	Intergovernmental Panel on Climate Change
IRA	Irish Republican Army
LCC	Loyalist Communities Council
LVF	Loyalist Volunteer Force
MEP	Member of the European Parliament
MLA	Member of the Legislative Assembly
MP	Member of Parliament
MRBI	Market Research Bureau of Ireland
NAMA	National Asset Management Agency
NATO	North Atlantic Treaty Organization
NDNA	New Decade, New Approach
NEET	not in education, employment or training
NHS	National Health Service
NI	Northern Ireland
NIA	Northern Ireland Alternatives
NIESR	National Institute of Economic and Social Research
NIO	Northern Ireland Office
NISRA	Northern Ireland Statistics and Research Agency
NPHET	National Public Health Emergency Team
NSMC	North South Ministerial Council
NTPF	National Treatment Purchase Fund
NUJ	National Union of Journalists
NWCI	National Women's Council of Ireland

OECD	Organisation for Economic Co-operation and Development
PPE	Personal Protection Equipment
PPS	Public Prosecution Service
PSNI	Police Service of Northern Ireland
PUP	Progressive Unionist Party
QUB	Queen's University Belfast
RAF	Royal Air Force
RHC	Red Hand Commando
RHI	Renewable Heating Incentive
RIC	Royal Irish Constabulary
RUC	Royal Ulster Constabulary
SAGE	Scientific Advisory Group for Emergencies
SDLP	Social Democratic and Labour Party
SF	Sinn Féin
SIU	Shared Island Unit
SNP	Scottish National Party
TD	Teachta Dála
TUNUI	Trade Unionists for a United Ireland
TUV	Traditional Unionist Voice
UCD	University College Dublin
UCL	University College London
UDA	Ulster Defence Association
UDR	Ulster Defence Regiment
UFU	Ulster Farmers Union
UK	United Kingdom
US	United States
UUP	Ulster Unionist Party
UVF	Ulster Volunteer Force
WCTU	Waterford Council of Trade Unions
WHO	World Health Organization

And remember that a Nation is a very complex thing – it never does consist, it never has consisted, solely of men of one blood or of one single race. It is like a river, which rises far off in the hills and has many sources, many converging streams, before it becomes one great stream.

ROGER CASEMENT (1905)

INTRODUCTION

I t is no longer a question of whether, but when and how Ireland and its people will be united. Since the Good Friday/Belfast Agreement (GFA) of 1998, the momentum towards Irish unity has intensified, propelled most dramatically in recent years by the departure of Britain from the EU. It has also been driven by economic and social progress in the South and by political and demographic trends in the North.

The challenges posed by the process of uniting two societies on the island – both with different traditions and diverse communities, contrasting health and education systems, and dual economies – are immense. They are, however, not insurmountable, and the benefits of reunification, as illustrated by the experience when divided countries have come together in other parts of the world, can be hugely rewarding.

The GFA, supported by a clear majority of people in both parts of the island, is a negotiated settlement underpinned in Irish, British and international law, which ensures that national reunification can only be achieved with the consent of a majority of people in the North. That commitment is balanced by an equally significant guarantee that the Irish people, North and South, can vote for a united Ireland in binding referendums. The decision to call a referendum will be made by the British government on the recommendation of its secretary of state for Northern Ireland when he or she considers that there is a real possibility

1

that a simple majority of people in the North would support a proposal for Irish unity.

With the GFA approaching its 25th anniversary in 2023, the public debate on the timing of a referendum is well underway. Discussions on how to prepare for the outcome of a decision by voters, North and South, in favour of reunification have also commenced. For several years, detailed deliberations on the constitutional future of Ireland in the wake of a positive vote for unity have been taking place among academics, in research institutes and universities, and, increasingly, in media and political circles on the island and abroad.

At the centre of these discussions is the key question of accommodating in a unified Ireland, the large numbers of people in the North who identify as British and unionist. By definition, these people oppose the breaking of the link with the UK and its political, legal and cultural institutions and traditions.

In the 2016 UK Brexit referendum, 56 per cent of those who voted in Northern Ireland (including a considerable number of those who had previously supported unionist parties) expressed their wish to remain in the EU; while across the rest of Britain, the majority of those who voted chose to leave. As protracted negotiations on future trade and other arrangements continued between the British government and the EU on the terms of their separation, the numbers of those in NI wishing to retain EU citizenship further increased, according to an opinion poll by The Detail news website in February 2020, eight months before the EU–UK Withdrawal Agreement was made.

The impact and disruption of Brexit on business, trade, farming, international travel and other aspects of daily life in the North became apparent following the implementation of the Withdrawal Agreement in the first weeks of 2021, and the concerns about the long-term benefits, or otherwise, of the UK decision to leave the EU continued to grow.

An opinion poll by LucidTalk, published in the *Sunday Times* in late January 2021, found that 47 per cent of respondents in Northern

Ireland wished to remain in the UK, with 42 per cent in favour of a united Ireland and 11 per cent undecided. Some 50.7 per cent said there should be a vote on whether NI remained in the UK at some point before 2025 (*Sunday Times*, 23 January 2021). A further poll by LucidTalk for BBC *Spotlight* in April showed that 37 per cent of respondents believed there should be a border poll within five years, with a further 29 per cent supporting a poll 'at some point after 5 years' (*Spotlight*, 20 April 2021).

The Protocol on Ireland/Northern Ireland – commonly known as the Northern Ireland protocol – agreed during the negotiations, allowed the North to remain within the EU free trade and customs areas, but business and farming organisations in particular, expressed real fears about their loss of revenue and income as a consequence of Brexit. Many NI citizens who previously identified exclusively as British applied for Irish passports in order to circumvent potential obstacles to their free movement for work, study and leisure in EU states under the new dispensation.

During April, there were protests in loyalist areas across the North, although these were much smaller than those during the conflict years. There were riots against the police; some vehicles, including a bus, were burnt; and there were attempts by gangs of young men to engage with nationalist youths across the peace line in west Belfast. The protestors raised objections to their partial detachment from Britain under the protocol and to their continued relationship with the EU under the terms of the trade deal. On 1 November 2021, another bus was burnt out in Newtownabbey, just north of Belfast, in protest against the continuing protocol.

Unionist political leaders unsuccessfully called on the British government to override the protocol due to the disruption caused in the early months of 2021 when there was a significant delay and reduction in the importation of, often essential, consumer goods from the UK into the North due to the bureaucratic and other difficulties arising from the Brexit deal.

By September 2021, a substantial increase was recorded in the trade of goods, in both directions between North and South, as manufacturers and other suppliers found new markets for their products and fresh sources of supply on the island. Imports from the North to the South increased by 60 per cent over 2020, while there was a 45 per cent rise in the opposite direction following the disruption to trade with the UK. Two months later, the Economic and Social Research Institute (ESRI) told an Oireachtas committee that imports from North to South rose by 90 per cent due to the withdrawal of Britain from the EU. This accounted for 5 per cent of total imports into the South, up from 1.5 per cent in 2015.

Just as Brexit was a catalyst for changing attitudes to a referendum on, and raised the prospects of, a united Ireland, the catastrophic and tragic loss of life and economic disruption wreaked by the coronavirus since it first emerged in early 2020 led to intense public debate in Ireland over the potential benefits of a single health service on the island.

The failure of the authorities in the North and South to develop an all-island response to the crisis was criticised by public health experts as gross negligence, resulting in many unnecessary Covid-related deaths and causing debilitating illness and suffering to tens of thousands of people. By early 2021, the death toll from Covid-19 of some 2,800 in the South and over 2,000 in the North exceeded the number who lost their lives during Troubles. A year later the number of Covid-related deaths was approaching 10,000 across the island, according to the CSO and the equivalent body in the North, the Northern Ireland Statistics and Research Agency (NISRA).

In addition, the introduction of progressive legislation to permit same-sex marriage and abortion over recent years has marked a change in the perception of the South as a socially-backward state, overly influenced by the hierarchy and teachings of the Catholic Church. The successes of the feminist and LGBTQ+ movements, and wider political and civic society, in the constitutional referendums on both issues built upon the radical departures of the 1970s and 1980s, when legislation to allow for divorce, contraception and homosexuality were first introduced.

By the 1990s, the dominance of the Catholic Church over the reproductive rights of women and the private lives of citizens was already diminished. This was not least because of the disclosures of appalling mistreatment, including sexual and other physical abuse, of children in its care, of women in mother and baby homes and other facilities, and of boys and young men in detention centres over previous decades in the South. Inquiries in the North revealed similar abuse in state and Church-run institutions of both main religions. This contributed to a gradual but significant weakening of Church control over people's lives; a reduction in the numbers participating in religious services and organisations; and a growing movement towards the secularisation of education, North and South.

These fundamental and ongoing social changes were mirrored by previously unthinkable shifts in political allegiance in the South, with a steady decline in support for the parties that had traditionally dominated electoral politics since the foundation of the state, a trend most evident in the results of the general election in February 2020.

In the North, election results since 2017 have reflected a narrowing of the gap in support for the larger unionist and nationalist parties and a substantial growth in the numbers supporting neither. In elections to the Northern Ireland Assembly, to local government and to the Westminster and European parliaments over recent years, the nationalist and other non-unionist vote has equalled and, on occasion, surpassed the combined support for the unionist parties.

As an insight into demographic trends for the overall population of the North, the figures for school, university and other third-level education enrolment suggest a continuing growth in the number of those who identify as Irish/Catholic/nationalist and a corresponding decline of those from the British/Protestant/unionist community. A September 2020 article in the *Irish Times* noted that 'The North's Department of

Education figures for the year 2019/2020 show that from nursery up to second level, Catholics made up 50.6 per cent of the schools' population … while Protestants made up 32.3 per cent'. The ratio is similar in the enrolments for university and other third-level education.

While demographics are an unreliable indicator of political choice, the 2021 census in the North is expected to confirm this trend, along with an increase in the number of people declaring their nationality as Northern Irish rather than Irish or British.

None of these trends can diminish or deny the prospect that a very large section, and possibly a majority, of people in the North who vote in a forthcoming referendum on Irish unity will reject the proposition and assert their wish to remain part of the UK. However, the economic, political, social and demographic trends post-Brexit, suggest that there is a greater likelihood now, than at any other period since the partition of Ireland, that a majority of people in the North will choose to sever its constitutional ties to the Britain and to join an agreed, unitary state.

In 2017, the EU Council of Ministers agreed that, if the people of Ireland, North and South, endorse a proposal for reunification, the new country will automatically be admitted to full EU membership. In advance of such an exercise in self-determination, as envisaged in the GFA, prospective voters should, at the very least, have an idea of the nature of the future constitutional, political, economic and social arrangements on the island.

In the event of a vote for unity, the large numbers of those who identify as unionist are entitled to certain assurances and guarantees, legally or constitutionally enshrined, which will protect their rights in this new Ireland. This includes their right to hold British and Irish citizenship, as set out in the GFA.

This right was reinforced following a legal action by Derry-born Emma DeSouza, who successfully challenged the insistence by the Home Office that she was a British citizen. DeSouza commenced the action after the Home Office denied an application by her US-born husband, Jake, for a European Economic Area residence card. She argued that, under the terms of the GFA, she was entitled to be recognised as Irish, and so held the same rights as all other Irish citizens – her husband was thus eligible for residency in the North. In May 2020, after five years of legal argument and in a significant climbdown from its earlier position, the British government accepted that all Irish and British citizens of NI will be regarded as EU citizens for immigration/family unification purposes.

Equally, the GFA states that those from both jurisdictions have a right to live, and see their children grow, in a country where all citizens can avail of fair and equal access to housing, health, education and other public services, to equality under the law notwithstanding their gender, race or religious affiliation and to work and live without exploitation or discrimination.

That is what the majority of people on the island decided when they voted, in May 1998, to support the GFA, which asserted that, whatever choice the people make in a referendum, it 'shall be founded on the principles of full respect for, and equality of, civil, political, social and cultural rights, of freedom from discrimination for all citizens, and of parity of esteem and of just treatment for the identity, ethos, and aspirations of both communities.'

Since that decision, the population of the South has increased by over 1.4 million, to 5 million people, while in the North it has reached over 1.9 million, according to figures from the CSO and NIRSA respectively. The number of non-Irish nationals living in the South rose to 645,500 by 2020, or just under 13 per cent of the total population and has made for a more diverse, multicultural society.

There are huge challenges ahead for those who want to create a fitting place for these, almost 7 million, people, and in convincing a majority in the North that a united Ireland will be in their best long-term interests. While the trends, as outlined above, suggest movement towards a unitary state in Ireland, there is no agreement as to when the mechanism to achieve this objective, a referendum, should be triggered. Nor is there agreement on what constitutional and political structure, and what sort of society, people will choose in a future border poll.

In the following pages, I examine what such a new Ireland might look like based on the opinions and experiences of various informed and engaged individuals across the island, in Europe and the US on the challenges involved in building a new Ireland. This will incorporate analysis on constitutional matters, the development of the all-island economy, new health, education and other public services, and what such fundamental change means for the diverse cultures and identities that inhabit the island. The work will also track the intensifying debate on the timing of, and preparations for, a unity referendum as it has developed since the decision by UK voters to leave the EU in 2016, and the impact of the Covid-19 pandemic on the health services in both jurisdictions since March 2020.

THE REFERENDUM ROADMAP

There is no agreement on when a referendum on Ireland's constitutional future should take place but a range of voices across political, academic and civic society, and in the media, agree that detailed preparations should be in place before any vote. Research institutes, universities, government bodies and political parties have already commenced that preparation in papers and reports that set out the different challenges presented by a referendum on unity, and for society in Ireland if it is passed. They include recommendations on the timing and wording of the referendums, North and South, and the need for prolonged discussion and open debate – through citizens' assemblies, parliamentary committees, a constitutional convention and other forums – about the implications of the vote for all people on the island.

The GFA sets out the strict parameters of the choice: the people of the North can decide to remain in the union with Britain or choose to become part of a reunified Ireland. If the North opts for the latter, the people of the South can agree to accept that decision and to make the necessary constitutional and other arrangements required to make it happen. The vote in each jurisdiction is decided on a simple majority of 50 plus 1 per cent of those who vote. Under the terms of the Agreement, and the UK's Northern Ireland Act 1998, which gave it legislative effect, the decision on when to call a referendum rests with the secretary of state for Northern Ireland. The Act states that the secretary of state will direct the holding of a poll 'when it appears likely to him [sic] that a majority of those voting would express a wish that Northern Ireland should cease to be part of the United Kingdom and form part of a united Ireland.'

In this respect, the GFA sets out a pathway for unity based on the concept that the people of Ireland, separately but concurrently, should decide their own future. It gives the power to the British government to decide a date for a referendum, while it also provides for a regular poll on unity to take place at a frequency of not more than every seven years. In other words, if the prospect of unity is rejected on the first occasion, voters can be asked to consider it every seven years until the proposal is accepted.

The GFA also envisaged a situation where devolved political structures, agreed during the negotiations for the peace agreement in 1998, could continue after a vote for unity. Thus, the power-sharing executive and the elected assembly that sits at Stormont in Belfast could continue to function after any such vote as a form of local or devolved administration, or for a transitional period, in a united Ireland. Similarly, the British–Irish Intergovernmental Conference (BIIGC), which is separate to and independent of the assembly and other structures of the GFA, could also continue to function as a mechanism for continuing co-operation of the two sovereign governments after a vote for unity.

The GFA does not prescribe the details of the new constitutional arrangements or political structures that would be put in place following a vote for unity. Neither does it, nor could it, specify how the post-unification society would deliver the basic requirements of its citizens in relation to health, education, transport or other public service provision, or on the range of policies, laws, rules and procedures that make for a functioning democratic society.

Instead, following a vote for unification, it will be left to the government of Ireland – which will have sovereignty after the referendum – in consultation with its citizens, to decide what should be done to ensure that the new, unified island maintains the confidence of its citizens in the institutions and laws of the new state. This also applies to the issues that would need to be addressed if voters in the North reject the proposal for a united Ireland and seek to remain part of the UK; then the responsibility would lie with the British government to oversee any required changes in its administration.

Research is continuing on the timing and form of the referendums, as well as on the potential constitutional rearrangements, political structures and policies that might be best suited to accommodate a vote by a majority of people in the North to become part of a united Ireland. However, it is agreed by all of those engaged in this research that the people who are being asked to exercise their right to self-determination should be informed of the constitutional, economic, political and social consequences in advance of the referendums. Some academics have asserted that, while the referendums must be held concurrently, that does not mean simultaneously, nor on the same day, as occurred when the GFA was endorsed by voters, North and South, on 22 May 1998.

On that occasion, voters in the North were asked to agree to the proposals contained within the proposed Agreement (they had received copies of the document in the weeks previous). Voters in the South were also asked to agree to the removal of Articles 2 and 3 of the Irish Constitution, which contained a territorial claim over Northern Ireland, and to replace them with a provision that only a decision reflecting the wish of a majority of voters in the North could end the union with Britain. This principle of consent was balanced by the right to self-determination given to the people of Ireland through concurrent votes, North and South.

Those entitled to vote will be determined by the two governments and some observers believe that the franchise could be extended, as was the case in the 2014 Scottish referendum on independence, to allow all those over the age of 16, and possibly Irish citizens living in other jurisdictions, to participate, given the historic significance of the poll for younger and future generations. Any such extension could require a constitutional amendment in the South in advance of the referendum on unity.

It is evident that the optimum way to a seamless or, at least, less disruptive transition to a unified Ireland is to ensure that voters have a reasonably clear picture of the constitutional arrangements and political structures that will emerge if they choose the unity option. For this reason, it would seem obvious that voters should know in advance what changes are required to be made to the Irish Constitution to facilitate unity, or indeed whether an entirely new one should be constructed. Voters should know in advance what guarantees will be put in place to ensure that the identity of those who will remain British citizens in a united Ireland is protected. Similarly, the GFA anticipated a bill of rights for Northern Ireland, which has not yet been introduced, which could then apply in any new constitutional arrangement.

While some will argue for a minimalist approach to constitutional change, there are others in both parts of the island in political, academic and legal circles, and in civic society, who see the referendums as an opportunity to continue, or accelerate, a more transformative process of social and political change, post-unification. The GFA envisaged such progress to a modern, pluralist society when it required the sovereign government, following unity, to exercise power on the basis of the principles of equality and parity of esteem of both communities. In order for this ambition to be realised, detailed and fact-based research over a significant period of time, and across civic and political society and opinion on the island, is required. Consideration should also be given to how existing rights can be expanded for each citizen, including those from all ethnic, migrant and other minority communities.

As the entire territory of a united Ireland will immediately become part of the EU, without any change to the Treaty of Rome, the new sovereign government will also be a party to the European Convention of Human Rights (ECHR) and the European Court of Justice (ECJ). These and other EU laws and institutions will underpin the human rights, equality and other legislative protections of citizens of the new, united Ireland. In this regard, the citizens of the new state will come under the legislative remit of both the sovereign government of Ireland and of the EU.

2

THE EVOLUTION OF AN EARTHQUAKE

T he decision by the people of Britain in the 2016 referendum to leave the EU unleashed a wave of anger and resentment in the North among the voters who had chosen to remain. An estimated 40 per cent of unionists and 85 per cent of nationalists were among those who voted to remain (The Conversation, April 2017). These included many engaged in farming and agriculture-related industries, which for decades have relied heavily on EU transfers from the Common Agricultural Programme.

When the assembly and executive collapsed the following year, in early March 2017, following the decision by Sinn Féin (SF) to pull out of the power-sharing arrangements, disaffection among nationalists escalated. Their ability to influence political decision making in the North diminished and their future outside the EU was being determined exclusively by the British government and the Westminster parliament.

The collapse of the institutions came amid recriminations over the involvement of senior Democratic Unionist Party (DUP) ministers in a scandal surrounding huge payments to its supporters from a Renewable Heating Incentive (RHI) scheme introduced by the British government. This followed an earlier controversy over the sale of properties in the North controlled by the National Asset Management Agency, an Irish government body set up to deal with the bad debts of the main banks in the South following the financial crash of 2008/09. The controversy implicated and politically damaged DUP leader and First Minister Peter Robinson, as well as some of his party colleagues in the NI Executive, and led to criminal charges against other individuals with close links to the organisation.

Nationalist and republican concerns were exacerbated when the DUP entered into a confidence and supply agreement with the British government and Conservative Party leader Theresa May, a few months after the collapse of the Stormont institutions, deepening a suspicion that the largest unionist party had little or no interest in restoring the devolved administration. Given that they were holding the balance of power at Westminster, and their open support for a hard Brexit, the DUP MPs were under no urgency to continue sharing power with SF and other parties in the North.

In the absence of political institutions, and amid growing fears about the impact of a no-deal or hard Brexit on the North, fresh voices emerged from within the nationalist and republican community about their lack of political representation and the uncertain future facing them and their children as Irish citizens. As a reflection of these concerns, Ireland's Future (IF), a non-party initiative of civic nationalists, emerged with an open letter sent by email to Taoiseach Leo Varadkar, on 8 December 2017 and published in the *Irish News* three days later. The letter was signed by almost 200 people, including prominent members of the business, academic, legal, arts and sporting communities across the North. It described the political pact between the DUP and the Conservative Party as 'a grave threat to political progress'. It noted the 'concerted undermining of the political institutions' and said the political crisis in the North was due to the failure of both governments to defend the Good Friday, Stormont House and St Andrews agreements made over the previous two decades:

The result has been a denial and refusal of equality, rights and respect towards the section of the community to which we belong, as well as everyone living here. The impending reality of Brexit now threatens to reinforce partition on this island and revisit a sense of abandonment as experienced by our parents and grandparents. The fact that a majority of voters in the north of Ireland voted to remain within the EU must not be ignored.

On the day the letter was delivered, 8 December, Varadkar, made an official statement with a commitment to the nationalist people in the North that their interests were being protected during the negotiations with Britain on its departure from the EU: 'Your birth right as Irish citizens, and therefore as EU citizens, will be protected. There will be no hard border on our island. You will never again be left behind by an Irish government.' Just weeks earlier, on 23 November, Tánaiste and Minister for Foreign Affairs, Simon Coveney, told the Oireachtas Committee on the Good Friday Agreement, that he 'would like to see a united Ireland in my lifetime, and, if possible, in my political lifetime'.

Both Irish government leaders were responding to the outbreak of anger among nationalists in the North at the absence of political representation since the collapse of the institutions, the increasing prospect of a no-deal Brexit, which could see the reintroduction of a hard border in Ireland, and the influence of the DUP at Westminster where it held the balance of power.

In return for the support of the DUP's 10 MPs, the May administration, it appeared, was prepared to jettison its responsibilities to advance significant provisions in the GFA in relation to human rights and legacy issues arising from the conflict, and on the promise of Irish language legislation and other commitments the British government had made since 1998.

After lengthy negotiations brokered by Coveney and Secretary of State for Northern Ireland Karen Bradley, a package of proposals that could have restored the power-sharing executive was rejected at the eleventh hour by DUP leader Arlene Foster in early February 2018. She rejected claims from SF that an agreement had been reached on contentious issues such as an Irish language act, marriage equality and a proposed bill of rights for NI, but it was widely suspected that the plug has been pulled on a deal at the insistence of the DUP MPs at Westminster.

The failure of this latest attempt to restore the institutions re-energised the campaign by IF, which set about widening its appeal across the nationalist and wider non-unionist community and refining its message. It found a growing audience, including among 'soft unionists' and people of no affiliation to either of the main political traditions. Many of these had voted against Brexit in 2016 and were deeply concerned about the direction the process of withdrawal from the EU was taking and its longer-term implications for their families and communities. IF reflected these concerns and also tapped into a deepening anxiety across the communities arising from the nature of the Brexit deal Theresa May was promoting and her stated intention to remove protections provided to Irish citizens in the North through the GFA and the ECHR.

Niall Murphy, a founding member of the group and a solicitor with Belfast firm KRW Law, represented clients seeking redress for suffering they endured at the hands of the British state, its army and police during the years of conflict. Among these were victims of collusion between the security forces and loyalist paramilitaries, including those killed and injured by an Ulster Defence Association (UDA) gang at Sean Graham bookmakers shop on the Ormeau Road, in Belfast in 1992, and those shot dead in an Ulster Volunteer Force (UVF) attack on O'Toole's pub in Loughinisland, County Down, in 1994. As a director of the board of the human rights group Relatives for Justice, Murphy was also concerned by the failure of the British government to address the legacy of official state collusion with loyalist paramilitaries and unresolved and illegal killings by British security forces. As a solicitor, he was particularly angered by the prime minister's proposals to remove the protections and legal recourse available to his clients, including a number from the loyalist community, from the ECHR.

The next major initiative of the embryonic movement was planned to coincide with May's attempt to push through her best attempt at a Withdrawal Agreement in the Westminster parliament in Autumn 2018. IF decided to convene a major gathering of civic nationalism, along with as many unionists and those of other political persuasions as were willing to attend, to demonstrate their opposition to May's proposals and the continued absence of political representation within the North since the collapse of the power-sharing institutions. In response to Coveney's and Varadkar's statements of support for nationalists in the North, Murphy and the small group of activists that led the IF initiative issued an invitation to Coveney to open, and to Varadkar to close the event: a conference to be held in Belfast's Waterfront Hall in October 2018. In the run up to the conference, discussions were held in Belfast with two officials of the Department of Foreign Affairs, Eamon Molloy and Fergal Mythen, who passed on the request to their colleagues in Dublin.

In reply, Coveney and his senior department officials requested that the conference be postponed given the sensitivity of the Brexit discussions between the British government and the EU and their concern that such an event attended by senior politicians, including the Taoiseach and Tánaiste, from Dublin would upset unionists. The Irish government officials argued that the unionists were already complaining about the 'backstop' envisaged in the deal negotiated by May, which would keep the North within the EU customs and trade area following Brexit. The compromise was designed to maintain a frictionless border in Ireland until alternative customs and other trading arrangements could be agreed in a final 'divorce settlement' and following a two-year transition period.

The Withdrawal Agreement and the Irish backstop would see the UK staying in a customs union with the EU while the North would also remain aligned with the EU single market for the purposes of certain rules and regulations. The DUP members at Westminster joined in the chorus of Brexiteers denouncing the perceived surrender of sovereignty by the prime minister marking the beginning of the end of the unhappy relationship between the party's MPs and Theresa May. On the day she travelled to Brussels to close the deal in late November 2018, May's main rival in the party, Boris Johnson, went to Belfast where he told cheering delegates at the DUP party conference that 'no British government could or should' agree to a border in the Irish Sea. 'If you read the Withdrawal Agreement,' Johnson said, 'you can see that we are witnessing the birth of a new country called UK(NI) or Ukni. Ukni is no longer exclusively ruled by London or Stormont. Ukni is in large part to be ruled by Brussels.' He warned that the backstop would separate Northern Ireland from the UK and repeated an earlier suggestion he had made for a bridge to be built between Scotland and Northern Ireland. 'We need to junk the backstop,' he told the receptive audience of DUP members.

The IF team acceded to Coveney's request to postpone the conference and instead published a second letter in the *Irish News* to the Taoiseach, reminding him of the commitment he had made to nationalists in the North in December 2017. They warned, again, of the dangers posed by a hard deal Brexit and of the resulting suppression of rights available to Irish citizens north of the border:

> The political institutions remain in suspension as political unionism continues to deny respect for our Irish identity and language, marriage equality, access to justice for legacy issues. As you know these rights are now taken for granted by citizens in other parts of these islands. The British Conservative government has rendered itself unable to effect any progress on these rights issues due to its dependence on the DUP. Brexit threatens to deepen the rights crisis and there is a real danger of serious erosion of current guarantees … there is a very real potential that partition could be

reinforced, and our country and our people further divided. This is a source of grave concern to all of us.

What was as significant as the content of the letter was the range and profile of the signatories, representing a large swathe of opinion across all sections of nationalism in the North and further afield. Over a thousand people, spanning the legal, academic, business, cultural and sporting voices across the nationalist community signed it, including actor Adrian Dunbar, Oscar-winning film director Jim Sheridan, Derry footballer James McClean, and an array of business leaders, lawyers, university professors, school principals, healthcare and other professionals. Among the sports stars were three Olympic medal holders and 30 senior GAA all-Ireland winners, while two other signatories also held Oscars and one had climbed Mount Everest. The names, published in the *Irish News* three days after the letter had been sent to the Taoiseach, had been collected through the network which the campaign was slowly, but organically, growing from their connections across civic society. According to Niall Murphy, after the letter's publication, IF was inundated with people asking why they had not been invited to sign up.

Two months later, on 26 January 2019, more than two thousand people, including many of those who had signed their names to the letter, gathered in the Waterfront Hall in the Belfast docks for the launch of IF. Representatives of the main nationalist political parties across the island addressed the enthusiastic audience along with other prominent civic society speakers. The Irish government was represented by agriculture minister and Donegal native, Joe McHugh, who was welcomed by the organisers but was several notches below their preferred choice in the pecking order of cabinet members. Fianna Fáil deputy leader Dara Calleary attended, while SF President Mary Lou McDonald and Social Democratic and Labour Party (SDLP) leader Colum Eastwood, also addressed the huge crowd.

McDonald called on the Irish government to begin planning for reunification and said it was 'irresponsible and arrogant' of it to dismiss any prospect of a unity referendum. She also said that the unionist community would have a home in a united Ireland: 'The Protestant, loyalist and unionist community are part of the fabric and diversity of our nation, and they must be part of [the] discussion in shaping ... and be partners in building a new Ireland – our shared and often troubled history can be reconciled.'

Eastwood told the packed hall that, while the time was not right for a border poll, unionists had nothing to fear from a conversation about Irish unity: 'My appeal to unionism is this. You need to convince us of your vision for the future and we'll try to convince you of ours, and then in time let the people decide' (*Irish News*, 28 January 2019).

The Waterfront event was a significant and historic moment in its successful assembly of the main strands of Irish nationalist and republican opinion across the island, even if the leaders of Fine Gael and Fianna Fáil chose not to attend. It was also the springboard for what was becoming an unstoppable campaign for a unity referendum and a debate on the future of a new Ireland.

IF followed it up with a successful meeting in Newry four months later, which brought together legal opinion and human rights campaigners to deepen the discussion and bring it to an audience in the border counties. High Court judge Richard Humphreys, who examined the implications of the Brexit vote for the GFA in his 2018 book, *Beyond the Border*, was among the speakers. Human rights lawyer Professor Colin Harvey of Queen's University Belfast (QUB), and an authority on constitutional change, also addressed the meeting.

The widening discussion, or 'the evolution of an earthquake' as Niall Murphy described the momentum for a unity referendum building among nationalist and others across the island on IF's website, encouraged the loose network involved in IF to formalise its structures, register as a company and to build a wider, national campaign. Their development coincided with the inevitable collapse of the May administration as the prime minister's efforts to advance her Withdrawal Agreement foundered on the rocks of her own party's hard Brexit enthusiasts and the intransigence of her former unionist allies at Westminster.

Following several unsuccessful attempts to get her bill through parliament, May announced her decision to resign in May 2019, less than two years into her premiership. She was replaced by Johnson, the arch-Brexiteer who promised to re-negotiate the Withdrawal Agreement, including the offensive backstop, much to the delight of the DUP.

The former chief whip, Julian Smith, was appointed as the new secretary of state for Northern Ireland and set about the, somewhat conflicting, tasks of restoring the devolved institutions while maintaining relations with the DUP, whose 10 MPs were still keeping the minority Tory government in power.

During his first meetings as prime minister with German Chancellor Angela Merkel and French President Emmanuel Macron, Johnson learned that, while prepared to listen to alternative proposals to the NI backstop, they had no intention of resiling from the EU position that there would be no return to a hard border in Ireland. 'The key elements of the Withdrawal Agreement and the Irish backstop are not just technical constraints or legal quibbling. They are genuine, indispensable guarantees to preserve stability in Ireland and the integrity of the single market, which is the basis of the EU,' Macron said after his meeting with Johnson at the Élysée Palace in Paris on 22 August 2019.

At a briefing with the Presidential Press Association before he met the British prime minister, Macron warned that the reinstatement of a hard border would threaten the hard-won peace in Ireland: 'There are still families whose children, brothers and sisters died in this conflict,' he said. 'To think of reviving that, because it suits us, would be irresponsible. I consider that Irish peace is European peace. We must not allow it to be threatened by a political and institutional crisis in Britain.' When asked by Lara Marlowe of the *Irish Times* at the briefing whether reunification and the integration of the entire island of Ireland into the EU would perhaps resolve the issue, the French president replied that it 'would solve all the problems, but it is not up to France'.

The solid support for the Irish government position by the most powerful EU leaders left Johnson more isolated as he ploughed on with his efforts to alter the Withdrawal Agreement and ensure Britain's scheduled departure from the EU by the end of October 2019. As reported by Pat Leahy in the *Irish Times*, when Johnson met Varadkar in Dublin in early September, the British prime minister insisted that he wanted a deal with the EU and hoped to find a way to resolve the backstop issue:

> I want to get a deal. Like you, I've looked carefully at no-deal, I've assessed its consequences both for our country and yours. And yes, of course, we could do it, the UK could certainly get through it, but be in no doubt that outcome would be a failure of statecraft for which we would all be responsible. So for the sake of business, for farmers, and millions of ordinary people who are counting on us to use our imagination and creativity to get this done, I want you to know I would overwhelmingly prefer to find an agreement.

For his part, Varadkar stressed that:

> The people of this island, North and South, need to know that their livelihoods, their security and their sense of identity will not be put at risk as a consequence of a hard Brexit. The stakes are high. Avoiding the return of a hard border on this island and protecting our place in the single market are the Irish government's priorities in all circumstances. We must protect peace on the island and the burgeoning success of the all-island economy. This is why the backstop continues to be a critical component of the Withdrawal Agreement, unless and until an alternative is found.

A week later, during separate meetings, Johnson met the same response from European Commission President Jean-Claude

Juncker and the Prime Minister of Luxembourg Xavier Bettel. He left Luxembourg with similar words ringing in his ear – that any new proposals must have the guarantees provided by the backstop contained in the Withdrawal Agreement. The British broadsheets, among them the *Daily Telegraph* where Johnson was once a columnist, were not impressed by the outcome. 'Luxembourg laughs in Johnson's face' the *Telegraph* reported, while the *Guardian* headline said simply, 'Johnson left humiliated'.

As the deadline for a Brexit deal approached without agreement on any alternative to Theresa May's backstop, Johnson appeared to concede that he would allow an extension of the negotiations in order to avoid leaving the EU without a deal. The concession was made in a submission for a legal action taken in Scotland, which asked the courts to require that Johnson seek an extension to avoid leaving the UK without a deal.

During the case in the Scottish High Court – taken by Scottish National Party (SNP) MP Joanna Cherry QC, Jolyon Maugham QC and businessman Vince Dale – lawyers for Johnson said that he would seek an extension under the terms of the Benn Act if parliament did not agree on a Withdrawal Agreement by 19 October 2019. The Benn Act, introduced earlier by Labour MP Hilary Benn, forced the Conservative government to seek an extension to the 31 October deadline if parliament did not pass a Brexit deal before then.

Following a hastily-organised and private three-hour meeting between Johnson and Leo Varadkar on 10 October at the Thornton Manor Hotel near Liverpool, both leaders insisted that a deal was possible by the end of the month. According to the Taoiseach, as reported by the *Irish Times*, the two leaders had found 'a pathway towards an agreement within weeks.'

The plan they discussed would see an all-Ireland regulatory zone for all goods, which would leave NI in the European single market. However, the arrangements would be subject to the consent of the devolved executive and assembly in the North, which would have to approve them in advance and renew that endorsement every four years. Given the unstable history of the institutions and the difficulty of achieving consent between the main parties when they were functioning, the proposals were very ambitious and also challenging for large sections of the Tory party and the DUP.

Varadkar also reminded the British prime minister that the deal had to be finalised with the EU negotiation team, led by the experienced French politician Michel Barnier, not with the Irish government. Barnier and his team, as well as Merkel and Macron, remained adamant that there would be no return to a hard border in Ireland. A customs border in the Irish Sea was emerging as the only acceptable basis for a deal with the EU and the Irish government.

As if Johnson needed reminding, DUP leader Arlene Foster repeated her opposition to any proposal that 'traps NI in the EU single market or customs union'. As the British and EU negotiators entered into a tunnel of final negotiations before the deadline expired, Foster warned that the 'DUP has always indicated that the United Kingdom must leave the EU as one nation and in so doing that no barriers to trade are erected within the UK.' The EU, she said, must accept that:

> the economic and constitutional integrity of the whole of the United Kingdom will have to be respected as we leave. As a consequence of the mandate given to us by voters in 2017, the DUP is very relevant in the parliamentary arithmetic and regardless of the ups and downs of the Brexit discussions, that has not changed. We will judge any outcome reached by the Prime Minister against the criteria above (DUP statement, Guardian, 17 October 2019).

Campaigners in the North noted that Foster and her party continued to oppose legislation on marriage equality, language and abortion rights that applied across the UK, while demanding respect for the 'constitutional integrity of the whole of the UK'.

From the other side of the Atlantic, a powerful and timely intervention came from Nancy Pelosi, the leading Democrat and speaker of the US House of Representatives. Addressing an event to mark the contribution of her fellow Democratic Party congressman, Richard Neal, to the peace process in Northern Ireland, Pelosi warned the British government that it would not be able to negotiate a much-vaunted post-Brexit trade deal with the US if the GFA was jeopardised after its departure from the EU: 'There won't be any trade agreement that violates the Good Friday Agreement,' she said, just days before a crucial meeting of the European Council in Brussels. 'Our message to the British government is: "Don't be misled into thinking there will be a US–UK trade agreement if the Good Friday Agreement accords are violated."'

Days later, the EU leaders approved the latest proposals put forward by British negotiators, which included only slight differences to the agreement reached with Theresa May some months previously. The new deal included an assurance that there would be no return to a customs border in Ireland, much to the disappointment and anger of the DUP, who pledged to object when it returned to the House of Commons for ratification.

Speaking alongside an obviously pleased Leo Varadkar, President of the EU Council Donald Tusk said:

> The key change in comparison with the earlier version of the deal is Prime Minister Johnson's acceptance to have customs checks at the points of entry into Northern Ireland. This compromise will allow us to avoid border checks between Ireland and Northern Ireland and will ensure the integrity of the single market.

With the end of October deadline looming for British departure from the EU, and no prospect of getting the new proposals ratified by parliament in the face of fierce internal Conservative Party as well as NI unionist objections, Johnson obtained a three-month extension of the Brexit negotiations and called a general election for 12 December.

On 1 November 2019, another open letter from IF to Varadkar was published, calling for urgent protections for Irish citizens in the North in the light of Brexit and the continued suspension of the devolved political institutions. The letter was signed by over 1,000 people from all walks of life, almost two-thirds of whom were from the South. The substantial chorus ranged from singer Christy Moore, poet Paula Meehan and musician Sharon Shannon, to hurler DJ Carey, Mayor of Boston Marty Walsh, and *Irish Times* columnists Fintan O'Toole and David McWilliams. A host of other personalities across business, trade unions, sport, culture and entertainment signed their names to the letter, which was printed over a full page of the *Irish Times*.

In the letter, the organisers of the IF network asked for a mature and reasoned debate in advance of referendums and on the constitutional future of a new Ireland, following a vote for Irish unity, in contrast to the shambles of the Brexit process:

> A clear majority of people in Ireland, both in this state and in the North, want to remain in the European Union. The majority of citizens in the North voted to remain in the 2016 referendum. This includes many unionists. In recent years, a conversation about Ireland's future, and the place of unionists in it, is publicly taking place. Irish citizens should continue to enjoy the rights which accrue from membership of the European Union as well as the full protection of the ECJ. It is the responsibility of the government to ensure that the democratic wishes and rights of Irish citizens are respected and protected, regardless of where they live on the island.

They made their first call on the government to convene a citizens' assembly in order to allow for a structured conversation about the manner in which constitutional and political change could be advanced and Irish unity achieved, as envisaged in the GFA. The request was inspired by the influence of citizens' assemblies on marriage equality and reproductive rights, which paved the way for the successful referendums on both issues over recent years: 'We ask the government to establish a citizens' assembly reflecting the views of citizens North and South, or a forum to discuss the future and achieve maximum consensus on a way forward,' the letter stated.

At a public meeting in Croke Park in Dublin later that month, speakers elaborated on the nature of the proposed citizens' assembly. It should be chosen from people across the island, representing all strands of opinion, gender, identity and geographic location who could, they argued, debate in a reasoned and informed environment what Irish society could look like after unity. It could allow for detailed discussion on the nature of an all-island economy, health service, education system and guarantees to protect the rights of all citizens in a new, shared Ireland.

Among the speakers were a former member of the Victims Commission in Northern Ireland, Patricia MacBride; economist Dr Seamus McGuinness of the ESRI; and Ailbhe Smyth, a leader of the successful campaign for the repeal of the eighth amendment of the Irish Constitution, which resulted in the introduction of legal abortion in the South. Chaired by Senator Frances Black, the meeting also heard Professor Colin Harvey outline the requirement under the GFA to hold a referendum on Irish unity and suggested that it could be called in 2023, the 25th anniversary of the 1998 agreement. He insisted that setting a date would focus minds, and the two governments, on the urgent need for preparation.

Patricia MacBride, a lawyer and commentator, argued that people needed to have an idea of the future arrangements in a shared island and that it was not a simple question of the government in Dublin taking over the running of the Northern Ireland state. Explaining the need for a citizens' assembly in a programme for the event, MacBride said that no one, including anyone in IF, was advocating for

a bolt-on of the 6 counties of the North to the 26 counties of the

South with responsibility for health, education, the economy and the welfare of citizens becoming the responsibility of the Dublin government overnight … A citizens' assembly is not a set of binary questions where people are brought in and asked to answer yes or no. It is a process that is focused on ensuring that democracy is truly representative and that the citizen is at the heart of the debate around political or constitutional reform.

She cited the recent examples of citizens' assemblies that took place from October 2016 to 2018 in Dublin and had considered topics including the repeal of the eighth amendment, climate change, fixed term parliaments, the ageing population and the operation of future referendums. MacBride submitted that it was technically possible to ensure a stratified random sampling of the population across the island to ensure that the assembly was representative of all strands of gender, geography, identity and opinion. A citizens' assembly should be sufficiently broad so that 'it allows for real, informed, facilitated discussion on the economy and inward investment, the health service, the education system, the protection of rights and many other aspects of life and society,' she said.

While there is no guarantee that the recommendations of a citizens' assembly will be adopted by the government, the process did lead to the May 2018 referendum and the vote to legalise abortion in the South by a margin of 66.4 per cent to 33.6 per cent. According to figures from electionsIreland.org, proposals to allow same-sex marriage in the South were passed by 62 per cent to 38 per cent in a referendum in May 2015, after a similar exercise and extensive public discussion and debate.

3

SHOCKS TO THE SYSTEM

The outcome of the 2019 UK election was a significant setback for the DUP and brought to an end the leverage it had influenced through the confidence and supply arrangement with the outgoing Tory government. It lost two seats, including that of its Westminster leader Nigel Dodds, who was defeated in North Belfast by John Finucane, a young lawyer and SF member.

Finucane – Lord Mayor of Belfast and a son of the solicitor Pat Finucane who was shot dead by loyalist and British agents in 1989 – benefitted from the SDLP's decision not to contest the seat. In return, SF gave Claire Hanna of the SDLP a free run to take another DUP seat in South Belfast while Stephen Farry of the Alliance Party won in the wealthy, largely pro-union, North Down constituency previously represented by independent unionist, Sylvia Hermon.

The SF vote was down on its 2017 election result, and it lost its seat in Derry to Colum Eastwood of the SDLP, but the careful voting arrangement between the non-unionist parties meant that, for the first time, the two nationalist parties outnumbered the unionists at Westminster: the DUP returned with 8 seats, while SF had 7, SDLP 2 and Alliance 1. The outcome was even more significant as it meant that a critical target had been reached in the conditions required for the calling of a unity referendum. When the number of votes cast for nationalist candidates exceeded those for unionist candidates in a general election, in the minds of many people the British secretary of state was obliged to at least consider whether to call a referendum or border poll on unity.

A comfortable election victory for Boris Johnson meant that he was no longer shackled in the continuing Brexit negotiations by the twin burdens of the DUP and the extreme Brexiteers within his own party, including the European Research Group. The consequences for politics in the North and for the growing debate on a unity referendum were profound. The immediate effect was a resumption of efforts, led by Julian Smith and Simon Coveney, to restore the suspended devolved institutions at Stormont. After weeks of discussions, an agreement entitled 'New Decade, New Approach' was signed off by all five parties in the assembly. It included commitments on Irish language legislation, and health reforms that guaranteed pay parity for nurses and an action plan on hospital waiting times. It also promised movement to improve the management of the education and justice systems and enhanced accountability for the conduct of ministers, civil servants and special advisers at Stormont.

By mid-January 2020, DUP leader Arlene Foster and SF MLA Michelle O'Neill were installed as First and deputy First Minister respectively, with equal powers, in an executive that also included representatives of Alliance, the Ulster Unionist Party (UUP) and the SDLP.

A month later, a general election in the South had, arguably, even greater significance in relation to a potential unity referendum, when SF emerged with more votes than either Fianna Fáil (FF) or Fine Gael (FG). The result, which defied all pre-election predictions, saw SF take 24.53 per cent of the popular vote compared to 22.18 per cent for FF and 20.8 per cent for FG, with other parties trailing well behind. The history-making swing to SF left the party with 37 seats, fewer than FF with 38, and with FG at 35. The result was all the more remarkable given that, just eight months earlier, in May 2019, SF had lost almost half their council seats and most of their MEPs, following a disastrous performance in the local government and European Parliament elections. As a consequence of those poor results, the party had adopted a cautious approach in the general election and was reluctant to run more than one candidate in most constituencies. Had it adopted a dual-candidate strategy, the party could have returned up to a dozen more TDs as it topped the polls in several constituencies with more than two quotas.

The result sent shockwaves through the political establishment and, in particular, within FF which had, with a large degree of complacency, expected to take up to 60 seats in the election and to be in a position to govern with a smaller party and some of the wide selection of independents returned to Dáil Éireann. The party leadership had underestimated the damage to its independence and credibility from its close association with FG during four years of a confidence and supply arrangement. Equally, both parties had failed to grasp how the continuing crisis in the provision of housing to a whole generation of young voters, and the growth of precarious, low-paid work across wide sectors of the economy, had transformed traditional voting patterns.

The mobilisation of young people in the 2015 and 2018 referendums on marriage equality and reproductive rights for women had raised expectations of what could, and should be, attainable in a modern, European democracy. The creaking public health system, inadequate childcare provision and FG plans to increase the pension age were also factors in the decisions of huge swathes of voters to desert and punish the large centre-right parties that had dominated Irish politics for decades.

The prospect of a referendum and of Irish unity, while promoted by Sinn Féin during the election campaign, did not feature among the primary reasons voters subsequently gave as the motivation for their unprecedented support for the party, but the idea was endorsed by a sizeable number of voters in an exit poll on election day, 8 February 2020. Some 57 per cent of voters polled said they thought there should be referendums on Irish unity, North and South, within five years.

The Ipsos MRBI poll commissioned by RTÉ, the *Irish Times*, TG4 and University College Dublin (UCD), revealed that 75 per cent of 18-to-24-year-olds and 62 per cent of 35-to-64-year-olds wanted a referendum within five years, falling to 47 per cent of over-65s, illustrating a distinct generational preference for unity, or at least a right to vote on it.

During the prolonged post-election discussions on government formation, the prospect of SF taking a prominent, if not leading, role simultaneously in administrations North and South weighed heavily on FF and FG. Both parties refused to enter discussions with SF, despite the similar numbers of seats won by each and the fact that at least two of the three parties would have to enter into a coalition in order to form a government.

Just weeks after the general election, another storm landed that was to have deep and lasting consequences, causing premature deaths among older people in care homes, overpowering the intensive care units (ICUs) of hospitals and stretching the already burdened health systems in both parts of the island.

Covid-19 fundamentally challenged the capacity of government and the public health service in both jurisdictions to protect the lives of citizens, as infections rapidly spread and large parts of the economy were closed down. The first confirmed case on the island was of a Belfast woman who had travelled home from Italy, the epicentre of the coronavirus outbreak in Europe, via Dublin airport.

By early March 2020, the hastily-assembled National Public Health Emergency Team (NPHET) in the South reported a doubling of cases within a week, bringing the total to 18, with another 4 cases in the North as the global figure neared 100,000.

On 12 March, as the first lockdown measures were adopted, Varadkar addressed the nation from Washington DC, where he was visiting President Donald Trump during the St Patrick's Day celebrations. Varadkar remained as Taoiseach until a new government was agreed and appointed and, in this temporary, caretaker role, was now facing the most challenging period since he took office in June 2017. 'We have not witnessed a pandemic of this nature in living memory,' he said. 'This is unchartered territory. We said we would take the right actions at the right time. We have to move now to have the greatest impact.'

Announcing a lockdown of schools, colleges, childcare and cultural institutions until 29 March, Varadkar also advised that indoor events of more than 100 people and outdoor gatherings of more than 500 should be cancelled. He said:

> In the period ahead, the government will deploy all the resources we can muster, human and financial, to tackle this threat head-on. Those resources are extensive but not unlimited. Healthcare workers have been at the forefront of this crisis since it started. They will be at the frontline of the crisis in the time ahead. We must do all we can to help them, so they can help those who need help the most.

The escalating crisis from the Covid-19 virus dominated public discourse as the first lockdown was introduced, while the government announced a raft of financial supports for individuals laid off from their jobs and for businesses forced to close.

The crisis also disrupted the discussions about a referendum for a united Ireland and a series of public meetings planned by IF across the country was postponed indefinitely. Its work was also affected when Niall Murphy contracted Covid-19 during a visit to New York, where he had been invited by the Brehon Law Society to attend Irish American events during the St Patrick's Day celebrations, and to discuss the emerging role of Ireland's Future in the unity debate. On his return to Belfast, Murphy was diagnosed with life-threatening respiratory symptoms and placed in an induced coma for several weeks. In the middle of the night on 30 March 2020, his wife, Marie, was informed that his chances of survival were '50/50'. As with many other patients, he attributed his recovery to the care of nurses, doctors and other frontline staff, but he also criticised the inability of the National Health Service (NHS) in the North to cope with the public health crisis. SF leader Mary Lou McDonald, was on a nationwide tour, addressing large rallies in Cork, Dublin and Newry, to demand her party's place at the table in government formation negotiations, when she was struck down in the early weeks of the Covid-19 crisis.

Notwithstanding the reassuring words of the Taoiseach in Washington, and the professional and scientific advice from the NPHET team led by Chief Medical Officer Tony Holohan, the weaknesses of the public health service in the South and its capacity to cope with an epidemic were quickly exposed. From the outset, the Health and Safety Executive (HSE) scrambled to get into the global market for ICU ventilators, testing kits and basic Personal Protection Equipment (PPE) for healthcare workers and the wider public. As the numbers of cases grew during the first surge, the years of successive cuts in the number of hospital, including ICU, beds and the failure to recruit sufficient nurses and doctors and other crucial frontline staff, came home to roost. The most vulnerable, elderly and sick people in nursing homes and other residential facilities, were the first hit as there was little or no protection in place to prevent the spread of the virus. Poorly ventilated and overcrowded care facilities hastened the spread. Many elderly people were infected when patients were released from hospital settings where the virus was on the rampage, into nursing homes without prior testing for Covid-19.

The cabinet decided not to activate its public emergency strategy, which would have deployed the resources of all the agencies of the state, including the health service, local authorities, government departments, gardaí and defence forces as set out in a report published in July 2017. Over 60 pages, the government report, entitled *Strategic Emergency Management: National Structures and Framework*, contained a detailed plan on how to respond to an unexpected crisis, including one caused by a pandemic. It recommended that the lead department, in this case the Department of Health, should immediately convene the National Emergency Co-ordination Group involving a 'whole of government' response to such an emergency.

Crucially, the government also failed to adopt an immediate policy of closing entry points to travellers from abroad. During March, almost 2,000 rugby supporters were permitted to land in Dublin from Northern Italy, the European epicentre of the Covid-19 crisis, where the coronavirus was already decimating its older population and overwhelming a modern and well-resourced health service. The supporters arrived in the city, even though the international game between Ireland and Italy that they had come to attend, had been cancelled due to the epidemic. Weeks later, hundreds of horse racing enthusiasts from Ireland mingled with many thousands attending the annual meeting at Cheltenham in a part of England already experiencing a rapid spread of infections from the virus. As case numbers soared, the government negotiated a €100 million a month deal to access privately-run hospitals and opened large step-down facilities for recovering patients and specially-commissioned mortuaries to cope with any overload of fatalities. Hundreds of thousands of patients on ever-growing waiting lists, including those awaiting treatment for chronic and life-threatening conditions, were unable to meet their consultants. Elderly residents of private care homes, many staffed by underpaid, undertrained and poorly-resourced workers, were dying at a rapid rate, while ICU units were almost overrun as numbers peaked between April and June.

Health and Social Care (HSC), the operator of the NHS in the North, was also overwhelmed as case numbers and deaths rose at a higher rate than in the South, and hospitals and healthcare workers struggled to cope with the pressure. A similar inability, or reluctance, in the North to curb the numbers of international arrivals intensified the spread of the virus, which was raging across the UK and stretching its NHS to the limit.

The failure, in both jurisdictions, to develop an efficient contact tracing system, which would have enabled the health services to track the source of individual infections and clusters of Covid-19 cases, severely hampered an effective response to the spread of the virus. While the numbers of deaths and cases in the North were significantly higher than in the South per head of population, the virus did not recognise borders, and it was evident that deeper co-operation was required between both administrations to delay and curtail its spread.

By the end of June, and as the first surge abated, the Health Protection Surveillance Centre (HPSC) in Dublin reported that there had been 1,475 confirmed Covid-19 related deaths and 25,462 cases in the Republic. In the North, there had been 551 deaths and 5,760 cases reported by the Northern Ireland Statistics and Research Agency (NISRA) at the end of June, as numbers of daily fatalities dropped to zero after the first lockdown. The scale of the crisis and the failure of the authorities, North and South, to agree measures to curb entry, or to enforce a strict testing and quarantining regime for those arriving at airports and seaports in order to stop the spread of the virus as other island nations had successfully done, was a matter of major public concern. The mounting death rates and the inability to seal off the country due to UK jurisdiction in the North, also led to speculation and debate as to the potential benefits of an all-island health service in the event of a unity referendum. The refusal of the main unionist parties to agree to any restrictions on entry from the UK, even as the virus killed many more in Britain than in any other country in Europe, was a significant factor in allowing its spread across the North and border counties during the first surge. This was the greatest public health emergency since the Spanish flu in 1918.

From the outset of the pandemic, Dr Gabriel Scally of Bristol University had called for an all-island response. Scally, a public health specialist, was born in 1954 in Belfast, where his father was a psychiatrist. As a child, Scally travelled each summer to Donegal where his father, who had previously been a GP, would cover as a locum for his uncle who, with his wife, ran a GP practice in Letterkenny. Scally's annual holidays to Donegal ended because his father, coming from the universal free

NHS culture, found it difficult to charge patients, while his uncle could not maintain his medical practice if he didn't. It was Scally's first insight into the contrast in public health provision on the island.

After attending secondary school in St Mary's in Belfast, Scally went on to study medicine in Queen's University in the city where he became active in student politics and served as a vice-president of the Union of Students in Ireland. His main interest was in public health and he spent two years training as a GP, including for a period in the village of Mullabawn close to Forkhill, in south Armagh at the height of the Troubles in the late 1970s.

On completing his degree, Scally did his post-graduate studies in public health in the School of Hygiene and Tropical Medicine in London and returned to work as a consultant in Belfast before his appointment as chief administrative medical officer of the Eastern Health and Social Services Board of Northern Ireland at the end of the 1980s. He subsequently took a position as a regional director of public health with the NHS in England, where he worked for 20 years.

Throughout his professional life, Scally has promoted the view that a universal health service, free at the point of use is the most effective, sensible and fair model of provision. 'The evidence base is perfectly clear from around the world that if you wish to get a fully functioning health service that deals with people equally and fairly, the only sensible way of funding it is out of general taxation. And free to everyone at the point of use,' he told this author in August 2020.

Before the arrival of Covid-19, Scally had carried out the investigation into the CervicalCheck scandal in the South and reported on the reasons so many women who developed cervical cancer had been provided with possible 'false negative' results following earlier smear tests for cancer. His report was widely recognised as a shocking and accurate portrayal of a dysfunctional service.

Scally was scathing at the lack of a coherent strategy to deal with the pandemic in either the Republic or the UK. He said he was the first to use the term 'Zero-Covid' as the most effective way to completely suppress the virus by making use of the advantage of living on an island. A member of Independent SAGE, a group of professionals in the UK with diverse medical expertise, Scally made an influential and effective intervention in the Covid-19 debate in both jurisdictions. He was among the first to call for an 'all-island' medical response, including a complete ban on foreign travel into Ireland:

> We were on the verge of suppression both North, South and in Scotland, and the fact we didn't fully suppress it was because we didn't try hard enough. We didn't put the resources into that goal. It's very hard to achieve something when it's not your goal. We're mopping up the floor here in this place, but we haven't fixed the hole in the roof.

Scally cited the failure to restrict arrivals from abroad at an earlier stage of the crisis as particularly negligent:

> At the time, Britain and Ireland were in a minority of countries across the world which did not impose border restrictions. The reason voluminous air traffic stopped was not because of Britain and Ireland doing anything to stop people waltzing in with viruses. It was because other countries stopped them. I've always regarded that as a failure.

The Covid-19 experience reinforced Scally's view that there should be a single, universal, health care system across the island of Ireland:

> One of the key cornerstones of the World Health Organization's international programme for development of health across the world is universal access. Achieving universal access across the island of Ireland is something that is a pretty fundamental building block, which is why I've been very pleased to see what is in Sláintecare.

Sláintecare, a 10-year plan for reform of the health services in the South, was agreed by the Oireachtas Committee on the Future of Healthcare in 2017. It proposed the establishment of a universal, single-tier health service, where patients are treated solely on the basis of health need. It also recommended that the health system should move 'towards integrated primary and community care, consistent with the highest quality of patient safety in as short a time-frame as possible'. It proposed the decentralisation of health administration and suggested that the ambitious reform programme should be led by the Department of the Taoiseach.

The South was the only country in western Europe that did not provide universal coverage of primary care, a situation that Sláintecare aimed to alter. In the South, over half of the population pay €50 for a GP visit. Those who arrive at an A&E department without a referral letter from their GP are asked to pay €100. Two-thirds of the population spend almost €150 per month on prescription drugs, on top of payments they make for other medical services. Those on low incomes (almost one-third of the population) are entitled to medical cards that provide free primary and hospital care. In recent years, the numbers of those with medical cards or GP visit cards has risen to more than 45 per cent of the population. In April 2019, it was announced that by 2022, free GP care would be extended to all children under the age of 12. Sláintecare also envisaged a movement towards free, universal GP services, comparable to the current NHS in the North.

A key challenge to both services, however, has been the unacceptable and damaging waiting times for the most basic of treatments, as well as for the most urgent of life-threatening conditions. In 2019, over 800,000 people were on waiting lists in the public system in the South, a figure which has continued to rise due to restrictions caused by the Covid-19 crisis. (By September 2021, the number had risen to 900,000 people, according to data from the National Treatment Purchase Fund (NTPF).)

Those who can afford to pay, or who have voluntary health insurance, can avail of private hospitals and can also gain more rapid access for diagnosis and treatment in the public health system. By developing a contract for consultants to work exclusively in public hospitals, Sláintecare also challenges the influence of the private medical industry over the health service.

In June 2020, Scally spoke with Monaghan GP Ilona Duffy and the late Professor Jim Dornan, in a video broadcast organised by IF about the ongoing pandemic, the failure to develop an all-island response and its impact on border areas. 'There is no point in having free ice cream for life if it takes a year to get a poke,' he said in relation to excessive waiting lists in the North during the broadcast.

While private health care is not as pervasive or developed in the North, the underfunding of the NHS and the creeping privatisation of health provision has fostered inequality between those who can afford to avoid ever-lengthening waiting lists by accessing private treatment elsewhere – including in the South, the UK or in Europe – and those who cannot afford to do so. However, the free, universal access to primary, community and hospital care by the NHS remains a significant benefit for citizens in the North compared to those south of the border.

Scally said that the government's role in taking over private hospital facilities – albeit at a cost of €100 million a month – to cope with the first surge of the Covid-19 crisis, was a form of nationalisation and an example of what is possible. Introducing a universal health service would require careful consideration and planning to meet the concerns of those who currently operate and use the private system, he argued:

> Better commissioning and contracting of services shows how a universal system would make use of private facilities all the way through to a nationalisation programme. It was interesting to see how the government moved very rapidly to nationalise the hospitals, in a sense, for Covid-19. I think there are a series of layers to that. There is the ownership of private facilities by

capital-based organisations, there are the interests of individual professionals in terms of their personal private practice and then there are the interests of the public who will worry that they will be giving up something that they hold dear, which is their ability to consult a doctor of their choice and get the treatment that they want at any time.

The pre-Covid public health service in the South costs almost €18 billion annually in public monies, while Northern Ireland Health and Social Services (commonly referred to as the NHS), requires about £8 billion each year. The North is the least resourced of the NHS regions across the UK and its deficiencies were highlighted when Covid-19 threatened to overwhelm hospitals and state-run care homes in the summer and autumn of 2020. In the South, the Covid crisis similarly challenged the health service and exposed its shortage of ICU and critical care beds as well as step-down facilities, and contributed to a tragic failure of supervision and protection for older people in nursing homes, as reported in the *Irish Times* in February 2021.

For Scally, the merging of the two services into a single universal health system in an all-Ireland scenario makes economic and political sense and would produce better economies of scale and outcomes for users. It is important, in his view, to concentrate highly specialised medical procedures and treatments but to have public health services available in every community. As he put it:

> The diffusion of medical health technology has changed the map of what can be done locally and in terms of the specialisation of services required in order to get better outcomes. The island of Ireland, in my view, is a really good size for a very well structured, highly efficient health service in which to operate.

Where previously community care was based on the old health board system, with public health nurses and centres located in towns and villages across the country, the GP system is now the favoured method for bringing care closer to the patient, including in the Sláintecare proposals.

In the North, a 2016 report by Spanish consultant, Rafael Bengoa, envisaged a similar future for healthcare services. It also proposed a consolidation of specialised treatments in regional centres of excellence. At the same time, it argued that many other services could be provided closer to people's homes, including in community-based GP centres, rather than in hospitals.

In both health systems, there is a movement towards multi-disciplinary teams, including pharmacists, mental health professionals, physiotherapists and social workers working with GPs to provide a more holistic approach to medical care. As with Sláintecare, the health service in the North, in the wake of the Bengoa report, adopted a policy of shifting care out of hospital and towards treatment of people in their neighbourhoods with a greater focus on illness prevention.

As a new wave of Covid-19 cases hit in the autumn of 2020, placing more pressure on the two health systems, Scally continued to publicly advocate for greater investment and resources in public health, including more public health doctors, in order to prevent the future recurrence of the devastation caused by the Covid-19 pandemic. He warned that a further surge, including of new variants, was likely and that an all-island response, including to inward travel, was essential to avoid many more preventable deaths. His advice was not always heeded. Neither was his view, shared by many other doctors and consultants, that a free, universal service built on the NHS model is the best fit for an all-island health service.

Professor John Crown, an oncologist at St Vincent's University Hospital in Dublin and former independent senator, agreed during an interview with the author that an all-island health service providing for a population of over 7 million people would be 'doable', notwithstanding the current dysfunctional nature of both systems, North and South. Other countries have excellent models already in place by way of example:

I'm a believer in socialised medicine but I'm not a believer in socialised medicine where everything is run by the government. What the government has to do is ensure a level playing field, to ensure through legislation and regulation that everybody has mandatory access to healthcare, to ensure rich people pay more for it than poor people do and to make sure that what everybody gets in the end is an equal and high-quality service.

The British model, however, is just to make sure that everybody gets an equal service and forget about the quality. As a result, the NHS has extraordinarily long waiting lists, only surpassed by Ireland. It has a very low doctor–patient ratio and mediocre outcomes. It's not a bad health system. It's just not an excellent one.

The excellent ones are Germany, France, Holland, Belgium. These are systems where government mandates that you must have insurance in one way or another. It doesn't own all the hospitals; it owns some of them. Under this model, people all have a universal social insurance entitlement which they can take at their choice to a government-run hospital, to a private hospital, to a university hospital, to a religious charity. Whatever it is, they take it where they want. The poor person would pay a whole lot less and the unemployed person would pay nothing for it.

Leaving aside the politics, an all-island health service would be sufficiently big with a population of seven million rather than just five million in the South to be very self-contained. People in Denmark, Norway or Sweden don't ever have to leave those countries to get healthcare and we wouldn't either. We'd be able to do everything, I would hope. We need fundamental reform in the system in the South. Trying to merge the two Frankensteins into one viable monster would be hard but not undoable.

Crown said that Sláintecare may succeed in taking private beds out of the public hospitals, but it will not eliminate the two-tier health system:

Sláintecare entrenches two-tier healthcare because it would be a totally separate public system and a totally separate private system. Under Sláintecare, the private system will thrive because people will leave the public system in droves. Private healthcare in Ireland is not only something some rarefied social elite have. Teachers, taxi drivers, guards, prison officers have private health insurance. It's not like England where [it's] only the top 10 per cent of the population that have it. What we call private insurance in Ireland is actually social insurance. It's the same thing that they have in Canada, only there they call it National Social Insurance.

In the same interview, Crown was scathing about the failure of the health authorities to deal with the waiting lists which are heading towards the one million mark and claimed that it is not an aberration but a business model:

The Irish health system is not underfunded, it's 'malfunded'. It's funded in a way that does not incentivise efficiency and equality. Instead, it incentivises inactivity because the hospital knows the patient on a waiting list does not cost anything. The patient costs the hospital no money until they come into the hospital and you start doing stuff to them. The waiting time is the business model of the system. The business model of the waiting list is to constrain the resource, make them wait.

It's more fundamental than saying it's somehow dysfunctional as a system. People have to decide; do they want the doctor who will try and get their treatment done relatively quickly and to a high quality, or do they want somebody who is being paid a salary who will say, 'you can go on a list and wait for it'?

It is interesting that the people that make that model all have private insurance. All the HSE administrators, Department of

Health civil servants, nearly all politicians have private health insurance. It doesn't affect them, that's part of the problem.

We've far too many small hospitals, far too many medical schools. A whole lot of things for historical reasons evolved in different ways and that's just the reality of where we are. Trying to get them to act in concert and to have a critical concentration of resources is not a bad idea. For some things it is probably good, but it doesn't again fix the fundamental problems which are access, inequality and waiting lists.

Crown also argued that the service in the South is well served by outstanding nurses, doctors and other healthcare professionals:

The problem is that they and their facilities are in such short supply that we prop up the bottom of most league tables for access to care. Waiting lists for tests, specialist appointments and operations are so long that in some cases the services effectively don't exist. Treatment delayed is treatment denied. Despite repeated warnings that our intensive care capacity was deficient, it took a pandemic to get action from the Department of Health and the HSE.

4

THE ECONOMICS OF IRISH UNITY

Just as the Covid-19 crisis challenged the healthcare system in both jurisdictions, it altered the narrative about the policies required for the recovery of the economy and the prospect for a united or shared Ireland in the future. By almost every measurement, the standard of living for people in the South is better than for those in Northern Ireland. That was not always the case, but over recent decades, life expectancy, average incomes, educational achievement and productivity in the South have considerably exceeded those in the North. Until 2005, life expectancy in the North was greater than in the South. By 2015, according to 2020 data from Ireland's Economics and Social Research Institute (ESRI), the people in the South were living longer and the gap in life expectancy was getting wider. By 2018, based on OECD estimates, women in the South were expected to live 1.5 years longer than those in the North, and men 1.4 years.

With an annual national output of over €360 billion, the economy of the South is over six times that of the North, which produces about £60 billion each year. The population of the South has reached 5 million people, compared to 1.9 million in the North (just 2.9 per cent of the UK), and has a vibrant, open economy, notwithstanding the economic damage inflicted by the recession and Covid-19.

On average, the people of the South produce and earn significantly more than those in the North, and the disparity is growing year on year. In 1911, Belfast had a bigger population than Dublin, had a larger industrial workforce and was a substantially bigger producer of goods and services. As noted in Bob Rowthorn's 1981 essay 'Northern Ireland: an economy in crisis', until the 1930s, the North was a net contributor to the UK economy and substantially wealthier, per head of population, than the new state in the South.

Since before the 1970s and the onset of the Troubles, the North has become one of the poorest regions in the UK and is hugely dependent on the annual subvention it receives from the British government to manage its public services. In the 1980s, 52 per cent of workers were employed in the public sector, including many in the police and prison service as the conflict intensified, compared to an equivalent figure of 22 per cent in the UK. According to the ESRI, unemployment rates reached 20 per cent (and over 30 per cent in Catholic or nationalist areas) as the North fell behind other regions across the UK.

The economy in the South went through recession with high unemployment rates in the 1980s, but its dramatic recovery and expansion in the following decade was not matched by the North. In the decades following the GFA in 1998, the growth rate in the North was less than a quarter of that in the more prosperous southern and eastern region of the Republic where 75 per cent of its people lived. Instead, it was closer to the poorest Border, Midlands and Western (BMW) region in the South with its 25 per cent of the population.

Foreign direct investment (FDI) by multinational corporations that produce high value goods for export has contributed to the stronger economic growth and productivity of the South, particularly since the late 1990s. The tax rate of 12.5 per cent and other generous incentives that allowed multinational companies to avoid paying the full tax levy, have also drawn FDI to the South. The increase of the rate to 15 per cent, as proposed by the Organisation for Economic Co-operation and

Development (OECD), along with action to eliminate the methods used by corporates to minimise their tax liabilities to other states, will reduce the annual, and disproportionate, contribution of international capital to the exchequer. As the South is the only English-speaking country in the EU since Brexit, however, its economy is likely to benefit from continued FDI that otherwise might have gone to the UK if it had remained in the trading bloc.

Rising standards in education, the English-speaking workforce and access to the EU market of 400 million consumers, have been key factors in the attraction of FDI into the South. Conversely, lower educational attainment has acted as a deterrent to high-skilled, high-value, export-oriented investment to the North, which contributes to the unfavourable comparison with the South in relation to gross domestic product (GDP) per capita. OECD estimates in 2018 showed that GDP per capita was $85,100 in the South and $36,700 in the North before the adjustment for the multinationals. After removing the influence of FDI from the accounts, GDP per capita was $51,900 for the South and $34,300 for the North. ESRI figures show that disposable household income, the money that families on average have to spend each year after essential costs are met, is also significantly different at $34,000 in the South and $29,400 in the North, a gap of $4,600, or 12 per cent, per household.

The subvention is the difference between the revenue raised and expenditure in the North in any year. It is provided by the government in Westminster, which sets and collects tax from citizens in the North. Expenditure is controlled by the UK government, which effectively decides how much is spent on public services, including health, education, social welfare, local government and security.

For many years, the debate on the cost of Irish unity focused on the issue of the subvention and whether the Irish exchequer could afford the estimated €10 billion that it costs the British government each year to run the North. In the years since the GFA, the subvention increased from less than £6.2 billion in 2002 to just under £9.2 billion in 2018. Even at

£10 billon, the subvention is only a fraction of the overall value of the Irish economy and amounts to less than 2.5 per cent of annual output of the South. Adjusting for the distorting influence of the multinationals, the subvention remains at less than 5 per cent of the total value of the economy in the South.

The subvention covers costs that will not become liabilities on the Irish exchequer after unification, including UK defence spending, debt interest payments and diplomatic and other international services which, along with other expenditures, could amount to 26 per cent of the total. These are non-identifiable items of current expenditure, which are estimates of the regional contribution of the North to wider UK spending and will not constitute part of the costs to the new Irish state of administration after unification.

Further, the UK will remain liable – morally, if not legally – for the cost of pensions it administered and to which generations of workers paid contributions over their lives in the North. According to the UK treasury, expenditure on pensions for public service workers in the North was £3.2 billion in 2017. During the debate on independence in advance of the 2014 referendum in Scotland, the UK government publicly conceded that it would continue to bear the costs of public sector pensions owed to retired workers there. Similarly, the EU took responsibility for the pensions of British citizens who worked for it before the UK exit in 2016.

Removing these liabilities will reduce the cost to the new Irish exchequer of replacing the subvention even further. These and other subvention-related factors – including the level of UK debt assigned to the North and what assets would be shared by the British – make it difficult to assess the real cost of unification to the Irish people. However, removing these liabilities will reduce the subvention to less than £5 billion from the current estimated cost of £9.2 billion and potentially much lower.

The cost of the subvention is relatively insignificant in relation to the overall finances of the Irish state, notwithstanding the legacy of debt which is outstanding from the financial crisis of 2009–2011 and the Covid-19 pandemic. It is evident that low productivity levels in the North created the necessity for the subvention in the first place. Rather than an argument for how well the North is faring, the subvention is, rather, a reflection of its economic failures and dependence.

It can also be argued that the economic and human cost of partition has greatly exceeded the cost of the subvention. From its formation in 1921, the Irish state struggled financially to survive and hundreds of thousands of people left the country in successive waves of emigration over the decades. The reality, of course, is that financial negotiations between Ireland and Britain following a vote in favour of unity could take several years and will, more than likely, involve a transition period during which operational and fiscal responsibilities would be gradually transferred. As ESRI economists Seamus McGuinness and Adele Bergin explain:

> A key aspect of the current debate around a border poll relates to the potential cost of reunification. We conclude that it is difficult to be specific about this as it is determined by a number of unknowns, including the length and nature of any adjustment or transition period, the relative role of both governments during that transition period in addressing some of the key issues … in reforming educational, industrial and regional policy, the relative success of such policies in raising NI productivity levels, the role and significance of the EU and USA in potentially reintegrating post-Brexit NI into the EU and assisting and promoting FDI to the region and the outcome of discussion on the issues of debt, assets and pension obligations.

As a result of the decision by the European Council of Ministers in 2017, a reunified Ireland would be a full member of the EU, which will have a stake and direct involvement in the financial and transitional arrangements and negotiations following the transfer of sovereignty from Britain. It can also be assumed that the US government – which helped to broker the GFA, has remained committed to its terms and conditions and has major economic interests on the island – will contribute financially to the new state following unity.

There will be a range of other economic returns from unification, not least the economies of scale that can be achieved from managing a society and economy of almost 7 million rather than two separate administrations of government. Further investment in integrated transport, energy, broadband and other infrastructural networks, particularly in depressed and previously divided border economies, can yield major advances in productivity levels and generate increased trade, business and employment across the island, as well as improving tax revenues.

The experience in other countries, notably of Germany in 1990, has confirmed the potential for a dramatic boost in the value of goods and services produced (the GDP) in the wake of unification. Canadian firm KL Consulting, along with academics from the University of British Columbia, estimated in 2016 that a unified Irish economy could generate an additional €35.6 billion in GDP within eight years of unification.

According to Intertrade Ireland, cross-border trade between small- and medium-sized enterprises in 2018 was valued at £6.5 billion, while the number of businesses trading between North and South was already higher than those between the North and the UK.

Economist and columnist David McWilliams said that preparations should be made for a referendum on Irish unity in order to release the potential of an all-island economy and revive the fortunes of what was once a thriving industrial centre in the north-east. When the two states were formed in 1921, one was heavily industrialised, with much better levels of education. The balance sheet 100 years later shows the complete failure of the North, which was twice as rich per head as the South in 1921 and is now twice as poor. The economy of the South is now six-to-eight times bigger on a GDP basis. Like many parts of the United Kingdom, the North has become infantilised by Westminster, McWilliams said in an interview with this writer:

> Only a country that issues its own bonds is an adult country. By that I mean, when you go out to the market and the Republic of Ireland says we want to borrow €20 billion tomorrow and the market says, ok this is your rating, you have an adult conversation.
>
> If you look at what is happening to Wales and Scotland and, of course, Northern Ireland in the context of the United Kingdom, there's an infantilisation of economics. The economy becomes a game of 'How much dole can I get?' The unfortunate thing is the answer to the union now, the only answer they have is, 'We will get more dole' and that is not a long-term way of living.
>
> Northern Ireland is a concubine economy, it exists to service and favour the central government of the union, and it's really, really bad for it. It's really bad for Scotland and Wales too. The United Kingdom is a series of regions which are dependent on the largesse of London.

Married to Sian, who is from a Protestant and unionist background in the North, McWilliams has witnessed over recent decades the steady withdrawal of younger, middle-class people from the unionist community:

> For the first 25 years of Northern Ireland's existence it was a net contributor [to the UK exchequer] so it was richer. Now what I see is this constant brain drain of my Protestant-born friends from the North and this unwillingness or a lack of interest in building a society there. They end up in Newcastle, Bristol and other parts of England and they don't come back. The Northern Prods, the middle-class ones just disappear.

In relation to the subvention, McWilliams agreed that it is minuscule in the context of the economy in the South:

> It's about 4 per cent of Irish GDP, it's not a big deal. You could raise a bond for that in the morning, you could raise today a perpetual bond to finance Northern Ireland for the next 100 years. Money is the least of the problems with the new Ireland. Money is never the problem. And it's not a lot of money. It's only peanuts in a €400 billion economy.

Taking the example of transport strategy, McWilliams said that it is possible to develop a mental map of what a new Ireland could be like following a referendum on unity:

> What is very important when you conceive of a new idea and a new country is new geography. What partition has been extremely good at is creating an unusual mind map in our minds of what Ireland looks like. For example, the idea of a Derry-to-Cork connection is abstract to most people. Whereas if you asked an Italian about a Milan-to-Naples connection, it would be something they can picture in their heads. They can picture the roads, the trains, how you get from A to B. In the same way in the UK: from Newcastle to London, people can picture it. The most unusual thing about Ireland is that our mind map of what our country looks like has been totally contaminated by the border.

The destruction of the railway network accelerated the process of rural decline in both jurisdictions and, along with the border, cut off large swathes of the west and north-west from their natural urban hinterlands. McWilliams continued:

> I don't think I've ever heard of an Irish person in my life talking about a road trip from Derry to Cork. When you change the

transport infrastructure, it forces upon people a new mental map of what the country looks like. If I were in power, the first thing I would do is move Dublin and Belfast port simultaneously to a port somewhere around Drogheda. Unification has to be something real so you have to say, 'We are preparing for this.'

In the future, the Belfast–Dublin conurbation will be home to more than half the people on the island. If you draw a line from around Wicklow town straight up to Ballymena and in from the sea around 20 miles, that corridor is going to be home to half the population. Your infrastructural thought has to go into that. Then you deal with the western corridor, which is Derry to Cork and west of that. Transport systems are much more than ways of travelling from A to B, they're actually extraordinarily unifying maps of how the country should look.

Partition has been very successful in dividing the economy as an entity and I think from that, everything else flows. Dublin and Belfast should be trading with each other every day but are not and Belfast should be trading with the likes of Cork but it's not, so all we have is this Dublin–Cork nexus. It strikes me that in the course of this new Ireland there will be a re-balancing, a more logical economy. The all-island economy is not as big as it should be and that's a function of the fact that the Northern Irish economy is totally and utterly dependent on the UK economy. Meanwhile, the North has yet to recover from decades of conflict and the destruction of many small businesses.

Don't underestimate how much the Northern small business [model] was destroyed by the Troubles. It was destroyed intentionally and wantonly and that takes a long, long time to get over. But business has always been a much more revolutionary and incendiary part of the political infrastructure and it does recover.

McWilliams predicted that there will be an all-island economy of eight million people by 2050, richer than the some of the wealthier regions of the UK:

> This will be an economy much richer than Manchester, much richer than many regions in the UK. If it adopts the growth model of the Republic, there's no reason to believe that it cannot compete and almost become like Connecticut or Massachusetts in the United States: a reasonably well-off part of the world which is centrist or maybe left of centre in its feel and is a successful civilised country.
>
> What we have is a story that is potentially the most interesting economic political story in Europe. There are more immigrants on the island than there are unionists. At most, the unionist population will constitute about 18 per cent of the entire (all-island) entity. This is not something to be afraid of. This is something to be worked with. I do happen to think that the model should be Switzerland. There are three big cultures in one country, and they don't particularly like each other, and they've remained very separate as cultural entities for many hundreds of years and the way in which they have lived together is profoundly devolved direct democracy. That's the way we've got to go, so the people in north Antrim who feel very threatened by this [unity] idea, should be given the opportunity to almost rule themselves.

5

EDUCATION IS THE KEY

E ducational performance, or the lack of it, is a major contributory factor to the low growth rate, productivity and income levels in the North. Since 2000, the North has continuously recorded the highest proportion of people with basic or no qualifications, and the lowest number of graduates of any region of the UK. The lower numbers entering third-level education in the North compared to the South is a further and dramatic illustration of the gap in overall living standards between the two jurisdictions. A comparison of attainment levels of 24- to 30-year-olds in 2015, showed that over 35 per cent of young people in the North were only educated to primary or secondary levels with less than 11 per cent in the South failing to advance beyond that stage. ESRI data from 2020 shows that only 40 per cent of young people in the North obtained post-secondary or third-level qualifications, compared to between 59 and 65 per cent across regions in the South.

The failure to integrate, and a selection system that excludes huge numbers of children from good education in their early teens, is a fundamental structural weakness in the provision of learning in the North. At age 11, about 30 per cent of children go on to grammar schools and will continue through the system. The remainder end up in schools of a lower standard and many tend to leave by the age of 16. As a consequence, only 74 per cent of children aged between 15 and 19 in the North are engaged in education compared to a figure of 93 per cent in the South. Most children in the South complete their Leaving Certificate or the vocational pathway known as the Leaving Cert Applied. There are no similar vocational platforms in the North and many drop out of education unless they have a defined route to university. Children from high-income, middle-class families who can afford private tuition are in a better position to pass the tests that allow access to grammar schools.

Unfortunately, a range of factors, including a restricted choice of subjects for children over 16, has driven many out of educational learning at too young an age. The education system in the South is also discriminatory against lower-income families with high pupil–teacher ratios, poor quality buildings and a lack of resources, but it achieves better outcomes than in the North.

For generations, from the age of four or five, children in the North have gone through a segregated system of education. Many, if not most, did not encounter children of another denomination until they finished primary school. Due to the segregation in housing between Catholic/ Protestant and unionist/nationalist communities, schooling has reflected the divide, particularly in working-class areas. As society has moved on, and over 25 per cent of people do not identify with any particular church or faith, a comprehensive review is underway in order to seek a single, widely acceptable and more integrated education system.

Before the Covid-19 crisis disrupted the programme, over half the schoolchildren in the North were involved in education partnerships, with up to 716 schools and about 85,000 students sharing classes. According to Professor Tony Gallagher of the School of Social Sciences, Education and Social Work at Queen's University Belfast, the shared education programme, which is supported by legislation, requires the authorities to encourage collaboration between teachers and pupils across the communities, including students attending different schools in their own uniforms. He told this writer:

The basic idea of shared education is to try and create a collaborative network where kids were moving between schools to take classes and the teachers were engaging with each other across the divide. I've seen prize nights in schools where you have kids from different schools in their own uniforms receiving a prize for shared educational activity in the school. You see kids with different uniforms in the same classrooms or the same corridors and that is a visual demonstration of our capacity to deal with difference.

One of the advantages of having separate uniforms is it makes it clear to everyone that this is going on; that people from different schools are collaborating and working together and it's terribly unproblematic. It's one of the unexpected pluses of the project. We'd have always thought of uniforms as a negative and this has been a plus. This is all likely to continue.

According to Gallagher, the independent review of education is expected to encourage more investment of resources and energy into the integration of schools. He pointed out that the movement towards integrated education has stalled since 2000: only 65 schools were based on the model of having a minimum of 30 per cent of students coming from a Protestant, and 30 per cent from a Catholic, background. While most of the integrated schools are in middle-class areas, there are others, such as Hazelwood College in north Belfast, which are close to interface areas with a history of sectarian tension.

The main teacher training colleges are also divided by religion and resisted the proposal for a single, non-denominational institute some years ago. An exception to Fair Employment legislation allows schools to select teachers who share their ethos by imposing a religious test before they are appointed.

The education system is also badly served by an academic selection process for primary school children (usually aged between 10 and 11), in which students face a series of transfer tests that will determine whether they can access a particular grammar or state-controlled school, which will, in turn, either lead them to third level and university, or leave them behind. About two-thirds of the children attending the state-controlled schools are from Protestant families. Most Catholic-raised children attend schools managed by the Council for Catholic Maintained Schools (CCMS).

As education minister from 1999 to 2002, the late Martin McGuinness of SF sought to abolish academic selection before the suspension of the power-sharing institutions. Later, his successor, Caitríona Ruane, proposed a similar move but was obstructed when the British government conceded to a demand by the DUP that it would retain the power to veto any such legislation on the issue at Stormont. Ruane sought a phasing out of academic testing at primary level – which had been abolished decades previously in the South and in most OECD countries – and got support from many school principals across the North, and from the Catholic Church hierarchy. There was, however, resistance from boards of management of second-level schools in both communities as well as from unionist politicians. As Gallagher explained, the situation has, if anything, worsened:

> Catríona Ruane tried to short circuit the system by ending the official tests, but because the academic selection itself wasn't banned, two consortiums of grammar schools established their own tests. Ironically, one is largely used by Protestant grammar schools while the other test is largely, but not exclusively, used by Catholic grammar schools. That alternative eleven-plus has operated from 2008. It's completely bizarre. We never thought that we'd end up with two eleven-pluses rather than one. These type of high-stake tests for kids that young has led to massive social class differences in terms of outcome. That's what we have in Northern Ireland.

The failure to remove academic testing for 11-year-olds also means that children with special intellectual needs are filtered through the selection system and excluded from access to their preferred schools. Many parents, from both traditions, are now sending their children to the best-performing private secondary schools, basing the choice on their child's prospects of getting to third level and obtaining professional qualifications rather than their religious ethos. As Gallagher put it during an interview with this author:

> There's always been a degree of crossover, particularly of Catholic parents sending their kids to, what they'd consider, the elite Protestant grammar schools. It's risen over recent years and there's probably about half a dozen Protestant schools who would have a significant minority of Catholic students. [There are] a couple in Belfast, and in different parts of the North.

The churches continue to wield a major influence on the running of both the Catholic and the largely Protestant, state-controlled education sectors. For many years, the Catholic Church provided the main civic institution for the minority nationalist community. Teaching jobs were an important route into the professions for Catholics, while the school curriculum encouraged a knowledge of Irish culture and language, which the state schools did not. According to Gallagher:

> Until relatively recently the Catholic schools [service], apart from the Church itself, was the only civic institution for the minority community. Teaching jobs were very important jobs for Catholics. These schools were one of the few places where you could openly express a sense of your Irishness in a society where there was lots of discrimination against Catholics.

Getting rid of the religious test in the hiring of teachers so that they can apply for jobs in any school would be a progressive move, he said, and would break some barriers between the communities. Creating a single teacher training system would also help, as the existing colleges for primary teachers in Belfast, Stranmillis and St Mary's, each serve mainly one tradition. Efforts to merge the teacher training colleges some years ago were unsuccessful and only about 20 per cent of student teachers at Stranmillis are from the Catholic/nationalist community while St Mary's teacher training college is almost exclusively Catholic.

Another difficulty has been the difference in the teaching of history. State-controlled schools and others emphasise British culture and comparisons rather than look to the South; indeed some do not teach the subject at all in order to avoid controversy. Recent improvements to the curriculum, however, have tried to tackle this divergence. As Gallagher explained:

> The curriculum we have now is quite good and there's a lot of teacher interaction around particular areas like history teaching or citizenship, so there's a lot of good professional development. There was a lot of collaboration during Covid as well where lots of schools and teachers were sharing resources and expertise.

Shared education has also helped to mitigate the imbalances and inequities in the A level exam system whereby second-level children in the North are forced to choose a small number of subjects for the final year. This has resulted in classes for popular subjects such as English and Maths being heavily subscribed, while minority subjects such as languages and science attract fewer pupils. Through the shared education initiative, schools have improved the numbers attending classes for these minority A level subjects.

Gallagher argued that, in a united Ireland, people of a Catholic/Irish background and other denominations, or none, will be in the majority with Protestant/unionists in a minority:

> In a potential united Ireland, and assuming you will have a

common school system across the island, the same principles must apply to protect minority rights and protect the position of a Protestant minority in terms of schools and education. If there's going to be an all-Ireland system, there will have to be some sort of acknowledgement of the Britishness of Ulster Protestants. You need to ensure you find some way to protect that.

One way is to make sure the curriculum for mixed schools has something to reflect this, as in their British history and identity. The other way is by allowing minority schools to operate as a way of providing some of that protection. The key thing is recognising that that is an issue that needs to be addressed and that there isn't a simple solution to it.

A transition period will be required to find a common education system and curricula that can be applied across the island, while also maintaining a choice for parents who want to raise their children in schools that reflect their ethos and culture. Among the most progressive and multicultural schools in the South are those in the Educate Together model, which provides for children of all religions and none. In the South, DEIS schools (Delivering Equality of Opportunity in Schools) have also helped to ensure that children from families living in disadvantaged communities are encouraged to attend and stay in the school system. The Gaelscoileanna, or Irish language schools, have allowed many thousands of children to learn through Irish and have grown rapidly in number across the North in recent years, while the demand has also grown in many communities south of the border. Gallagher said:

You're not talking about radical change overnight. It's also important to recognise some of the consequences of the social divisions, the class divisions within the system. Most children may not be able to access private schools. It's better to try and bring as many schools as possible into the system but, as part of that, trying to ensure they don't use mechanisms that are exclusive.

In the longer term, the goal would be to have an education system that is genuinely inclusive, has as few barriers to people as possible [and] that also is geared towards trying to provide as many opportunities for success as possible. One of the challenges we have in the North is that we have an exam-heavy system that's very focused on the very traditional ways of doing things. It's almost as if the purpose of education is to squeeze as many qualifications out of a young person as possible because the only privileged route that we talk about is getting to university. Less than half of young people go to university, so we should be thinking about everyone else.

For Jarlath Burns, principal of St Paul's High School in Bessbrook, County Armagh, which is in the Catholic maintained education sector, academic selection in the North seems to be all about the preservation of an elite grammar school system in both nationalist and unionist communities. A former captain of the Armagh GAA team, Burns is critical of a system which discriminates against children with special needs and is obsessed with examination and learning by rote. In his view, a lot of the anxiety and mental stress suffered by young teenagers is a consequence of examination and testing pressure. The oversubscribed, 1,700-pupil St Paul's, he said in an interview with this author, offers a completely different educational experience where the happiness of the child comes first. 'The biggest challenge facing education is how to end the hegemony of the grammar school. Middle-class Catholics and Protestants have the loudest, most articulate voice in education. If we removed the unfair selection system, the *raison d'être* for elite grammar schools would no longer exist,' he said.

St Paul's is a mixed gender school in a predominantly Catholic and nationalist community, and the pupils have a strong say in how it is run, said Burns. It provides an extremely broad curriculum, ranging from extremely academic to vocational, and its pupils have a record of high achievement in GCSE and A level exams. In a recent inspection, it received 'Outstanding in All Areas' and is seen as a prototype for a possible future model of education. It is a Catholic school but you don't have to be a Catholic to attend, he said. There are pupils of every faith and creed and non-believers, while local Protestants have their own smaller, state-controlled schools a few miles up the road, both of which rely heavily on the educational and recreational facilities at St Paul's for support.

Since he became principal in 2013, Burns has adopted a policy of reaching out to the Protestant and unionist community of south Armagh:

> In an area where nationalists dominate, we have devoted a lot of time to reaching out to the Protestant community, which suffered over the years in south Armagh. We have taken confidence-building measures to assist them including by bringing the Orange Order and the PSNI [Police Service of Northern Ireland] former chief constable George Hamilton to talk to our pupils. It would be a disaster for the Protestant community if their schools were to close, and they have depended on St Paul's for resources to ensure that does not happen.

It is therefore common to see pupils from Newtownhamilton and Newry high schools walking the corridors of St Paul's and accessing some subjects that are not available in their own schools. Burns believes this is a more realistic way of sharing education, rather than moving to a fully integrated model. He has also fought to ensure that the ethos of the school is inclusive and has encouraged pupils from St Paul's to attend the annual Pride event in Newry; not, he said, to show how tolerant the school is, but to celebrate its diversity:

> When we marched in the parade for Pride in Newry in 2015, some of the more right-wing elements [of] the community expressed disappointment and protested. We wanted to send out a message

to the LGBT pupils in our school that it was not a question of simply tolerating or accepting them, but of celebrating our diversity and our humanity. It was controversial, but I contacted the CCMS – which controls Catholic schools – before the event and their reply was, 'You are the principal, it is your decision.'

The Catholic hierarchy has spoken out against academic selection, which, it said, has led to the unfair distribution in post-primary schools of children with the greatest needs. Burns explained that academic testing resulted in a situation where many grammar schools have tiny numbers of pupils with special educational needs compared to St Paul's and others in the controlled sector.

Special needs pupils include those with a range of diagnosed conditions – from attention deficit disorders to autism, Asperger's syndrome to dyslexia – who in previous generations would have been dismissed as 'bold' or unruly children. These are the children who are filtered out by the discriminatory testing of 11-year-olds. As Burns said, 'It is a question of values which, in our school, are built on integrity, truth, compassion and kindness. We never give up on a pupil. We believe there is always something special in every child.'

With a daughter and a nephew teaching in the South, Burns has been given an insight into the educational systems in both jurisdictions, which leads him to believe that the challenges of constructing an all-island education system are considerable, but not insurmountable:

I wouldn't start from where we are now in either jurisdiction. The system in the South, while still superior to that in the North, is also not without fault. The pressure on young people to achieve is crazy. I was struck when it was explained to me that there is only an optional oral exam in Junior Cert Irish. The pressure of the Leaving Cert with so many subjects in such depth, is quite surreal.

We need a completely new model of education. A united Ireland should not be the North welded on to the South. We have to reimagine how we do education. We need to understand that young people do not exist solely for the purpose of school, but should be allowed to live happy, carefree lives, enjoying the outdoors and [getting] involved in sport, music, reading for pleasure, poetry and the arts.

In our school, up to the age of fourteen we do not impose excessive homework on the pupils. We try and make them enjoy the experience of education and, during this time, we work on building their resilience. We wonder why mental health is such a huge issue with teenagers. It is due to the pressure they are under. Instead, we teach our junior pupils about their local history and geography. We set our own curriculum. At their age, we were picking blackberries and climbing trees, not buried in homework.

He argued that in a new, all-island education model there should be a move from content-based to skills-based learning and an emphasis on problem solving and information literacy:

Our education system currently produces well-qualified people with few skills or common sense and this is the natural outcome of a focus on exams rather than actually learning. Teacher training should be streamlined and current obstacles to young graduates from the North teaching in schools in the South, eliminated.

The powers of the boards of governors and trustees, which promote the unfair system of academic selection in the North, and the private fee-paying secondary system, which only wealthy people can afford for their children in the South, has to be challenged.

Of course, a united Ireland won't be a Utopia. There will always be those with money [who] can get access to private education or healthcare. But that does not mean we cannot try to create a fairer and better system of education for future generations.

Burns accepted that it is probably ambitious to assume that immediate and profound change could occur within the Irish education system within the context of a united Ireland. The wheels of educational change turn slowly and while most seem to be agreed on the nature of the problems, there is little consensus on how to fix them, particularly the high number of pupils who leave education in the North with no qualifications whatsoever. This, he said, is a direct consequence of the elitist nature of post-primary education there.

As a pragmatist, he suggested that a lengthy 'settling in' period would have to occur, which would not see the necessary changes in either jurisdiction immediately but would set a date five years into the future when the brand-new education system would click in, countrywide.

This system would see all children transferring at 13 from primary schools to their local, regional, non-selective school, whose admissions criteria would not be set by the school, but by the education authority. Each school would have an emphasis on transferrable skill acquisition and would have meaningful vocational pathways for pupils to prepare for apprenticeships or trades as well as university or institutes of technology. He would offer a post-16 choice between a five subject or three subject option, which would mirror the Leaving Certificate/A level model. Both of these systems have their advantages and disadvantages, but he prefers the A level system which, he argued, prepares pupils more effectively for third-level study.

In the South, proportionally more students attend third-level but many teachers and educationalists share Burn's criticism of the Leaving Cert programme and the stress it imposes on young people competing for the limited number of places in their preferred university courses. There is still a massive deficit in the number of young men and women from working-class and deprived communities in the South entering universities, compared to those from wealthier backgrounds and with private schooling. The DEIS schools in the South have helped to keep vulnerable children, and many from poorer backgrounds, in school for longer and provide more options for vocational and skills training.

Aíne Hyland, a leading educationalist and emeritus professor at University College Cork, has long promoted an education system that is inclusive from early childhood to graduate education, where no child or young person is an outsider. In an interview she described her ideal system, in which 'children and young people of all backgrounds, social, religious and ethical; race, colour and ethnicity, including refugees and asylum seekers; sexual orientation; and those of all abilities and (so-called) disabilities will be equally respected.'

She has called for additional resources to be provided to bridge the gap between those from disadvantaged backgrounds and their more advantaged peers. Provision for certification and qualifications, in a context of lifelong learning, should be flexible, allowing learning to occur in a wide range of contexts and environments. 'Assessment at the end of formal schooling will be reformed to remove over-emphasis on end-of-final-year examinations without any dilution of standards. Equality and excellence can co-exist!' she argued.

In the South, almost all young people (more than 90% of the age cohort) remain in full-time education until the end of senior cycle when they sit the Leaving Certificate or similar applied tests. The South has one of the highest completion rates of second-level education in the world, and one of the highest rates of transfer to higher education.

According to Hyland, however, the Leaving Certificate examination is set and marked in such a way as to discourage creative, imaginative and 'non-conformist' answers and to encourage stereotyped and pre-prepared answers. She said:

> I believe that we shouldn't throw out the baby with the bathwater, but we need to seriously rethink how the Leaving Certificate

assesses, examines and certifies. The current examination must be reformed. It should include orals and practicals, portfolios, continuous assessment, CBAs [classroom-based assessments] – which would account for at least 50% of the marks and should be completed and submitted well in advance of the final exams.

In the North, there is particular concern at the numbers of young people from more deprived areas in both communities leaving school early and disappearing from formal education. Too many young working-class Protestants and Catholics in Belfast and other urban centres are not in education, employment or training (NEET). Across the North, ESRI estimates that 26,000, or 13.2 per cent, of those between the age of 16–24 years were described as NEETs in 2020. The position of young Protestants is compounded by the experience of their parents who are part of a generation most directly affected by the deindustrialisation of the economy since the 1970s. The once skilled and semi-skilled Protestant workforce was decimated by the decline in traditional manufacturing, textiles and shipbuilding, in what was once the main centre of industrial production on the island.

These young Protestants are excluded from decent jobs and careers, are fearful of the future, and angry that their parents' loyalty to the Crown has not been rewarded by those who urged them to risk their lives and freedom to protect the union. The existence of an alienated, under-educated and financially dependent section of the population in loyalist and unionist communities in the North is recognised as the most likely source of violent opposition to the integration of both parts of the island. Since the GFA, efforts have been made through state and EU support programmes, and projects supported by philanthropic and other funds, to engage the youth in these communities in education and training and away from the still-functioning loyalist paramilitaries.

Among those who are trying to improve the prospects of young Protestant working-class youth are some former members of the UDA and UVF. They are now fighting the systemic unemployment, poverty and the illicit drugs culture that have pervaded their communities. In some cases, they are in direct conflict with former associates in the same loyalist paramilitary organisations who are involved in illicit drugs and other criminal enterprises in the North.

Tom Winstone was a member of the Young Citizen Volunteers, the youth wing of the UVF, when he and Billy Hutchinson – a leader of the UVF while in jail and, later, a co-founder of the Progressive Unionist Party – shot dead two young Catholics who were walking to work along Belfast's Falls Road in October 1974. Half-brothers Michael Loughran and Edward Morgan had let their father take the last seat in a black taxi before they headed off on foot to their jobs as labourers. At the time, Winstone and Hutchinson believed they were protecting their community and their British identity by shooting the two Catholic men. He does not believe that now. Since his release from prison, Winstone has spent his life trying to prevent other youths from going down the same road. A father and activist, he has devoted his energies to improving the living conditions for one of the North's most impoverished communities who have seen little of the promised investment which was to flow from the peace agreement.

As co-directors of Northern Ireland Alternatives (NIA), a community-based restorative justice organisation working within grassroots loyalist communities, Winstone and his colleague Debbie Watters gave this author an interview in which they described their work with young people over the past 30 years as an effort to promote justice, peacebuilding and reconciliation. The key to change, in their view, is education. In July 2020, they spoke about their work with young people in east Belfast and with republicans and former IRA members in poorer areas of the city. They insisted that one of the greatest challenges facing their communities remains the failure of the education system in the North and the intergenerational impact of unemployment and poverty among loyalists. Winstone said:

The results are getting better by the year. And the opportunities are there. It's not so much the young people, it's their parents that don't have enough faith in education to push their kids to go on to further higher education; or not enough of them.

It's not just about changing the mindsets of the young people. It's about changing the mindsets of their parents and maybe even their grandparents to say, 'They have to have a better life; they have to have better opportunities than we had and what we went through.' Otherwise, we're just going into this spiral of forever looking over our shoulder rather than looking ahead.

Many parents with few or no qualifications perhaps do not have the tools to help their children through education, so NIA has tried to teach basic learning skills to early school leavers in the east Belfast community. As Winstone put it:

There's not enough emphasis put on the help that those children and their parents need. We see it ourselves with young people coming into our place [NIA], kids who left school without qualifications. We are there for them, to put the arm around them and try and help them. Here, they get their basic English, Maths or whatever, and now some of them are going on to third-level education and getting employment – otherwise no one would have taken the opportunity to help them. Inner-city Belfast is no different from inner-city Dublin in that regard.

The change in Protestant communities will come with a different mindset among the present generation of parents, Watters argued:

It's about giving extra resources to schools. But we can't just blame the schools for the low level of achievement, we have to start at the home. We have to give the tools to those people who need it to help their children to go on to bigger and better things. Now, this could be a generation or two away, but it's what is needed.

Brexit, she said, has further fractured the unionist family and has simultaneously promoted a discussion about the place of working-class Protestant communities in a new Ireland: 'People within working-class Protestant communities are more open to the debate now because of Brexit in terms of what would our place in a new Ireland look like. I think there are conversations that people are entertaining now that they never would have before.'

In her view, Brexit exposed a divide within unionism between middle-class Protestants who want to remain in the EU, and more traditional voters who followed the DUP and Ulster Unionist Party (UUP) in supporting the leave campaign. Working-class loyalists voted overwhelmingly for Brexit. 'I wanted to remain part of Europe,' Watters said. 'I'm still a unionist but I had no party that was representing my voice. The unionist family wasn't strategic enough around Brexit, and Alliance got the vote,' she argued, referring to the collapse of the DUP and UUP votes in areas where substantial numbers of their supporters shifted to the Alliance Party in the December 2019 Westminster election.

Winstone also voted to remain in the Brexit referendum, in contrast, he said, with his UVF associates and most people in his east Belfast community.

> I voted to remain but you should not read too much into this. People went where they went for that particular reason, and I would not assume that they would be in favour of a watered-down union. I'm slightly different to most unionists and loyalists. I class myself as Irish but I'm Irish/British. I'm happy in my own skin saying that.
>
> I think the difficulty that you would get now for even those that are voting Alliance, or maybe softer unionists going for a united Ireland or a new Ireland, call it what you wish, are the antics of

Sinn Féin. Unionist people would be voting against it even if it was Utopia simply because they [Sinn Féin] are voting for it.

I'm a Democrat and whatever the democratic voice is, that's what it's going to be, but there's an awful lot of discussion taking place around all the issues, and I'm not talking about orange and green issues. I'm talking about bread-and-butter issues: hospitals, work, pensions, all of those things that would need to be sorted out.

Can Ireland afford to be united? I don't think so at the moment. Will Britain chip in to get rid of us? Possibly, to a degree, but I'm not sure the two things would marry up. What Britain could contribute and what Ireland could contribute and maybe get from Europe or wherever, I don't think the numbers would match up.

Trying to convince people that they would be better under a new Ireland, is going to be a big, big sell. It used to be 'Rome rule' that we were frightened of. Ireland's a different country now than it was 30 years ago. There's no doubt that they're more progressive down there in Dublin. But we are still wedded to this fear factor. This debate would have to be done in a way where people can explain what accepting this new Ireland is going to do for them, what safeguards there's going to be. A lot of young unionists and loyalists are more worried about their unionism than they are about their way of life.

'Loyalist' is a word used to describe young working-class Protestants, but in Winstone's view, it is often used in a way to denigrate his community:

I don't like the word 'loyalist', it's a dirty word for a unionist. It keeps us separate from the good people when you're classed as a loyalist. But those young loyalists, let's call them that, are more interested in their cultural identity than they are in their education and that's just what we see here on a day-to-day basis.

Their cultural identity, Winstone said, centres around celebrating their past:

> It's being able to collect their bonfire wood; being able to march up and down the road; and being able to celebrate something that happened 300-odd years ago. Because that's all they've been taught, it's all they know. And I'm speaking as someone who was a young loyalist at one stage, not knowing anything different because we weren't taught it. Obviously, it's slightly different today than what it was 40 years ago, but you still get that mentality within households and within families.

Promising young loyalists that they can celebrate their historic occasions in a new Ireland may not convince many who already see their right to parade and light bonfires to celebrate the victory of King William of Orange in 1690 as being restricted under British rule.

'We're part of Britain at the moment,' Winstone said. 'We're not in the new Ireland and yet there are certain things that you're not allowed to do, so how could they be any better off under this new Ireland? That's the argument these young loyalists would go with.'

While he accepted that Orange Order marches through communities that do not want them and burning fires in a way that endangers lives is not acceptable, he said that many young loyalists feel their identity is under threat.

For Watters, those fears are compounded by the growth of SF, North and South: 'If they can't do reconciliation up here, how could we be assured they would do reconciliation in a new Ireland? Our experience here is that the commitment to reconciliation is solely verbal,' she asserted.

For all this hostility, the people with whom NIA work most closely in working-class areas of the North are republican activists. The organisations that are trying to ensure that young people do not get involved in violence, and which have promoted training and education in their communities, have often been funded by the same non-government sources, including Atlantic Philanthropies (AP), the charity funded by US businessman and peace broker, Chuck Feeney. Former loyalist and republican prisoners have benefitted from the AP programmes and regularly meet up. As Winstone said:

> There is probably more discussion on the ground between the warring factions than between the politicians. But it doesn't mean we agree. Just because we're speaking to each other and we're not shooting each other doesn't mean to say we're in agreement. I think there's been more discussion going on over the last few years than there was over the last 20 years, but they are still difficult conversations.
>
> We had Atlantic Philanthropies funding, which allowed us to be totally independent; to grow the organisation our own way and challenge the system. That American philanthropic money really allowed us to do our own thing for the first 15 years of NIA. That's probably why the politicians didn't want to come near us. If the government departments are giving you money, you feel like you owe them, whereas we didn't feel like we owed them and we didn't have to play their game.

One of the obstacles to their development have been political and media assertions linking NIA to illegal organisations. In order to build trust and strengthen their relationships within the Protestant working-class community, NIA has engaged with the UDA and UVF, but that does not mean encouraging or endorsing them. As a former member of the UVF, Winstone has a clear picture of where the loyalist groups currently fit in the complex, wider context of the North. The armed political campaign is over, although some of his former associates are engaged in criminal activities using the name of one or other of the main loyalist organisations, just as criminals in nationalist and republican communities use similar flags of convenience:

> Some of them are involved in criminality on both sides, but they are doing it for their own needs, for their own back pockets. They are not doing it on behalf of an organisation. Some of those that were maybe on the fringes, or those that didn't go home and put the feet up, are still actively involved in things that they shouldn't be. They're doing it for their own wee cabal, or whatever you want to call it.

Genuine former activists on both sides, he claimed, are usually the ones that try to protect the peace lines and divert young people from getting involved in violence, whether it is over disallowed parades, flags or bonfires: 'They try to take them on a different route. Those others that are involved in criminality want those young people to get involved in violent activity because it takes the heat off them. Others like the sound of their own voices and the publicity they attract.'

Watters and Winstone reserve particular scorn for politicians in the DUP who campaigned for Brexit without realising the consequences, including bringing the prospect of a united Ireland closer. As Winstone explained:

> Probably one of the unintended consequences of the vote is that we are a step closer to a united Ireland. Hundreds of middle-class unionists applied for Irish passports because they want to remain part of Europe and they want to have the benefits of Europe.
>
> The DUP never thought through the unintended consequences of their actions. Those people who went for Irish passports are in some way saying that their identity is not one dimensional. I think that's the key to all of this. Brexit highlighted that identity is not about one single issue. People have had to rethink what their identity looks and feels like.

What needs to be done is [have] an open and honest discussion so that, and I'm choosing my words carefully here, the hate-mongering people on both sides don't come up with a bogeymen scenario. We're talking about facts rather than *maybes* and *what might be* and that type of thing.

But as Watters put it, 'Just because someone either carries an Irish passport or recently acquired an Irish passport doesn't mean they're going to vote for a united Ireland.'

6

A 'WATERY PROD'

Glenn Bradley is a chartered member of the Institute of Directors (Ireland) and the Institute of Purchasing and Supply, and until March 2021, he was chair of the Northern Ireland Business and Human Rights Forum and a board trustee of the Community Foundation for Northern Ireland. He has developed a reputation in corporate governance relating to business and human rights within global supply chains and is a leading and respected ethical trade activist and trainer. He is also a former UUP official, with 10 years' past service in the British Army, and he shares the view that the Protestant and unionist people of the North are on the road to a united Ireland. The political leaders of unionism are dangerously in denial, he said.

Bradley grew up in the unionist Woodvale area of west Belfast, close to the current peace line, and was witness to daily armed violence on his doorstep. Joining the army, he said in an interview with this author, was his response to Irish republican aggression directed on his community and family:

When I was 16, I just wanted to hit back at the IRA, so I naively joined the army thinking I would get the best military training possible and [would] come back to Northern Ireland and take the fight to the 'RA. It didn't quite work out that way because the army, in its infinite wisdom, sent me on operations in 1985 in the Middle East, and so it was a case of frying pan to fire. However, being outside the goldfish bowl of incestuous Northern Ireland, my world view diametrically changed very quickly.

Bradley realised that armed conflict was not unique to his own place of birth and that its origin was more complex than the inherited narrative he had been fed while growing up. Post-army, he joined the UUP and was a junior member of its talks team during the negotiations for the GFA in 1998. He has remained an unapologetic 'peace processor' and supports the Belfast/Good Friday Agreement.

He was, however, disillusioned by the failure of political unionism to embrace wholeheartedly the actions required to create actual parity of esteem. 'No one seemed to wish to break down community barriers and look at generating social cohesion or equality that enhanced wellbeing,' he said.

As a consequence, he helped to forge an alliance with other businesspeople, community activists (including former loyalist and republican combatants), victims and faith groups:

> The objective was to create a safe space to engage and come together to focus on the future and attempt to generate a shared, united, interdependent group of influencers who practice respect for diversity and whose example could benefit everyone on the island as a constructive role model.
>
> There is mounting evidence that unionists are no longer in a majority and referendums on the constitutional future of the island will take place within a decade. The British government will leave very soon after any decision by voters in the North to join a new, constituted Ireland.

This process, he said, has been dramatically hastened by what he described as the 'disaster of Brexit'.

Bradley is convinced that the ordinary people are light years ahead of the politicians in that daily conversations have begun and, he argued, it is primarily the task of the Irish government to prepare:

> The lesson from Brexit is that any future constitutional change should be carefully planned. The Irish government – indeed broad nationalism, because creating a new Ireland is not a republican project – needs at the very least to have a roadmap of how constitutional change will actually come about. It was 1990 when the British government said it had no selfish or economic interest in the North so we're well down the timeline in the notion that the British government will go at some point, and I personally have no doubts that they want to go.
>
> At the time of the Anglo-Irish Treaty during the War of Independence, nobody then, British or Irish, actually fathomed that Westminster would still have a foothold in Ireland in a hundred years' time. Post a referendum result for constitutional change, I believe the British government's departure will be like their departure from India: sharp and short. I don't believe it will be like Hong Kong, which was a long process because Britain did have selfish and economic interests, all the things that they've formally stated they don't have for Northern Ireland. They'll say to political unionism, 'We're gone in two years, sort this fucking mess out yourselves.' And they'll just pull out. That's another reason why I believe the Irish government really needs to up its game in the thinking of this change management solution.

The British establishment, in his view, has little economic interest in the North, as big landowners have long departed. The same insurance, banking, retail and other corporates that have a commercial presence in

Belfast or Derry also operate in the South, so British investment is not based on sovereignty. There is little of strategic interest unless you count the numbers of young, mainly working-class Protestants, who join the British Army from Ireland.

> Something like 15 per cent of the British Army's recruitment comes from Northern Ireland. One of the reasons for that is because we turf out, percentage wise, the largest number of uneducated kids per region in the UK. The reason so many kids from here join the British Army is because they've no other job opportunity or community role models and the majority are predominantly working-class kids from loyalist areas. I say that as someone who came from a loyalist area and as a former soldier myself.

Bradley blamed a lack of constructive leadership for the current crisis in unionism, specifically former DUP leader Arlene Foster and her successor Jeffrey Donaldson, who, he said, since they left the UUP to join the DUP in 2003, surrounded themselves with 'a cabal of self-righteous powermongers and Orange supremacists'. They are the least likely people to support the prospect of deep-rooted constitutional change through democratic all-island referendums, no matter what was agreed in the GFA all those years ago, Bradley claimed.

He also suggested that preparations should be made by the South for an entirely new constitution:

> As someone who is engaged in the game of change management constantly in business, change doesn't scare me. The choice at a border poll is a binary one: remain in the UK, retaining the dire status quo; or do something positively different. If it goes to something different, to leave the UK, that has to be ratified in the South and immediately negotiated. The problem is there is no precision [from] anyone. For a start, it would require substantial changes to the Irish Constitution, which in themselves would

require a referendum beyond the border poll. It is incumbent upon the Irish government to have at least a draft paper of what the roadmap of transition is. Its primary function is to come up with the concepts and the specifics. I can understand why they're reluctant, but they at least need to have draft policy papers. This free-stater partitionist mentality that Northern Ireland and its people are 'up near Iceland and detached from us' has to end.

Bradley said that, while the British government, which is already facing a referendum in Scotland in the coming years, may decide to quickly depart Ireland following a unity vote, there will need to be a prearranged transition period in which the power-sharing structures in the North will continue to function, although it will come under the ultimate control of the Oireachtas and the Irish government. He also predicted that the EU and US governments will support the emergence of the new political and constitutional entity on the island:

> I believe that the Northern Ireland executive will continue functioning in some guise, for a period of absorption, for want of a better description. In my opinion, that should be at least 15 years. The Dáil will assume certain responsibilities. Given that Europe publicly backs the reunification of Ireland, I don't think there would be any issue with it covering the current subvention from Britain for a period.
>
> I think the EU would bite your hand off to do that and cover the cost for up to 50 years. As someone who has already accrued a full UK state pension that I'm entitled to at 67, the British exchequer is going to have to make sure that my pension (and many others) is available in the new state, whether by calculating it and sending a lump sum to the new government, or [by] whatever other fiscally-responsible way is agreed. In addition, healthcare is a primary concern: will there be a new all-Ireland NHS?

Those are the type of bread-and-butter things that really need to be specific, measured and thought out seriously. We wouldn't see the EU being unfriendly, I don't believe America would be unfriendly, and the British government will also have to be responsible for its obligations to people and its mostly unwelcome presence in Ireland over centuries.

It is evident that leadership is required within unionism to face the reality that its numbers are dwindling, and its younger people are deserting the main parties in droves, including, Bradley said, his own two sons:

> My oldest son is 32 and my youngest son is 28, both born of a father who was raised in the loyal Irish tradition and in a family considered loyalist and unionist. Yet neither vote for a unionist party, neither consider themselves to be unionists. Both have a British and Irish passport, but that's more to make travel easy for them, and if they are asked, like their father, they say, 'I'm Irish. I'm from Belfast in Northern Ireland, but I'm Irish.'

They are of a generation, he insisted, who could be persuaded to accept constitutional change if it served their interests:

> Unionism is dwindling and I don't just mean the sheer force of numbers. Many have turned their back on the pro-union cause, put off by blood-and-thunder politics and the denial of rights available elsewhere in the UK. Many others go along with the status quo because that's what they were born into and it is all they know. But could they be persuaded to accept change? I absolutely believe so.

He has spoken to senior British ministers who accept and support the idea of getting out of the North. He mentioned one senior politician who was quite candid in private discussions over recent years that the issue is one for the people of Ireland to resolve:

> On flights to the UK I have invariably found myself sitting beside prominent British politicians. Being a known figure through business, trade and public appointments, I have had quite candid, honest and open conversations [with them]. My lived experience is that the English view us as one people, and one senior parliamentary figure convinced me of that. He said, 'You are all Irish, you really need to sort this out yourselves.' I said, 'Well with the greatest respect, I'm also a former British soldier and served in the army on operations in Northern Ireland. I don't believe that the British government is as clean as you might like them to be.' They were never a referee here and indeed they convoluted the situation.

> Simple historical facts, like people who spoke Gaeilge having their hair set alight by British soldiers, created inherited resentment and there are lots of other examples of poor British policy heaping suffering here. And to be fair, this English MP said, 'How far do we need to go back in history? Let us deal with the here and now. And the now is that you are all Irish people. Just as I am an Englishman, someone else is a Welshman and someone else is a Scotsman. This is an internal Irish difficulty that ultimately needs to be resolved between yourselves.'

> He said that [neither] he nor the government had any selfish, economic or strategic interests and asked me, 'What more must we say in order for people in unionism to take up a leadership position and begin preparations?'

In his discussions with unionists about their fears of losing their British identity, Bradley has referred to his personal and family connection with the former British colony in Asia:

I know India very well, and not just from a business or leisure travel perspective. My great-grandfather was a Connaught Ranger. My paternal granny was born out in old India when the Connaught Rangers served there. When the British withdrew from India, the birthright of all the Anglo-Indians wasn't affected. I believe that in a new Ireland, anyone's birthright as a living British citizen will not be negatively affected. The Good Friday Agreement will prevail and those who desire to retain British citizenship will be able to hold a British passport.

And when they ask about the tricolour, I say, 'Who's to say the tricolour will prevail as the national flag of Ireland? Who's to say it won't become the provincial flag or another design? Who's to say those changes won't come about? Why can you not accept that the orange part of the tricolour represents us and say, well that's me I'm on that and I'm an equal partner?' The key is that when we get into the specifics of what might follow a referendum for change and a British government decision to withdraw, the persona of a unionist changes because it's no longer about maintaining the constitutional union with Britain. It is about maintaining a pro-British political and cultural tradition in the wider context of a new Ireland and some unionists do see this.

Bradley was most scathing about criminal elements of the loyalist paramilitaries who exploit their communities, and the DUP which has used them as voting fodder. In the spring and summer of 2021, criminal groups fomented riots against the police involving some very young people in deprived loyalist communities across the North. Bradley does not believe that they would enter or sustain a campaign against the British government, or indeed the security forces in a new Ireland. Their sense of betrayal, in his view, derives from the ill-considered Brexit policy pursued by the DUP and some other unionist parties:

The biggest blight on unionist working-class communities are criminals using loyalism as a flag of convenience and the DUP elite who do shag-all for the people but exploit them as voting fodder. In the wake of a referendum result for a new constitution, who are these so-called 'loyalists' going to fight? Are they going to fight the British government? Are they going to fight the British or Irish army? Are they going to fight the police? I'm not saying that there won't ever be backlash violence, but I don't think that armed action would have the will of the people backing it and so a prolonged campaign couldn't happen. Let's face it, many of the loyalist organisations of today are crime gangs with many associated with drug running and dealing, so [if] a counter-policing or army response would interfere with their criminal empires, these people may soon realise the futility of violence in the situation they face; that is, [that] no amount of violence or blood-and-thunder rhetoric will make Britain stay.

Bradley pointed out that many other former loyalist combatants are involved in authentic reconciliation and community work and cited the Resurgam Community Development Trust in Lisburn, those involved with the East Belfast Mission, Restorative Justice, and named other projects that have 'completely transformed from paramilitarism to be excellent role models for community service'. He argued that we are in the endgame of a disastrous partition:

I'm very conscious of the Indian experience where, when partition happened, it was followed by violence. But in Ireland, we've already been through the partition trauma when the British drew an imperialistic line on a map in 1921. It has already been demonstrated that the line was altered to create gerrymandering in Northern Ireland. But the other largely unspoken aspect is that partition created two bastard states: one committed to marching rights in the north, and the other committed to religious rights in the south.

Partition failed a great many people in both jurisdictions and that failure is felt the length and breadth of this island. It largely led to the civil uprising of 1969 and the subsequent violence of the Troubles, involving all stakeholders in the conflict. However, I do feel there's no going back to those days. People are more informed, and digital or social media makes events live. If we take the evolving peace process and British government comments and actions from 1990, I believe this really is the end game of British government failures in Ireland.

Bradley accepted that there is a huge economic deficit between the North and the South. He argued that some of that could have been avoided if all signatories to the GFA had convinced the British government to invest hugely in the economy of the North, and particularly in its most deprived areas:

> At that time, and as a member of the UUP, I wish unionism had gone to Blair and said, 'All the money you're about to retain from security, we want that invested into the Northern Ireland economy for the next 25 years.' Now, imagine if that had happened: the differentials in the economy between North and South would not have widened so much. We would be on an almost equal economic footing as the South. We absolutely slept-in at the time of the Good Friday Agreement in not realising just what it would cost to 'operate government and maintain peace'.

Bradley's uncle was an off-duty, Royal Ulster Constabulary (RUC) officer who was kidnapped, tortured and killed by the IRA. He was abducted in September 1990 as he crossed the border, coming home from a long-weekend fishing trip with friends in County Kerry. The exact circumstances leading to his death remain unclear and Bradley claimed there exists rumour and growing indications that his uncle's death was a result of the determination by some in the British security apparatus to protect the identity of one its agents in the IRA. He said the legacy of that dirty war will persist unless those responsible are confronted before the British government announces its departure from the North:

> I believe once they say, 'We're out,' that will be that. Some of the problems we encounter are the legacy of the apparatus of various British security departments, some who still operate here. My own uncle, Louis Robinson was an RUC officer, kidnapped, tortured and killed by the IRA on the border in September 1990. It is said that a British agent in the IRA, being operated by a unit within the British Army, was the one that killed him.
>
> If accurate, you had a British agent making the decision that a British servant of the Crown who was a police officer should die, and the potential that his army handlers knew about it all along. It is mind-numbingly painful to get your head around such a myriad concoction of abuse of power and it makes me have utter compassion for all who have suffered during the conflict. If I'm asked today what I am about, I reply, 'I'm about no more suffering. I'm about parity of esteem in practice. I'm about desiring a fiscally-responsible government that will deliver in an equal and equitable way for all the people of this place we call home and I will operate to improve citizen wellbeing.'

Whatever about the organisational strength and political coherence of loyalism, the current climate of uncertainty over the future of the union and their British identity can make life difficult, and even dangerous for those in their community who are open to Irish culture, language and sporting traditions.

Linda Ervine, a sister-in-law of former UVF leader and founder of the Progressive Unionist Party, the late David Ervine, has attracted a hostile reaction from a small, but vocal, minority ranging from social media abuse to threats of violence as a consequence of her teaching and cultural work, including the Irish language classes she runs in east Belfast, and her presidency of the recently formed East Belfast GAA. The club has grown rapidly since its formation in early 2020, with more than 1,000 members competing in hurling, football and camogie. When interviewed, Ervine said:

> The membership is a mixture of Catholics and Protestants, but we don't ask about people's religion when they join. It's probably more Catholics, but again it doesn't matter. You've got Catholics who have been born and brought up in east Belfast and who've never had a club of their own who maybe had to play for other clubs. There are Catholic people who have come to live in east Belfast who may have been involved in GAA in their hometowns, including people who have moved to Belfast for employment or for university.
>
> You have Protestants from east Belfast who have never ventured into a GAA club, who maybe watched it on TV or had a secret interest and now they've got a chance to play. You have Protestants who travel in from outside east Belfast for this opportunity to get involved in something new.

The club has made every effort to be inclusive and to encourage members from the Protestant and unionist community, as illustrated by its invitation to Linda Ervine to become its first president. The invitation came as she was recovering from Covid-19 in the early months of 2020.

> While we were in lockdown, I saw a message reaching out to anyone in east Belfast who would be interested in playing Gaelic games. It gave me a feeling of hope, that Northern Ireland was beginning to move beyond the division which has impacted so much of our everyday lives.

I sent a private message wishing them well. After a few messages back forth, I was very surprised when they asked me if I would consider being the president of this new cross-community club starting in east Belfast.

I didn't have to think too long before agreeing to be part of what I regarded as a positive new initiative. I was immediately attacked online for my decision and every 'sin' committed by the GAA was thrown at me. I was still dealing with the effects of Covid and felt neither physically nor mentally able to cope with the negativity that suddenly surrounded me. I have to admit that part of me considered walking away, but this would have reflected badly on the club.

The club, however, has gone from strength to strength. It has been given the use of pitches by local schools and other GAA clubs while they try to raise the funds and obtain land to build their own, and Ervine was proud to see players wearing the black and yellow colours with the words 'East Belfast GAA' across the front of their shirts. The motto of the club 'Together' is written in Irish, English and Ulster Scots with symbols of the shamrock, thistle and Red Hand. Ervine said, 'At Christmas [2020], we had an awards night and, because of Covid-19, it was all done online. When the host welcomed everyone, he had the Down GAA flag, the tricolour and the Union Jack behind him.'

As Irish language development officer with the East Belfast Mission, Ervine has brought hundreds of people to its language courses since she took up the position in 2011. She said:

Numbers are extremely healthy, even online. We started off at beginners and we now have eight people at university, five people doing degrees and three doing diplomas in Irish. Five of them are Protestants. Another one of our learners is a mature student who is now doing a PhD in history and politics at Queen's. He told me he achieved this because he got involved in education by coming to the Irish classes with us, so there are just some fantastic stories.

Her work with the Irish language and the GAA has drawn criticism and she was concerned that she would become a focus of greater hostility when anger among some members of her loyalist community deepened as debate about the protocol and a border poll intensified throughout 2021. She is convinced that a referendum is inevitable and that a repeat of the shambles, lies and confusion surrounding the Brexit vote would be a disaster.

There is a myriad of opinion within the unionist community from the really hardline of, 'We'd rather die in our own blood than get on our knees,' to more liberal views, and even people who are in favour of a united Ireland. I personally am not pushing either way and I suppose I'm happy enough with the status quo. I am both Irish and British so it doesn't hold a fear for me. I'm not signing up for either flag because I belong to both constituencies, if that makes sense …

I'm not going to be swayed by a flag of any colour. I want to look at the practicalities and what's going to work for me as an individual and [for] my family. For example, the NHS: though it is imperfect, it's one of the best things about the British state, so I would want a continuation of some sort of free healthcare. I would also be concerned about the fact that we do get help from Britain. There are a lot of people in civil service jobs, so what happens to them? What happens to people's employment?

I'm in my late-fifties now, so by the time it comes along I imagine I won't be long off pensionable age. I'm only going to get a tiny British pension, but how does that work with benefits in the South? … If we do go into a united Ireland, do we keep some sort of devolved power? Will Stormont still exist or will it be all ruled from Dublin?

Will there be a period of changeover? Will that be gradual, rather than waking up one morning and we're part of the rest of Ireland. Will there be an opportunity for people to keep that dual identity we have at the moment, which is not only British or Irish, but British *and* Irish? Will that continue for those who choose to do so? …

But the biggest worry hanging over me would be the violent reaction that could happen if the vote goes that way.

In her view, the threat of violence will come from existing or new loyalist groups, although, in her view, at present they are largely run by older people with little political power or influence in the community, unless it is through criminal intimidation or the sale of illicit drugs:

I don't fear the protests over flags, or more recently against the NI protocol, because we've seen so much of that over the years. It flares up and it dies down. It is people getting angry and a way for them to vent and express their feelings. It tends to be loud and it's generally peaceful, it's a bit disruptive but people have every right to do that.

I would be more concerned about the more sinister forces who, even though small in number, could cause havoc and problems. In a personal context, although it's not rational, it's people like me who could become targets. To some of those people, I represent the Irish language and I would just be an extremely soft target because I live within this community. I would have personal fears in a way that I wouldn't have had before because I was anonymous. I have lost that anonymity, unfortunately.

At the same time, she has reason to suspect that many unionists will support a united Ireland, when the referendum comes around:

I would imagine that a small or a growing number of people from the unionist community will vote in favour of a united Ireland.

That has to do with Brexit and practical reasons. Then you'll get a lot of people who are not happy about it and then the ones who are violently opposed to it.

The loyalist paramilitary groups are very tiny and extremely irrelevant really to everyday life. They're old men who, in my opinion, don't really have any influence anymore but who need to keep shouting about the past because that's where they were important. They don't have a great importance because today's society is changing and people are expressing different views.

I don't know whether a referendum, if it didn't go the way certain people wanted it to go, could be enough to light a flame. We know that can happen so easily in Northern Ireland. I don't think people really foresaw 1969. There were rumblings, but they didn't know it was going to be 30 years of war.

She accepted that the power of the UDA, UVF and other loyalist groups today is not comparable to the situation in 1974 when they brought down the power-sharing executive. Neither did they enjoy the same support of influential elements of the British government and security forces, as they did all those years ago. Indeed, she, too, suspects the British government may already be planning its departure from the North:

I would imagine the British government is already in talks with the Irish state. Before we ever get to a referendum there'll be a lot of backroom talks and preparation, trying to get the right people on board. I'd say there'll be a big lead-up into it. Rather than the British state being in cahoots with loyalists, it would be in cahoots with the Irish government this time so it's going to be a very different scenario.

As with others observing and working with loyalist youth, the theme returns to education. It is from a well of despair that the recruits to any future campaign of loyalist violence will be drawn. As Ervine said:

All aspects of health, wellbeing [and] employment are affected by people's lack of education. We have various issues in Protestant working-class areas, and in Catholic ones too, with addiction, alcoholism, drug abuse and violence. The Troubles and sectarianism have overshadowed the real problems. There is absolute despair among people.

Her experience of the independence referendum in Scotland in 2014 gave her an insight into the factors that can influence dramatic constitutional change:

My husband and I were in Scotland the week before the referendum and it was especially interesting for us, coming from Northern Ireland. We were in Lewis and Inverness and Glasgow and all around the place getting opinions from different people. There certainly wasn't a religious divide. You had neighbours, one for yes and one for no.

A lot of people we talked to gave the same answer. Their heart said Scotland, but their head said UK because they were frightened. A lot of them said, 'If I was younger, I'd vote for Scotland and independence.'

Now people I know who had voted to stay have totally changed their views. They feel they were misled by the government at the time and now would vote to leave. It's inevitable that Scotland will go that way. It seems to me very certain. That will obviously impact us here in Northern Ireland too.

It's also a real wake-up call for people here. For the people who have a very close relationship to Scotland it's a kind of tension. They're mad loyalists here and yet there's a family member or a close friend in Scotland who's saying, 'I want independence.' That must blow their minds because you still have that loyalist element in Scotland, too.

According to Ervine, the Brexit experience has caused a lot of DUP voters to reconsider their preference, particularly since the promises made by the party have not materialised, the union has been weakened and there are empty shelves in the shops:

> That isn't going to bode well for the DUP and I hope that when it comes to election time, people will remember. Before the Brexit referendum, the DUP said that everybody else was scaremongering, that there would be no border in the sea, and that will not be forgotten. I hope that people are starting to catch on to themselves and realising that these people are bloody harmful.

In her own area, Ervine has witnessed changes in people's voting trends, although most support the DUP. Their MP, Gavin Robinson, is among the few senior DUP party members who has suggested that it should engage in debate about a forthcoming unity referendum, if only to ensure that it is defeated. Ervine said:

> He is one of the saner ones. I vote Alliance although they wouldn't tick all my boxes. I like the Green Party as well, but Alliance has a bit more oomph. For me they're the only show in town at the minute. If someone puts a leaflet through my door and there's a flag on it, I'm not voting for them. That's the first thing that's going to switch me off.
>
> What bothers me is, with all the issues that we have here in Northern Ireland – poverty, lack of education, lack of opportunity, housing – we can't even get talking [about] or dealing with those problems a lot of the time because some people are too interested in shouting about referendums and flags and parades, all the periphery and nonsense. That's where all the money and attention and energy goes.

Her children, who are in their thirties, she said, are not interested in protests over flags or protocols and are embarrassed by them:

> My children were brought up in a working-class Protestant area. They're in their thirties now and they're extremely liberal. They're not interested in the whole flag thing – in fact they're embarrassed by it. None of them are pushing for a united Ireland but none of them are particularly afraid of it either. They're just not overly interested.
>
> They were annoyed about Brexit, and they'd rather stay in Europe. I think they're typical of a lot of young people. We have all these liberal young people who will eventually, I hope, go to the polls and make a big impact on the politics here. At the minute, they're staying at home so we're not getting their opinion really. They're so disenchanted with the whole thing; it's boring to them. They're looking at the nonsense on TV; they're switched off by Sinn Féin and the DUP. I suppose they don't feel that they have a voice and they don't feel that they can make a change. But until they get involved in the process, nothing will change.

Denzil McDaniel is someone who recognises the necessity of change in the North. Born in Enniskillen, he spent several years working in the civil service before a change of careers led him to journalism. In 1973 he joined the Enniskillen-based *Impartial Reporter* where, in the early '80s, he was appointed deputy editor, and then, in 1987, editor.

'I took over as editor in January 1987 and the bomb in Enniskillen happened the following November,' McDaniel recalled at interview, referring to the IRA's 1987 Remembrance Day bombing in Enniskillen that killed 11 people, including one police officer, and injured 63.

McDaniel grew up in the town, initially in a mixed estate before his family moved to an exclusively Protestant area, and his time in the civil service – which like most state-run organisations across the North in the late 1960s employed a majority of its staff from the Protestant community – showed him, among other inequities, the systemic discrimination in housing and other areas of life for the local Catholic population. Working in the social welfare section where he assisted people with their supplementary benefit payments, he witnessed the scale of rural poverty among Catholics and nationalists in Fermanagh.

Unionist politics dominated in the North, even in places like Fermanagh where the population was more evenly split or with a slight Catholic/ nationalist majority, he said. He witnessed first-hand the widespread and undemocratic practice of gerrymandering – whereby local unionists manipulated the boundaries of electoral areas to maintain their majority – when the local council built a housing estate in a place called Donagh, close to the border with county Monaghan. McDaniel said:

> It was just a small hamlet, but the unionist-controlled council decided to build houses there because, if they built them closer to the more built-up nationalist areas, it would have meant that the unionist politicians would have lost their electoral majority. They moved five or six miles down the road and built a housing estate for Catholics in the middle of nowhere, so they were able to maintain political control.

By the time he entered journalism, McDaniel acknowledged his Protestant background but did not identify as a unionist. He recalled:

> The *Impartial Reporter* in the early days would have been considered a unionist paper but I started doing things which hadn't been done before when I took over the sports coverage in the late 1970s. I started to cover Gaelic games and I would have reported on local government and then the Bobby Sands election in 1981.

During McDaniel's first decade there, the paper enjoyed a consistent

readership across the communities, selling about 14,000 copies weekly –
mainly in Fermanagh with its 19,000 homes; in south and west Tyrone;
and some across the border in Monaghan. It had to tread carefully in a
part of the country where unionists and nationalists were evenly balanced
in numbers but where control of local government and administration
had long rested with the former. As McDaniel explained:

> It was a difficult balancing act because you had to report everything.
> You had to form relationships with the new and increasingly
> influential Sinn Féin and yet you still had to go and visit homes of
> UDR [Ulster Defence Regiment] men who had been killed. I think
> you really just had to keep your integrity and keep communicating
> with everyone and treating everyone fairly and the same. We kept
> a middle line and, interestingly, the backlash came over GAA
> coverage. Even up to the time I left, in 2012, you would still pick up
> the odd comment like, 'The paper's been taken over by the Gaelic,
> all the GAA coverage.' You would still get those comments.

For McDaniel, the discussion about constitutional change cannot take
place too soon and indeed has already commenced among traditional
unionist voters, although at a more discreet level:

> I don't speak for unionism, but I get the sense from them that
> there's quite a wide variation of opinion about engaging in this
> discussion on constitutional change. I think there's an absence
> of realism in unionism. They know change is coming but they
> imagine it's years away. We're very much into short-termism.
>
> When Micheál Martin says there will [be] no border poll in
> the next five years, unionists think, 'Well that's kicked down the
> road for another while. We don't have to worry about it now.' They
> imagine five years is just a lifetime away …
>
> But there is no such thing as a majority anymore in Northern
> Ireland with the number of Catholics/nationalists close [to], if not

exceeding, the number of Protestants/unionists demographically.

People who don't want change tend to be the older demographics, whereas if you look at the under-30s, and these are likely to include younger unionists, they are either 'don't knows' or they are open to a united Ireland. There's a higher percentage of support for a united Ireland among young people and a higher percentage among people who are very unsettled by Brexit.

The significance of the 56 per cent of voters in the North who did not want to leave the EU also illustrates the concern among unionism of the resurgence of English nationalism, McDaniel said:

The rise of English nationalism, which has been exposed by Brexit, has greatly concerned unionists in the North at a grassroots level. They have always been told that Westminster isn't really interested in them and that's more obvious now than ever with Brexit. Scottish independence is also now closer than ever. Suddenly, unionists are looking at a London government and a Tory leadership that are totally insensitive to them and the potential break-up of the United Kingdom. Internally, they are not a majority anymore. So all of that drains on them and many are asking, 'Where are we going here? What arrangement can we make?' I think that is happening very much at grassroots level and it's not reflected in what unionist leaders or what the unionist media are saying.

Unionist [leaders] don't generally tend to have these discussions in public because they don't want to look as though they're divided, when actually, in fact, they *are* very fragmented. If unionists or Protestants go public with doubts, they tend to be castigated by the naysayers like Jim Allister or Jamie Bryson. For years now they've tended to keep the head down and talk about it privately and not publicly.

McDaniel also recognised the element of fear among Protestants who are reluctant to discuss their future because they might be ostracised within their community:

> It's not always a physical fear but a great line someone threw at me once was, 'You're a bit of a watery Prod.' It's easier to keep your head down. But the discussion is going on. There are people within the unionist parties who realise that things have to change.

This is most clearly reflected in comments by former DUP leader, Peter Robinson, that unionists need to prepare for a border poll: 'Robinson is saying, "We have to be careful, we have to be strong and settle the union because if a border poll ever comes, we need to win it."'

McDaniel believes that many unionists, including politicians, recognise that they need to control whatever change is coming. They have proved through the GFA that they can do deals with nationalism and actually run the North together. It may not be just a choice of staying with the UK or getting taken over by the South. There may be other options, and those kind of debates are going on, McDaniel said:

> The fear in unionism is that they don't want to engage because of what they see as a pre-determined outcome in which they're being taken over by the South, and that's where the danger comes with a border poll. I can understand why Micheál Martin would want to try and reassure them and to say it's not happening for at least five years.

However, McDaniel believes that Martin's strategy will not work as it will only delay the necessary discussion on the island about the inevitability of a unity referendum and the nature of the new Ireland that might emerge:

The debate needs to happen, and the talk needs to start now. It's not just a simple border poll, let's throw it out there. What does a united Ireland look like? How do we engage unionists in that debate? To kick it down the road and say that it is not happening will just disengage unionists further. That is where Micheál Martin's position falls down.

He insisted that within unionism and loyalism there is a sense of, 'We know it's coming, we know the writing is on the wall, but we're going to spin it out as long as possible.' Even though they talk to republicans and work with them on a community level, McDaniel concluded, there is still an angst towards Sinn Féin:

It's almost saying, 'We're not going to let that lot tell us our future after what they put us through.' We'll talk to you privately but with regards to coming to a negotiation about a united Ireland, even if we think it's inevitable, you're going to have to wait.

7

EVERYBODY ON THE TRAIN

F ive months after the February 2020 general election, and following prolonged negotiations, a Programme for Government was agreed between Fianna Fáil, Fine Gael and the Green Party. Micheál Martin was elected Taoiseach on 27 June.

The two larger parties ended a rivalry that was rooted in the decision 98 years earlier when the Dáil, in January 1922, narrowly voted to accept the Anglo-Irish Treaty. Over nine decades, FF and FG had alternated as the main parties of governments in the South and were driven by conservative social and economic policies, heavily influenced by the teachings of the Catholic Church. The formal coalition of the two parties was their response to the emergence of Sinn Féin as a major political force – SF had won the popular vote with a radical programme of change in economic, health and housing policies – while the 12 elected members of the Green Party made up the numbers to form an administration.

The historic coalition heralded the long-awaited prospect of the potential merger of FF and FG. Prior to the decision, Éamon Ó Cuív, the grandson of de Valera, was quoted in the *Irish Times* in June 2020 as warning that if his party entered coalition with FG 'we will hasten the demise of our party and once again create a political system with two large parties, but that Fianna Fáil will not be one of them'.

As part of their agreement, Micheál Martin as incoming Taoiseach, agreed to stand down in December 2022 to make way for the return of Leo Varadkar, or whatever FG leader is in place at the time, as head of government. Varadkar became Tánaiste and minister for enterprise, trade and employment, while FG retained the finance, foreign affairs and justice portfolios. FF members took responsibility for public expenditure and reform, as well as for the particularly challenging departments of housing, health and education. Green Party leader Eamon Ryan became climate, communications and transport minister, and deputy leader Catherine Martin took on responsibility for tourism, arts and culture, sport and the Gaeltacht.

The Taoiseach faced the immediate challenge of coping with the continuing threat to public health from Covid-19 and an unexpected bump in the road when he was forced to sack his, just appointed, agriculture minister, Barry Cowen. It followed the disclosure that in 2016 the Offaly TD – and brother of former Taoiseach, Brian Cowen – had been disqualified from driving after being stopped by gardaí who discovered he was under the influence of alcohol. To make matters worse, Martin also endured the refusal of the party spokesperson on justice, Jim O'Callaghan, to accept the position of minister of state in the new government. O'Callaghan was expected, at least by those close to him, to be offered the position of justice minister or attorney general but the former was filled by a relatively inexperienced FG TD, Helen McEntee, and the latter by Paul Gallagher, who had served in the role in previous FF-led administrations.

The Programme for Government included a proposal to create a new unit within the Department of the Taoiseach 'to work towards a consensus on a shared island', as envisaged by the GFA. It pledged to work with the NI Executive on a range of cross-border initiatives, including the extension, from the border at Aughnacloy, County Monaghan, of the A5 motorway from Dublin to Derry. It also proposed the extension of the Ulster Canal from Clones, County Monaghan to the Upper Lough Erne in County Fermanagh, and the construction of the Narrow Water

Bridge from Omagh in north Louth to Warrenpoint, County Down, as well as upgrading cross-border greenways. It envisaged deepened cross-border co-operation on crime between the PSNI and the Garda, while the programme said it would develop 'an all-island strategy to tackle climate breakdown and the biodiversity crisis.'

The commitments followed early government formation discussions between FF and FG, from which emerged the proposal to set up a unit to promote a united Ireland and to advance previously agreed infrastructural developments and wider North–South co-operation. In the subsequent discussions on the Programme for Government, the Green Party argued that the words 'shared island' were more acceptable given its broad membership in the North, even though many of them support a united Ireland. It was agreed that this shared island unit would be driven from within the Department of the Taoiseach, although foreign minister, Simon Coveney was reported to be wary of any transfer of responsibility for the North from his department.

Speaking in the Dáil in early July, Martin confirmed that the policy of the new government was to develop a stronger North–South relationship, but that a referendum on a united Ireland would, in his view, be 'divisive' and 'partisan'. He rejected a call by SF president Mary Lou McDonald for a referendum on unity and an all-island approach to develop the economy and the health services.

The Taoiseach insisted that the correct approach for the future was to develop an accommodation so that 'we can all live in peace and harmony and not to try to dictate to one tradition about what the solution is going to be. As reported in the *Irish Times*, he added that the GFA was based on British–Irish, North–South and relations within Northern Ireland, and that:

> irrespective of what may emerge in the future, it is my view that these three sets of relationships will have to underpin any future arrangements …

The over focus on the border poll was too divisive and too partisan and ran counter to what SF wanted to achieve. That is my view. I favour a different approach. For example, I favour a stronger North–South dimension now.

He accused McDonald of adopting 'a more territorial, majoritarian approach whereas I prefer to develop a more consensus approach'. In response, McDonald said that both Brexit and the Covid-19 public health crisis had:

> reshaped how people think and talk about reunification … No longer is Irish unity discussed only in aspirational terms, it is now increasingly regarded as a common-sense approach and essential to the prosperity of all of our people. I say that because growing our green economy requires an all-Ireland approach. Protecting and building public health services and protecting public health itself requires an all-Ireland approach, as does strengthening our agricultural sector and defending rural Ireland. All of these things must be all-Ireland in nature.

In her first confrontation with the new Taoiseach, the leader of the opposition made it clear that the issue of a referendum for Irish unity would be her party's priority during the Dáil term. She argued that the establishment of the Shared Island Unit fell far short of what was required to prepare for constitutional change:

> Will he establish an Oireachtas joint committee on Irish unity? Will he convene an all-island representative citizens' assembly, or such an appropriate forum, to discuss and plan for constitutional change? Will he initiate the process for a referendum and get clarity on what the thresholds for triggering such a referendum might be?

In response, Martin repeated that the SF leader was trying to enforce a solution on unionism:

> The agenda for the future on this island is how we engineer and develop an accommodation where we can all live in peace, harmony and reconciliation on the island and not to, at the outset, try to dictate to one tradition or one group what the solution is going to be, which seems to be the agenda the deputy is pursuing.

In further exchanges with Aontú TD, Peadar Tóibín, the Taoiseach conceded that the Shared Island Unit was established in response to the growing calls for a referendum and the need to prepare for an eventual majority vote for unity: 'That is why we are setting up the Shared Island Unit, to go through the nuts and bolts,' said Martin. 'What would an all-island health service look like? How would the political structures work?' Martin also speculated on the continued existence of an assembly in Belfast in a future united Ireland. Having gone further than intended in his remarks, which he said were a matter for 'longer debate', Martin said that Tóibín had 'provoked me into saying that'. (www.oireachtas.ie, 8 July, 2020)

Within days of his appointment as Taoiseach, Martin spoke to the first and deputy first ministers, Arlene Foster and Michelle O'Neill, by phone and planned a meeting in Belfast to discuss shared priorities on combatting the spread of Covid-19, some joint infrastructure projects, Brexit and other issues. He said he also intended to meet the leaders of the North's other parties. However, the Covid-19 crisis upset his plans in an unexpected way. His first visit to the North as Taoiseach was postponed in the wake of a breakdown in the relationship between Foster and O'Neill following the deputy first minister's attendance at the funeral of senior Sinn Féin and IRA figure, Bobby Storey, in late June.

Storey died unexpectedly while undergoing surgery for a lung transplant in England and, on 30 June 2020, more than 1,500 party members and supporters, led by senior Sinn Féin members and former IRA prisoners, attended his funeral in Milltown Cemetery in west Belfast. During the funeral procession, dozens of stewards enforced a distance between those walking behind the coffin but the huge crowd that assembled at Milltown was not so easily managed. Prominent party leaders and members, including McDonald, Pearse Doherty, Conor Murphy, Gerry Adams and deputy First Minister Michelle O'Neill, were among those criticised for breaching social distancing guidelines and Covid regulations concerning attendance at funerals. The DUP, UUP, SDLP and Alliance parties supported a motion in the executive calling on O'Neill to apologise for attending the event. According to a BBC News story in July 2020, Arlene Foster asked O'Neill to consider 'stepping aside' pending a PSNI investigation, and their daily joint press briefings, which included updates on public health advice on Covid-19, were suspended. O'Neill refused to step down. She apologised to anyone who was hurt or offended by the funeral but not for her attendance which, she said, was in a personal capacity and not as deputy First Minister.

While the Storey funeral briefly destabilised the power-sharing Executive, the Taoiseach downplayed the alleged breach of Covid-19 guidelines by the deputy First Minister, stating that:

> We have to be careful of not being overly judgemental of people's behaviour, we all have to strive to do the right thing in respect of the public health advice ...
>
> Where there is a breach that upsets members of the public, I think people should put their hands up and say, okay, I understand the anger, I understand where you're coming from in having a problem with what I did, and I think we all learn lessons then from that and then we have to move on.

Martin, O'Neill and Foster eventually had their meeting – held in Stormont on 16 July – and the three leaders agreed to convene a meeting of the North–South Ministerial Council, the first in over three years, in Dublin Castle at the end of that month. Martin also met with British Secretary of State for Northern Ireland Brandon Lewis and other party leaders.

Speaking after his engagements, Martin repeated his warning that a border poll would be 'very, very divisive' and insisted that his preference would be to explore the economic, social and political issues that would enable us to share the island in a peaceful way. 'I will be an engaging, understanding Taoiseach, trying to keep people together and trying to move forward on the economic front in particular and also in terms of getting projects over the line that we have been talking about for some time,' Martin told a press conference after his round of meetings.

Arlene Foster who, before the visit, had welcomed the distinction between previous governments in Dublin talking about Irish unity and Martin's shared Ireland approach, said the discussions around 'areas of mutual interest' were productive. 'As two jurisdictions sharing an island, it makes perfect sense that Northern Ireland seeks to build a positive relationship with our neighbours in the Republic of Ireland,' she said. (The Executive Office, 16 July, 2020)

Michelle O'Neill said that the discussion with Martin centred on the Covid-19 pandemic and the need for a joined-up approach to it across the island, and also about 'the potential implications of Brexit and the pressing concerns this raises. I set out the need to work together to protect the needs and interests of people and businesses across this island.' (The Executive Office, 16 July, 2020)

The first visit by the new Taoiseach to the North took place after the traditional Orange celebrations around the Twelfth of July, which passed off quietly, not least because many outdoor parades and gatherings were suspended due to Covid-19. However, this relative calm did not necessarily reflect the mood within political unionism. There remained a continued unease about the NI protocol the UK government proposed to the EU during Brexit negotiations in October 2019 and the increased likelihood of an Irish Sea border for goods, including medicines and live animals, travelling between the UK and the North. After the 'Betrayal Act', as it was described by leading members of the DUP and UUP, was passed by a comfortable majority at Westminster some weeks later, their lack of influence in parliament was cruelly exposed. It was a swift descent from holding the balance of power and enjoying an alliance with the Brexiteers. It was all the more humiliating given the enthusiasm for Johnson at the DUP party conference in Belfast in December 2018 when he promised, according to a *Newsletter* article in October 2019, that 'no British government could or should sign up to putting a border in the Irish Sea'.

The rumblings within the two main unionist parties about 'the betrayal' and potential threat to the constitutional position of the North grew louder by the month. By the summer of 2020 they were talking openly about the threat to their identity and citizenship presented by an Irish Sea border. Former DUP leader Peter Robinson told unionist commentator Alex Kane in an article for the *Irish Times* that, 'unless significantly amended, the present deal would tilt the political axis from primarily east–west to north–south'. Reg Empey, a leading UUP negotiator for the GFA and a member of the House of Lords, was quoted in the *News Letter* in September as warning of the inevitable 'constitutional consequences' if the protocol remained as the North's 'centre of gravity could gradually move in a Dublin/Brussels direction'.

Under the radar, younger loyalists, under the influence of factions of the UVF and UDA, organised rallies against the protocol, although the renewed spread of Covid-19 disrupted and delayed their plans. As the centre of power within the DUP shifted from their increasingly impotent MPs at Westminster to the MLAs in the revived assembly in the North, senior figures, among them Arlene Foster, sought to downplay the dangers posed by the protocol and indeed to promote its possible benefits.

When the Johnson government confirmed in late May that an Irish Sea border was likely to emerge if a Brexit deal with the EU was agreed at the end of the transition period in December 2020, DUP minister Edwin Poots spoke of its potential benefits: 'We'd have the advantage of actually having access to the single market and to the UK market and make NI an attractive place for inward investment.' A June 2020 *Irish Times* article noted that other senior unionists even suggested that, if the protocol had such beneficial economic consequences, it 'might reduce the vote for unity in a future border poll'. As agriculture minister, Poots had responsibility for implementing the protocol in relation to the movement of animals and produce if, and when, it came into place.

The spread of Covid-19 across the North, and the inept handling of the crisis by the British government, disguised the extent to which the fear of constitutional betrayal was exercising the minds of many unionists and loyalists. As the numbers of cases began to rise significantly, and hospital ICU units were filling up in a second wave of the pandemic, the focus of the Executive and Assembly was on reducing the mounting death toll.

The turmoil within the main political unionist parties, and the divisions widening in the DUP leadership in particular, were never far from the surface as the consequences of its own endorsement of Johnson's deal with the EU became apparent. Its refusal to engage in the debate about the North's constitutional future also became more questionable.

In an assessment of political unionism in *The Irish Times*, Denzil McDaniel asserted that the interests of unionism were not necessarily reflected in the shifting positions of the party leaderships, and that the assurances of Micheál Martin that there would be no referendum on unity for the foreseeable future should not be taken for granted:

> Unionist leadership resists the idea of a border poll, claiming it would be divisive, and [they] comfort themselves in the belief that they would win it anyway. They will take comfort in the new Taoiseach Micheál Martin's assertion that there will be no unity

referendum, but it would be a mistake for them to bank that and be complacent about his assertion that the future is about relationships …

It's important to note that no single voice speaks for unionism, it is not one homogeneous monolith … many grassroots unionists are increasingly disillusioned with Westminster.

Even though a sort of cognitive dissonance allows them to somehow live with a border down the Irish Sea, there can be no denying an increasing lack of trust in London and English nationalism within a creaking United Kingdom.

For this reason, McDaniel argued, there should be a concentrated effort, including by the Irish government, to debate and prepare for an alternative solution and that 'simply tagging the six counties on to the present 26 is not an attractive proposition for many, including some traditional nationalists and republicans in the North'.

He also asserted that, according to a number of opinion polls, more people in the North profess to be neither unionist nor nationalist, 'and yet we hear no plan to address ordinary unionist fears, no imaginative plan to give Northern Protestants a vision of how a shared island would protect and respect a way of life they cherish, a culture and identity that's important to them, or address their worry about losing the NHS and a standard of economic living'.

He cited the former member of Seanad Éireann, Ian Marshall, as an example of a diverse voice who was arguably more progressive and pragmatic than many in political unionism and who, McDaniel said, 'wasn't a voice for unionism, but a unionist voice'.

It was a pointed reference that reflected the dismay among many people in both communities in the North, at the failure of the incoming Dublin government to reappoint Marshall as a senator. In what he described as a 'huge insult', Marshall said in late June that he learned on social media that the government was not going to nominate him for a second term. A senator since 2018 and a former president of the Ulster Farmers Union (UFU), he said that 'many in the unionist community in Northern Ireland felt let down by the decision. But that's politics.'

From south Armagh, Marshall was born in 1968 into a Presbyterian family a few miles from Markethill and grew up on a farm during the height of the Troubles. He recalled to this author:

> I grew up in the eye of the storm during the very dark days of the Troubles, knowing nothing but division and mistrust. Growing up in a mixed community, people invariably had to work with each other, live beside each other, get on with each other, trade and do business with each other. I attended a Protestant primary school, interacting and mixing with Protestants in social circles and sports clubs. It was very much along green and orange sectarian divides. I went to grammar school in the Royal School Armagh, which was a Protestant grammar school. You went to either a Protestant or a Catholic school. You mixed with only Protestant or Catholic friends. It was a case of 'ne'er the twain would meet' until you got to third-level education. Many of my friends never met a Catholic until they went to Queen's.

It was a situation that would later make his tenure as president of the UFU all the more challenging. In his area of south Armagh where the military conflict – between the British army, security forces, loyalist organisations and a well-organised IRA with substantial support in the nationalist community – was most intense, the UFU tried to maintain cross-community engagement, and represent everyone. As he put it:

> They made very strong efforts in my time from the 1980s to make sure that you parked your politics at the door, that the organisation was about farm businesses and families. They worked very hard to encourage people from all parts of the community to get involved.

It was a very highly-charged environment in south Armagh, coming from all directions, and it was particularly difficult to keep your farm business profitable. The one thing that tended to unify people was the necessity that, to make money and keep their businesses, they needed to work together. It's a great leveller, pounds, shillings and pence.

Marshall grew up only a few fields away from the farm of James Mitchell in Glenanne, where a gang of up to 40 UVF members, many also serving in the British Army's Ulster Defence Regiment and the RUC, stored weapons and explosives and organised attacks on the nationalist community, causing up to 120 deaths in the mid-1970s. It is widely accepted that the 'Glenanne Gang' also assisted in the planning and execution of the Dublin and Monaghan bombings in 1974 and the killing of three members of the Miami Showband in July 1975, and was responsible for the deaths of six young Catholic men – three each from the Reavey and O'Dowd families – on 4 January 1976. A day later, republicans killed 10 Protestant workmen at Kingsmill crossroads, not far from the Reavey home in Whitecross.

Marshall described the mood at the time:

This was happening on our doorstep. We knew some of those actors in that whole business. I was about 8 years old when the Kingsmills and Reavey atrocities happened. I remember after the Reavey deaths as a child listening to adult conversations about 'three IRA men' murdered and the feeling of 'there's a fight back here'. We all know the true background to that story now and the reality of what it was. When the Kingsmill atrocity happened at that very same time, I remember thinking, this is ethnic cleansing going on along the border, where Protestant farmers were being shot in their milking sheds and their houses and their yards, many of whom were part-time RUC/UDR men.

When you look back through the lens we have now, you can see that level of mistrust between communities. It's quite easy with the benefit of hindsight to see a culture where the 'powers that be' were quite happy to see Protestants murdering Catholics and Catholics murdering Protestants, and the last man standing would be befriended. To think that we were managing businesses and bringing up families with that level of distrust within the community was unbelievable.

Marshall recalled how land was only sold 'one way' in Armagh: an unwritten rule that land could not be sold across the religious divide. You might get a black wreath, a bullet in your letterbox or a death notice in the newspaper if you were suspected of selling to 'the other side', he recounted:

There were people out there who were quite happy to make sure that that crossover didn't happen: the real threat of what could happen if you let land go 'the other way'. There were cases where an ambulance was sent to a house of a farmer thinking of selling land the other way but there was no emergency. It was a warning shot to say, 'We're watching, make sure you do the right thing.'

When he began to observe events in a wider, international context, Marshall realised that the North was not such a unique and isolated conflict:

I had always thought, in my naivety, the Northern Ireland question was very much isolated and specific to here. Civil unrest and human rights issues were on the agenda in many parts of the world in the late '60s and early '70s. When you look at it in chronological order and put everything in context at this time, it was wrong on all sides here.

Marshall campaigned against Brexit and publicly challenged the DUP for misleading voters in the North in relation to the promised benefits of leaving the EU. As business development manager at the Institute for Global Food Security at QUB, Marshall was acutely aware of the interconnectedness of agricultural production on the island, and between the two islands:

> Over generations we have built an industry that's inextricably linked North and South. Around 400,000 lambs go from Northern Ireland down South every year; 25 per cent of our milk is processed south of the border; we have 10,000 pigs a week that move across the border. We have businesses in processing that operate across the two jurisdictions.

The potential to develop business, trade, tourism and health services is threatened by the departure of the UK from the EU, which is damaging the interests of everyone on the island, he said.

In his opinion, as someone who has retained close contacts with former loyalist paramilitaries and has regular discussions with SF members in Dublin, these groups have more in common than dividing them:

> When I'm talking to loyalists in east Belfast, they're focusing on all the same things that the republicans want: let's improve the education of kids, let's open up opportunities, let's drive tourism and foreign direct investment, let's encourage business. They're miles ahead of political unionism because these guys know the demographics are changing. The difficulty they have is that no one is telling them where they fit.
>
> Political unionism is reluctant to get into discussions on a 'shared island' because they see it as a Trojan horse for a united Ireland. However, some unionist leaders might engage in conversations that encompass the north, south, east and west parameters of the GFA.

Marshall also maintains that unionist distrust is a reflection of their inherent fears and insecurities, including about the Irish language, and is often based on concerns over an erosion of their culture and identity:

> It was my 86-year-old grandmother who had to remind me that the bible was translated into Irish by the Presbyterians. 'Learn your history, the Irish language is about all identities,' she would say. She talked about the place names that are derived from Irish. In addition, it wasn't until I went to the Seanad in 2018 that I learned the history of the Irish flag. I never knew the flag represented green for nationalism, white for peace and orange for Protestantism.

For many unionists and loyalists the Irish flag is merely an emblem draped over coffins at paramilitary funerals, and has no significance or meaning for them.

Marshall is convinced that Irish unity could happen but only when unionists see that it would be in their interests. He believes that there are 'visionaries' in SF who recognise this, but there are many others who antagonise unionists on social media and elsewhere:

> Irish unity happens when you create a situation where unionists see advantages and want to be there. The strategic move by republicans would be to say, 'Here's something that will be better for you than where you currently are.' I am critical of those who say, 'It's not if but when Irish unity is going to happen, so if you're a unionist you're just going to have to suck it up. We'll get a nice padded corner with soft furnishings for you and we'll look after you. Don't worry, It'll be all right.'
>
> If we can learn anything from Brexit, it is the need to inform people, frontload these conversations now and ask these questions. Republicans argue that the train to Irish unity has left the station. My question is why on earth would any unionist get on it? There's more likelihood that they'd blow up the track than get on the train.

What we need to say is that the train on this *conversation* about the future is leaving the station, but the destination is unknown. We need everybody on the train. It's time for open minds, strong leaders, and to move away from identity politics.

8

WAITING FOR A REFERENDUM

Arguably the most prolific, insightful and influential academic contributor to the debate on Irish unity, and the constitutional and political issues that arise from the GFA, is Cork-born, Professor Brendan O'Leary. He is a founding member of the ARINS project (Analysing and Researching Ireland North and South), a joint initiative between the Royal Irish Academy and the Keough-Naughton Institute for Irish Studies at the University of Notre Dame in the US. O'Leary also participates in the Constitution Unit based in University College London, is author of the three-volume *Treatise on Northern Ireland* and is currently Lauder Professor of Political Science at the University of Pennsylvania. He is a member of the Friends of the GFA, which includes academics, lawyers and politicians in the US. Previously O'Leary was a political adviser to the late Mo Mowlam and to Kevin McNamara when they served as shadow secretaries of state for the Labour Party in Britain.

In a review of the *Treatise* volumes, historian Breandán Mac Suibhne summarised a number of myths that O'Leary demolished in his sweeping and devastating analysis of the Northern state since partition. Among them, Mac Suibhne wrote in a review published in the *Irish Times* in July 2019, were the assertions made by other writers and historians in Ireland and elsewhere:

that British intelligence defeated the IRA; that the IRA alone caused the Troubles; that internment worked; that the civil rights movement was predominantly hijacked by neo-Trotskyists; that the Stormont regime was a 'normal' British local government; that the conflict was overwhelmingly sectarian rather than national or ethnic in character; that integration could have worked, at any time, but for papist resistance; that the southern Irish were never interested in reunification; that unionists were always willing to accept power-sharing – they just did not want any role for the Irish government; that the Good Friday Agreement was 'Sunningdale for slow-learners'; that 9/11 led the IRA to decommission; that the RUC did not need to be reformed out of existence; that loyalist violence was simply reactive rather than proactive; that British policy has always been consistent, since 1921, 1925, 1949, 1968, 1972, 1979, 1985 or 1998 – that is, depending on the proponent's selective illusion.

That is some list – and far from exhaustive. For example, O'Leary gives the lie to the lazy notion that the South was the evil Catholic twin of the North: Protestants were not actively displaced by political decisions from high-status positions in the public or private sectors or the professions in the cities … No parallel occurred to the systematic gerrymandering or active disenfranchisement in the North. There was no banning of minority political parties. Protestants were treated as equal citizens, with full private cultural rights, and their religious institutions did not experience discriminatory public policy.

In his final volume of the *Treatise*, entitled *Consociation and Confederation*, O'Leary concluded that the reunification of Ireland is on the way and that it will have economic benefits for people in the current North and the current South. He predicted that a referendum on unity will happen within the next decade and, like others, has argued that those aspiring to Irish reunification should ensure that the necessary and detailed preparations are done and that the political conditions for success are in place before it is called in order to ensure that they prevail. He insisted on the importance of reaching agreement on, or at least a concept of, the constitutional arrangements of a new, all-island polity before its political, including devolved, structures are framed.

I interviewed O'Leary in the summer of 2020 for this book. He maintained that the task of preparing for a referendum and the outline of future constitutional and political and policy arrangements had been undertaken by academics, activists and commentators but that did not absolve governments of their responsibilities. 'I agree with the fundamental idea that, unless you know the expected constitutional structure you can't have a coherent discussion of various public policy configurations. You have to work out the likely constitutional configurations and then discuss the various public policy ones that would follow,' he said. He was concerned that there is little appetite on the part of the governments in Dublin and London or in Belfast to engage in formal discussions on these and other issues in the short term:

> Starting in London, they don't want Scottish independence so they can hardly openly begin to plan possibilities for Irish unification. In Dublin, the 'shared island' approach and the competition with Sinn Féin, the priority of recovering from the pandemic and of stabilising the Northern government collectively freeze initiative. In the North, as always, even the very mention of the question polarises, and in any case, the North has no independent authority to develop and prepare for a referendum.
>
> So that means, in my view, that the bulk of the preparatory work in the period ahead falls to the academy [university and research institutes] and to civil society. I am pleased to see that there are multiple initiatives in this domain and there should

be. The idea that there is only one way forward is absurd. It is essential that the academy provides a forum for all sorts of ideas and rigorously evaluates what is useless and what is feasible.

The ARINS project has brought together a range of academics in the fields of political science, economics, constitutional law, history and some of the humanities to explore three essential questions: preparation for Irish unity; the implications of Brexit; and the possibility of a reform to the union between NI and the UK. At the launch of the project in early 2021, O'Leary set out in an article for the *Irish Times* the rapid changes, post-Brexit, which have made it essential that voters in a referendum 'have an informed and properly clarified choice'.

O'Leary said that demographic trends have now transformed the cultural balance of population in the North and have placed Protestants in a minority. He cited recent elections, which have altered the political landscape: the vote for the main unionist parties is now less than the combined vote for others. In elected councils across the North, almost half have a majority of pro-unity members and the other half have a pro-UK majority. In the Assembly, there are equal numbers of pro-unity and pro-UK MLAs. In the Westminster parliament, members from NI also divide evenly between the two camps. These do not include independents or members of parties that do not designate themselves as unionist or nationalist.

O'Leary predicted that elections to the assembly in May 2022 will return a majority of nationalists and non-unionist candidates, with a member of SF elected as first minister. Brexit and the Northern Ireland protocol agreed with the EU have further weakened the union and its supporters, while the prospect of Scottish independence poses an existential threat to the UK and unionism as a coherent, political force, O'Leary said. The number of those in the North who wish to remain in the EU continues to grow and includes a significant number of Protestants who previously supported unionist parties. This dynamic is central to the momentum building towards a united Ireland. In the same article O'Leary argued:

> To resume full citizenship of the European confederation, many northerners have taken out Irish passports. Up to half the population have them, while the number taking out UK passports has slid. Later, they may support Irish unity to return to the European Union – not to Pearse's, Cosgrave's, or de Valera's Ireland.
>
> Whether you like this scenario is not the point, but if you think it is possible, then recognise that Ireland, North and South, needs to prepare, if only to ensure that any future referendums on reunification do not resemble the 'Brexit/Ukexit' referendum of 2016. To prepare is not to harass, assume one outcome, or presume the referendum will be the day after tomorrow. Preparation can be open, peaceful and pluralist, ensuring multiple voices are heard, and available to constant correction.
>
> Voters in reunification referendums must have an informed and properly clarified choice. The onus to clarify rests with the South. All parties in the Dáil must decide between offering a precise model of unification or offering a detailed constitutional process that would follow affirmative votes for unification.

These must include, he argued, some outline of 'the power-sharing securities needed for people of British identity and citizenship'. He wrote:

> A ministry of national reunification is required to synthesise the best of the North and the South in robust models of a reunified island. It must engage unionists, nationalists and others – the latter and 'soft nationalists' will be the pivotal voters in the North. It must organise citizens' assemblies, and it will need to oversee a united Ireland transition fund.

On the question of a referendum, O'Leary accepted that a vote must be taken concurrently by voters North and South. However, he did not agree that concurrent means that it has to be simultaneous or taken on the same day. Indeed, he argued that it makes more sense for people in the South to vote only after the decision on unity of those in the North is confirmed, not least because they will be voting on different issues. In the North, it is a binary choice between remaining in the union or joining a reunified Irish state. In the South, the vote will involve agreement on making the required constitutional changes to incorporate any decision made by voters in the North to become part of a united Ireland. He wrote that:

> Concurrent means that you and I make a decision on the same subject. It doesn't mean we have to make it simultaneously. I think the case for an interval is straightforward. If the North has voted 'no' to unity and on the same day the South has voted 'yes' and voted for an enormous number of contingent amendments to the constitution, the Southern electorate has been put through unnecessary potential change. It would depend on the scale of what the South wanted to modify to make unification work. They may go for a completely minimalist programme but they could also go for an extensive programme of change.

In short, O'Leary's article contended that it would make no sense to have people in the South vote in a referendum which sets out the changes required to the Constitution to allow for unification, if voters in the North had rejected the proposal for Irish unity.

In *A Treatise on Northern Ireland, Volume 3: Consociation and Confederation*, O'Leary also expanded on the constitutional order that could emerge from a vote for unity. Under this scenario, the power-sharing executive, assuming it is in place at the time, can lead the negotiations on behalf of the people of the North. 'The greater the breadth of cross-border and cross-community presence in that executive, the better the prospect that care will be taken to address Protestant and unionist concerns and concerns widely held across Northern Ireland,' he said.

The British government will be involved in these discussions in relation to its assets and liabilities, including state pensions, in the North. O'Leary also envisaged the possibility of more than one referendum involving voters in the South, with the first a simple choice on whether they accept the decision of the people of Northern Ireland to end the union with Britain and join a reunified Ireland. In *Treatise Vol. 3*, O'Leary considered the possibility of a confederation

> in which two sovereign states are joined together in a common state, jointly establishing a confederal government with delegated authority over both of them for specific functions. This process would necessarily involve the recognition of Northern Ireland as a state proper. The confederation would represent Ireland in the EU and internationally; it would have all-island institutions, which would certainly include a common court, but could also include an army with constituent territorial units and probably a confederal police, devoted to investigating serious crime, though its powers could be delegated to a joint body.

O'Leary has since expressed his preference for a unitary state with a possible devolution of powers to the North for a period. In a discussion with this writer in late 2021, O'Leary said that a confederation would be incompatible with the GFA and EU membership. He went on to say that a united Ireland is, however, a logical and rational development for the people on the island. A unitary state, with the possible devolution of some powers to a regional assembly in Belfast for at least a transitional period, is his preferred outcome. A confederal model, involving an independent status for the North would be incompatible with the GFA and with EU membership.

He argued that those advocating for a unitary state, as opposed to a confederation, may insist that the referendum results can be implemented within the existing terms of Bunreacht na hÉireann (the Constitution of Ireland). Article 15.5.2 allows for regional assemblies, which would see the assembly currently based in Stormont continue, with representatives elected from existing constituencies in the North.

Meanwhile, politicians who currently fight elections for the Westminster parliament, including those who do not take their seats, will take their place in the Dáil. There are a myriad of issues, including those pertaining to the primacy of the Irish language (in Article 8 of the Constitution), the flag or flags that should be flown, the national anthem, and the reconstruction of the Senate, which, according to O'Leary, would have to be resolved. But essentially this process would involve the effective abolition of the North as a political entity. The most recent parallel to this would be the reunification of Germany in 1990, whereby the German Democratic Republic (East Germany) was absorbed, within a very short period, into the Federal Republic of Germany (West Germany).

In *Treatise Vol. 3*, O'Leary wrote:

> Either Bunreacht na hÉireann is extended to all of Ireland on the German model or Northern Ireland is kept as a devolved unit inside an otherwise unitary and centralised Ireland as is allowed for under the existing Good Friday Agreement.
>
> These two arrangements each have respective difficulties. Northern Ireland being preserved may not be desired by all Northern Republicans and Nationalists to put it mildly. After all, Republicans fought for the destruction of Northern Ireland not for its maintenance even though they have, since 1998, worked the institutions of the Good Friday Agreement.
>
> Secondly, the devolved Northern Ireland model would create on an enormous scale what is called the 'West Lothian' question in

Great Britain. The West Lothian question refers to the fact that a Scottish member for West Lothian in the Westminster parliament gets to vote on all matters affecting the UK but the English Member of Parliament does not get to vote on matters devolved to the Scottish parliament.

Now that kind of issue arises in any system of what is technically called 'asymmetrical devolution'; in other words where you have devolution to one part of the state but not to others. In Ireland, it would be a particularly severe problem because the size of the North as a proportion of the overall state is roughly one-third and that would mean that for the all-Ireland parliament the influence of the Northern deputies would be dramatically more extensive than those of their Southern counterparts. They would be shaping Southern policy as well as being in control of the North.

While this could be resolved by confining votes on domestic questions in the South to deputies from there, it would hardly achieve the type of political unification of the entire island for which people would have voted in the referendum, O'Leary argued. There is also the issue of maintaining the executive, which currently exists in Belfast as a devolved decision-making administration within the UK.

The Irish Constitution allows for a degree of political devolution to local or regional structures subordinate to central government. It does not allow for a subordinate executive, however. While some constitutional lawyers have argued that the institutions, including the executive, established under the GFA could remain in place if the Irish Constitution was amended, O'Leary does not agree with this course. In his view, a devolved administration based in Stormont or elsewhere, would not have executive powers as that would undermine the elected government of the country. In his concluding chapter of *Consociation and Confederation*, O'Leary wrote:

Northern nationalists, notably Sinn Féin and its supporters, may become the key players in deciding whether the Northern Ireland Assembly is restored, and, in due course, whether and when there will be a referendum on Irish reunification. The later such a referendum is held, in the author's view, the greater the probability that there will be a decisive vote for Irish reunification. Sinn Féin enthusiasts will seek an early referendum, but they would be unwise to do so. Waiting for the referendum will, however, become the new canopy under which Northern Ireland politics unfolds.

A new ministry for Irish national reunification and reconciliation would not be premature. Its first planning agenda should include a long constitutional convention to address the new institutional configurations, territorial order, and protections of minority rights that would be required to make a success of reunification, and how Northerners could participate in the remaking of the island.

Warnings of a loyalist backlash or forelash will rent the air. Yet, if and when a referendum is won by advocates of Irish reunification, it is most unlikely that British regiments will be deployed in de facto alliance with loyalist militias – as occurred in 1920, and again after 1970. An Ireland, moreover, that has prepared its constitution and its institutions with proper, prudent, and consultative foresight may be able to reunify with its lost counties with minimal threat to any human life. Though other malign vistas cannot be excluded – including those that start with premises based on Albion's record of treaty breaking – the one just briefly sketched seems far likelier than at any previous time in this author's life.

In 2019, as part of UCL's 'Working Group on Unification Referendums on the Island of Ireland', chaired by Dr Alan Renwick, O'Leary, along with several other academics – John Garry, John

Coakley, James Pow and Lisa Whitten – conducted their own version of a citizens' assembly in Belfast, in order to assess public opinion on a united Ireland across the communities in the North. Their findings were published in 2020 in an article titled 'Public attitudes to different possible models of a United Ireland: evidence from a citizens' assembly in Northern Ireland'.

The day-long citizens' assembly exercise involved a cross section of the population who were asked about their preferred models of unification in the event of a referendum favouring Irish unity. Forty-nine members (out of 50 invitees) of the public were selected on the basis of age, gender, socio-economic group, region and community (political/religious) background to ensure a balanced and representative group of citizens of the North. Notwithstanding the relatively small sample (citizens' assemblies held in the South over recent years usually have around 100 participants), the outcome was informative and perhaps surprising.

The attendees listened to presentations by the moderators, Garry and O'Leary, engaged in discussions and then indicated their informed views on two possible models of a united Ireland: The first was the 'Integrated model', defined as 'an integrated united Ireland, essentially a unitary state in which Northern Ireland ceases to exist, being absorbed into an all-island polity governed from Dublin's parliament and executive, overseen by its courts'; the second was the 'Devolved Northern Ireland /GFA model', defined in the article by Garry et al. as 'a united Ireland in which the bulk of the arrangements of the GFA are preserved but transferred to Irish sovereign authority: Northern Ireland continues to exist, albeit now as a devolved entity within a sovereign Ireland, with a continuation of its current power-sharing arrangements and with the current powers of the Northern Ireland Assembly and Executive intact'. Participants were also provided with alternative arrangements that could be expected in a united Ireland, including the prospect, however unlikely, that the new Ireland could re-join the British commonwealth, with the Crown as symbolic head, as permitted under Article 29 of the 1937 Irish Constitution.

In the report, the moderators explained how the participants, including those from a Protestant/unionist background, supported the integrated model over the devolved NI/GFA model:

> At the start of the day support for a united Ireland with a devolved Northern Ireland on the lines of the GFA was much higher than support for an integrated united Ireland. But, by the end of the day, support for a united Ireland with a devolved Northern Ireland had declined to the same level as support for an integrated united Ireland. This change in support was most pronounced among Protestant participants. Although perceived as ostensibly a 'soft', inclusive, or compromise option, some thought that the transferred Good Friday model was unlikely to work politically because the power-sharing arrangements were not functioning, and in their view showed little promise of reliable functioning; the different policy powers in the different parts of the island were judged likely to cause confusion; and, indeed, some thought that because this model is neither the status quo nor a fully-fledged united Ireland, it is unlikely to satisfy either nationalists or unionists and would hence prompt further acrimony and conflict. Relatedly, other participants saw such an arrangement as transitional – a 'semi-skimmed' united Ireland– one that would not last.

While the exercise represented a snapshot in time of the opinion of a limited number of participants, it revealed how considered decisions and recommendations can emerge after detailed presentation and discussion of various options. It also illustrated that those engaged took into account the real political climate and dynamics at the time of the deliberative exercise, March 2019, when the power-sharing executive and assembly at Stormont were in suspension. The moderators also based their exercise on a unity referendum, where the outcome was calculated on a vote of at least 50 plus 1 per cent, North and South. They also suggested that 'the appropriate sequence of referendums would be to start in the North, followed by one in the South, but if and only if the North had voted for re-unification'. This is a departure from the model adopted for the referendums on the GFA itself, which were held on the same day in 1998.

It was explained to participants that the GFA envisaged that existing rights to retain British or Irish citizenship, or both, will remain in a united Ireland, including those embedded in the ECHR and other EU law. The Common Travel Area between Britain and Ireland would probably remain. The British–Irish Council – linking the governments of Ireland and the UK with the devolved administrations in Scotland and Wales, as well as Jersey, Guernsey and the Isle of Man – would continue. The BIIGC, at which the two governments address matters not within the remit of the devolved administration at Stormont, would also remain in place, albeit with the British government representing the interests of its citizens in the new Ireland. This would be a reversal of the situation before unity whereby the Irish government has 'a special interest' in representing the interests of Irish citizens in the North. In a post-unity situation, the balance of power will shift from the British to the Irish governments, including the ability to convene the intergovernmental conference.

After outlining these elements of continuity in the post-unity situation, the moderators then set out the most significant changes that would take place after unification and how these would apply in the integrated and devolved models under discussion. The opposing perspectives on the cost of Irish unity were also laid out with one side arguing that the South could not afford the North or to match the annual subvention from the UK. The other side argued that a united Ireland, as a rich and developing economy, with income per capita higher than in the UK, could easily integrate the North, which would also benefit from joining with a 'more dynamic, high growth economy', particularly in the wake of Brexit. The participants were asked to make an assumption that, in the short term, a reunited island would make only a small difference economically for the North, with some people becoming better off and others worse off, but with no dramatic change to levels of wealth. However, a major change would be that the currency across the island after unity would be the euro.

As a consequence of a vote for unity, the new political entity would bring the entire island into the EU and under its laws. The North would no longer be part of NATO, as Ireland's policy of military neutrality would come into effect. It was assumed that Dublin's membership of the Partnership for Peace and security co-operation with other EU states would continue. The Irish Defence Forces, which could incorporate members of the British Army who come from the North, would be the Irish army.

Similarly, the Central Bank would now apply its powers across the entire island economy as would the Supreme Court, which would be expanded to include a representative set of judges from the judiciary in the North. The Oireachtas, comprising the elected members of Dáil and Seanad Éireann, would continue to make laws, including the setting of tax levels, although they would now include representatives from the North sitting in an all-island parliament.

The President of Ireland would immediately become the head of state, while other more 'mundane' institutional changes were also predicted as part of the citizens' consultation. These included that people in the North would now pay their television and other licence fees to the Irish state broadcaster RTÉ rather than to the BBC, and the British honours system of knighthoods, CBEs, MBEs and other awards would no longer apply. The national sports teams, including the competitive field games of rugby, hockey and others which are already run by all-island federations, would represent Ireland. It was noted that soccer was a major exception in this regard.

Participants were given a guide to the likely make up of an all-island parliament with an estimate that one in six representatives would come from the 'cultural Protestant' tradition. It envisaged that the largest parties would likely 'be FG, SF and FF with the DUP, UUP, Alliance, Greens and other left-wing parties sharing the cultural Protestant vote'. The SDLP was not named in this potential future scenario for the purposes of the citizens' assembly exercise.

The report continued:

> Very importantly, in an integrated Ireland, one would expect the southern parties to organise in the North and some northern parties would seek to recruit voters in the South. There would be a quick move towards an all-island party system – a visible transformation in the eyes of most citizens. There would be a big change in the organisation of public services, policies and security in the North. There would be a common civil service: judging by what has happened in other reunification processes there would be a fusion of the civil services; the Northern Ireland civil service would be integrated into the Irish civil service. There would be some rationalisation (implying job cuts) where there would otherwise be duplication. Some civil service jobs would require competence in the Irish language as at present in the South, but that would be a selective requirement, not ubiquitous.
>
> In this model, there would be an integrated health service. The same system that exists in the South would extend and apply in the North, no doubt, with transitional arrangements to allow for the different model that has applied in the North since 1945. There would be common provision for Catholic schools, Protestant schools, and non-denominational primary and secondary schools, similar to the model that applies in the North at the moment, with equal funding for each set of schooling arrangements. Universities and higher institutions of third-level education would be part of the same system, and subject to the same regulations. Over time there would be a single welfare system, a common set of pension arrangements in the public

sector, and common regulation of private sector pensions, and the same kinds of benefits would apply throughout the island.

Finally, the convenors offered two possible models of government for the new island which would, most likely, be put to voters in a referendum: an integrated united Ireland and a united Ireland with a devolved Northern Ireland, with the former proposal winning most support among participants.

9

THE HUME LEGACY

By late July 2020, the rate of deaths from Covid-19 had fallen significantly as the first wave of the coronavirus abated, with the total number in the South at 1,764 and case numbers of 25,869. The numbers being treated in hospitals were at their lowest level since the virus peaked during the spring, and there was optimism that schools would reopen in time for the new academic year. Deaths from Covid in the North reached 600 in early August and there had been almost 6,000 cases. There was worrying evidence that case numbers were beginning to rise more rapidly, at least in part due to the easing of the lockdown restrictions during the summer months. The South allowed travel from just 15 'green list' countries without arrivals being required to quarantine for two weeks. People in the North were allowed to travel to a total of 59 countries without having to isolate on their return.

This was the subject of tense exchanges in the Dáil between the Taoiseach and Mary Lou McDonald in advance of the meeting of the North South Ministerial Council (NSMC), when the latter accused Martin of adopting too passive a stance in relation to the issue. She said that he should seek an agreed strategy on international travel with the NI Executive and called for a 'single island system of protection' as the only way to get ahead of the virus. 'We do it for animal health, why on earth don't we do it for human health?' McDonald was quoted in the *Irish Times* in July 2020 as asking.

Martin responded that it was difficult to achieve a joint, all-island approach given the wide difference in numbers on the green list between both jurisdictions and said that a 'a reality check in terms of what's possible and what is not possible' was required, accusing McDonald of 'political positioning' and 'sloganeering'. The discrepancies in the regulations between North and South were discussed days later at the first plenary meeting since 2016 of the NSMC between the new government and the leaders of the NI Executive, but the calls by opposition politicians and public health experts, such as Dr Gabriel Scally, for an all-island, and far more restrictive, approach to international travel were ignored.

The death of John Hume in early August served to remind people of the key role he had played during the conflict in the North, particularly through his lobbying of senior members of several administrations in the US and his work in Europe, where he served as an MEP for many years and raised significant investment and peace funding for the North.

Hume's death also refocused the attention of many people on his concept of an agreed island and the success of his initiative with Gerry Adams, along with then Taoiseach, Albert Reynolds, in getting the British government to formally declare in December 1993, that it had 'no selfish strategic or economic interest in Northern Ireland'. The statement was included in the Downing Street Declaration, which laid the basis for an IRA cessation of hostilities in August 1994, and also set out the road map for the negotiations that led to the GFA. The contribution from Hume and Adams detailed the route that republicans and nationalists sought towards a united Ireland through self-determination.

The legacy of partition and the foundation of the NI state in 1921 were among the subjects raised when, on 13 August 2020, Micheál Martin met Boris Johnson, for the first time since becoming Taoiseach, at Hillsborough Castle in the North. With the pending centenary looming, Martin said that he and Johnson accepted that they had 'different perspectives on these big events'. As reported in an *Irish Times* article from August 2020, the Taoiseach said:

> History for me is about enlightening the generations to come and current generations. It's not about trying to prove a point. There will be different perspectives in relation to obviously the centenary commemoration of 1920 and 1921 in respect of the island of Ireland, both in the Republic where we will be doing our centenaries and likewise in the north.

For his part, Johnson accepted that there were different views of history but asserted that the foundation of the NI state was 'something obviously to celebrate, because I love and believe in the union that makes up the United Kingdom, the most successful political partnership anywhere in the world. Whether you call it a celebration or a commemoration … it's very important that it should be marked.'

At an earlier meeting with Johnson, deputy First Minister Michelle O'Neill insisted that partition and the new state were built on 'sectarianism, gerrymandering and an inbuilt unionist majority' and had failed; the Taoiseach was asked by reporters whether he agreed with the description. He had never been 'an advocate of partition', Martin said, but the narrative had moved on. 'That is what the Good Friday Agreement was about,' he said, 'it was about transforming the narrative around the North–South relationship. We actually have moved a long way from where we were.'

Both leaders made reference to Hume, whose death had delayed their meeting for a week, and his contribution to peace making between the two islands, although there was no mention of what the former SDLP leader would have made of Brexit, was the main topic of discussion at Hillsborough. With negotiations between the EU and UK suspended for the summer break, the Taoiseach said he was hopeful for a productive outcome when they resumed in September.

The growing sentiment among nationalists in the North on the need for constitutional change, particularly in the wake of what many considered the potential of a no-deal Brexit by the end of the year, was not assuaged by these expressions of hope from Dublin.

In September, IF co-founder, Niall Murphy provided a lengthy interview to the *Irish Times*, as part of a week-long series of articles on a shared island. The Belfast solicitor was still recovering from his battle with Covid-19, which saw him in an induced coma for 16 days after he had contracted the virus during a trip to New York in March.

His near-death experience deepened his respect for those who had cared for him during his illness in Belfast, he told the newspaper, and reinforced his view that a future health service in a united Ireland should be based on the universal care model provided by the NHS. However, his time in hospital also taught him about the immense pressure nursing and other medical staff were under as ICUs, emergency wards and other under-resourced healthcare facilities came close to collapse at the height of the first wave of the crisis.

Murphy said he believed that if unionists and others are to be convinced that a united Ireland would be in their best interests, they should be assured that a future all-island health service would adopt the best practices and principles of the NHS. 'It would be a declaration to those who live in North and who cherish the NHS that that's how it's going to be, going forward,' he said.

Murphy described how IF had emerged following the collapse of the NI executive in 2017 when the very ill deputy First Minister Martin McGuinness resigned in response to a sequence of scandals – including the NAMA Project Eagle and the so-called RHI Cash for Ash controversies – as well as sustained and ill-judged comments directed at nationalists by senior DUP MLAs and MPs. A GAA and Irish language activist, Murphy was a co-founder of Gaelscoil Éanna in Glengormley in north Belfast. He recalled how nationalists were appalled by remarks made by Arlene Foster in 2017 in response to SF insistence on an Irish language act: 'If you feed a crocodile it will keep coming back and looking for more,' she said at the time, in reference to the refusal of her party to facilitate Irish language legislation. DUP MP Gregory Campbell went further and insulted Irish language enthusiasts and the wider nationalist population when he jokingly phoneticised *Go raibh maith agat* (the Irish words for 'thank you') as 'Curry my yoghurt' in a public comment.

Murphy, a father of three, recalled how the December 2016 decision, by then DUP Communities Minister Paul Givan, to slash the Líofa Gaeltacht Bursary Scheme – which finances children from low-income families in the North to learn Irish in the Donegal Gaeltacht – was an insult too far for many nationalists in the North. The amount involved in the withdrawal of the scheme was not hugely significant, but the removal of the £55,000 allocation was seen by those who cherished the Irish language as the final straw, and it prompted McGuinness's decision, announced a month later, to leave the power-sharing government, he said.

In a subsequent investigation by news website The Detail, published in late April 2017, it emerged that Givan had been warned by senior department officials that the cut would mean the majority of applicants, who were children from deprived backgrounds, would be unable to afford the learning experience. A Freedom of Information query found that the department official had recommended a reduction in the size of the grant, but that Givan had responded six days later with the words 'no scheme'. The fund was restored weeks after the decision, but it was too little and too late to alter SF's decision to leave government.

Murphy told the *Irish Times* that he supported setting a date for a referendum on unity, while he also called for the establishment of an all-island citizens' assembly and detailed preparation by the Irish government in advance of any poll. He welcomed the establishment of the Shared Island Unit within the Taoiseach's department as a step towards such preparation and said that IF would engage with it, if invited: 'We think there is possibly more that could be done but it is a step nonetheless and we want to engage with it as enthusiastically and progressively as possible.' In the same article he also stressed that IF was involved:

> in private consultations with civic unionism, and we have invited political unionist representatives to attend and speak at our events ...
>
> Any constitutional settlement on this island must involve input from unionists because they live here. It's their island too, it's their home. They are neighbours. I have no exalted position on this island over anybody and nor does anybody over me.

Born in 1976 and raised in Glengormley, County Antrim, Murphy was just over 20 years old when the GFA was signed but had already experienced trauma during his formative years when members of his local GAA club, St Enda's were killed and injured, and the clubhouse attacked, by loyalists during the conflict.

The 72-year-old club honorary president, Sean Fox, was killed by the UVF in October 1993 at his home in Glengormley, close to the club grounds. The UVF claimed that it had interrogated the pensioner for an hour before they shot him. Fox lost an eye when a bomb exploded in a pub in the 1970's. The father of four was an Irish speaker who taught language classes in the club. Murphy recalled him as a popular figure.

Murphy was a family friend and neighbour of 36-year-old Gerry Devlin, a father of two, who was killed by the Loyalist Volunteer Force (LVF) at the entrance to St Enda's in December 1997. The manager of the club's senior football team, Devlin was shot by the same weapon used in other killings and shootings of Catholics in mid-Ulster. Gerard Lawlor was another club mate who was shot dead by the UDA in July 2002, apparently because he was wearing a Glasgow Celtic shirt. Murphy is acting for the Devlin and Lawlor families in their legal action against the British state and for alleged security force collusion in the killings.

Murphy's *Irish Times* interview also noted that he did not accept the argument that talk of a unity referendum might result in the resurgence of loyalist violence, at least not on the scale of that armed campaign that led to such killings in the past: 'I don't think anybody has an appetite for that,' he said. 'Ulster loyalism might find itself at odds with English nationalism. English nationalism has imposed an economic border in the Irish Sea. Irish nationalism didn't. English nationalism has delivered an economic united Ireland and will impose it.'

By September 2020, the IF group had held discussions with the main political parties on the island, with the exception of the DUP and the UUP, although there were tentative, informal engagements with senior figures in the latter organisation. It had its first formal meeting with then Taoiseach Leo Varadkar and Tánaiste Simon Coveney in February 2018, during which the prospect of a border poll and preparations for unity were discussed. Among those also present were the secretary general of the Taoiseach's department, Martin Fraser, and Varadkar's senior adviser, Brian Murphy. Niall Murphy, Brian Feeney and former member of the Victims Commission in the North, Patricia MacBride, were among the large IF delegation.

The atmosphere was noticeably colder at a subsequent meeting with Micheál Martin, later in June 2018. According to Feeney, the Fianna Fáil leader 'went off the deep end' about those promoting a referendum and openly campaigning for Irish unity. Martin was accompanied by his adviser, Pat McPartland, a native of County Armagh who was known for his harsh criticism of SF over many years. At the time, the FF leadership was deepening its partnership with the SDLP in the North, having stepped back from the suggestion of a merger of the two parties. On the same day as the engagement with Micheál Martin, IF also held what Niall Murphy described as constructive meetings with then Labour Party leader Brendan Howlin, leader of the Green Party Eamon Ryan, as well as with Mary Lou McDonald of SF.

IF continued to build its internal structures and resources, including its registration as a company and the formation of a board, as well as appointing independent senator Frances Black as chairperson and Niall Murphy as secretary. Its plans for a nationwide series of rallies, including in Cork, Galway and Derry, were put on hold following the outbreak of Covid-19 in early 2020, but it continued to build a network across the island, as well as in the UK and the US, where it also registered as a company, over the following months.

During the spring and summer of 2020, IF produced a number of online webcasts involving prominent figures discussing a future all-island economy and health service and on the issue of worker's rights in a new Ireland. It also published well-researched documents on the economics of unity and the constitutional challenges to be faced through the referendums envisaged in the GFA.

IF continued its campaign of promoting discussion on preparing for a referendum with debate and analysis on the challenges facing the Irish people in forging an agreed island; in the development of an all-island economy, health and education service; and a society acceptable to those of a British identity. As the year progressed, tens of thousands of people watched interviews with a range of politicians, economists, health professionals, trade union and business representatives discussing the benefits of Irish unity in videos produced by IF and broadcast across YouTube and other social media. Its spokespeople and support base clearly represented a broad canvas of opinion and was beginning to attract an audience across the political and community divide, including among younger, non-aligned, voters. IF members played a significant role in raising, and responding to, the growing discourse on Irish unity in Ireland and the UK in media, academic and political circles.

For nationalists in the North, but also across the rest of the island and among Irish Americans, the conversation reflected a steady and rising tide of expectation that a united Ireland, based on the principles of equality embedded in the GFA, was achievable as a lasting solution to the failure of partition. It was no longer possible to dismiss the calls for a united Ireland as just a SF rallying cry; or to reject those calling for an Irish government White Paper on unity, a citizens' assembly and detailed preparations in advance of a referendum, as unreasonable.

For its part, SF had been producing researched arguments for a united Ireland for some time and it set out a vision of unity in its document 'Towards a United Ireland' in 2016, the year of the Brexit vote. This included a critique of partition and outlined the prospect of a new Ireland 'in which the rights of all citizens are respected and which delivers prosperity, equality and inclusion.' Two years later, it produced an economic analysis, 'A United Ireland – Better for Jobs, Enterprise and Research', which projected how unity could unlock the potential for huge economic growth, generating jobs and an improvement in living standards across the island, in particular for border regions that had suffered as a result of partition.

In 2018, the party published 'A National Health Service for a United Ireland', which proposed an all-Ireland, universal healthcare system, accessed on the basis of need, free at the point of delivery, funded by progressive taxation and with fair pay and decent working conditions for healthcare staff. At SF's ard fheis in Derry in November 2019, Dr Seamus McGuinness of the ESRI presented his latest comparative research on the economies, North and South, and the disparities in income, life expectancy and other quality of life measures.

In July 2020, the Irish government announced the Shared Island Unit, while its political allies in the SDLP launched a New Ireland Commission, which proposed to examine constitutional issues, economic policy and the provision of an all-island health service. Launching the initiative, SDLP leader Colum Eastwood said that the changing circumstances, including Brexit, had made the case for unity more compelling. He was reported in the *Irish News* that month as saying, 'Look at what's happening across these islands with Brexit, Scottish independence and English nationalism; it is incumbent on all strands of political thinking to at least have a conversation about what the future looks like'.

During 2020, academics from Belfast, London and the US commenced their first online consultation on how the referendums as required by the GFA should be conducted, and without prescribing any preferred outcome. The UCL working group sought views on the methodology and arrangements for the referendums while, during the same period, the ARINS project, involving researchers from universities North and South, and in the UK and US, began their detailed research into various aspects of constitutional and political change. Professor Colin Harvey of QUB and IF, and High Court judge Richard Humphreys continued to promote the importance of engagement with citizens, including unionists and loyalists, on the legal reconfiguration of relationships and rights in various articles and debates.

As these researchers and advocates continued their separate projects, all had in common an acceptance that detailed preparations were required, led by the Irish government, but involving all political parties and sectors of society on the island, in advance of a unity referendum. By early 2021, there was a uniformity of views that Brexit was the catalyst for historic and constitutional change in Ireland, and a substantial amount of research work was underway into how it could come about.

10

POLICING IN A NEW STATE

B rendan O'Leary set out a template for a united Ireland in his *Treatise* and for the citizens' assembly participatory forum he carried out with John Garry in Belfast in 2019. He envisaged, theoretically, its constitutional and political structures, legal and policing requirements, health, education and other public services and the integration of the two administrations.

What it could not do was forecast the challenges and obstacles posed by those with the responsibility of making the integration process work, or identify the less visible opponents of change who exercise power in the various institutions of government, North and South. Among the more contentious issues confronting those tasked with designing the future united Ireland is how to ensure public support for the forces of law and order in the new dispensation.

Former PSNI officer, and now retired businessman, Sam Thompson said that there were many in the Protestant and unionist community watching the sun setting on the North as it celebrated its centenary. It may not be a completely flawless sunset, however. Thompson insisted that most unionists will accept the outcome of a vote for Irish unity but that there will likely be some violence from their community if certain, sensitive issues are not resolved in advance of the referendums. There are many licensed and legally-held weapons in unionist homes and, the PSNI has estimated, a considerable number of illegal firearms and other munitions under the control of loyalist groups across the North.

Thompson is based in Bangor, County Down, part of what is often referred to as the gold coast of the North because of its relatively wealthy population. He said at interview with this author that the prospect of unity is dawning on many within his community:

> I think the majority of unionists and loyalists would probably accept that the game is up and that it is time to sit down and get the best deal you can. When push comes to shove, I think there would be some violent opposition and the question is how much?

Much depends, he noted, on whether the so-called legacy issues are resolved between the two governments in advance of the border poll, particularly in relation to the potential prosecution of former members of the security forces for conflict-related deaths and other offences:

> If the whole thing is about revenge and humiliating unionists and prosecuting former UDR men and RUC men, it's not going to be accepted. All these issues of the past need to be resolved once and for all and just can't be carried over. The Irish government is going to need to be involved in that and agree not to change what is finally hammered out with the British.

The policing of loyalist and unionist areas will be a sensitive issue during discussions for a united Ireland, Thompson predicted:

> Even if it wasn't organised, you could have rioting and stuff like that. This brings us on to the whole policing thing. I can't see how the Garda could start policing areas like east Belfast and the Shankill Road [in west Belfast]. It would be very easy in places like south Armagh and southern Fermanagh.

There might also be small, organised groups who will attack the new policing service, including its members from the South, he suggested:

> In unionist communities, there would probably need to be some sort of continuation of the PSNI. It might be called some other name, in which you have a proportion of gardaí. Certainly, in unionist areas you couldn't draft in a southern police force and expect them to take over. People up here got used to a lot of police casualties during the Troubles, but I really don't know how people in the Republic would react to two or three guards getting killed every month.

Deploying the Irish Defence Forces in parts of the North could lead to a reverse of what happened soon after the British army arrived on the nationalist streets of Belfast and Derry:

> You've seen what happened with the British army if you put soldiers in situations they don't really understand. When they're getting a lot of heat and abuse from the locals, all it needs is a few of them to react badly. To a lot of loyalist people that would seem as alien to them as the British variety would be to nationalists. There are people, for example in the Shankill Road who have never crossed the border and have no intention of doing so. I don't think people in the Republic really quite understand that. I think some of them would be amazed that there are areas like parts of north Down and east Antrim where Catholics comprise less than 10 per cent of the population. East Belfast would be similar.

The dissident republican threat is likely to disappear but loyalist resistance to a new constitutional order can be expected to fester and sensitive policing will be required. Before partition, the island was policed by the Royal Irish Constabulary (RIC), which had widespread community support until the first decade of the twentieth century, which saw the rise of militant republicanism and the War of Independence. As Thompson recounted:

> The whole thing about policing in Ireland is that the police are seen to represent a status quo which people don't like. I remember talking to my grandfather many years ago. He grew up in the early part of the twentieth century and all the police on the Shankill Road were from places like Tipperary. Having a lot of people from Cork and Tipperary and other parts of the South policing unionist areas isn't anything new.
>
> The difference then of course was that the unionists on the Shankill Road didn't object to the existence of the RIC. I think there will need to be an overlap or some sort of mixture of guards from different areas. In the likes of south Armagh, you could have almost 100 per cent garda whereas around the Shankill that might drop down to around 10 per cent. There have always been Catholic police officers in those areas, but they've mostly been from Northern Ireland.

Brexit has revived the constitutional question after decades of stability for unionism since the Good Friday Agreement. Thompson said further compromise, indeed co-existence in a unitary state, is possible for the majority of unionists as long as their identity is recognised and they are not discriminated against:

> Brexit sort of woke it up again. Irish unity can be done if unionists can be reasonably comfortable and lead their lives in Northern Ireland where they don't feel in any way that their identity is second class. It may not necessarily be the most desirable, but a tolerable state of affairs. That's what you need to get for unionists. They might realise, 'I'm not living in the United Kingdom any more but at least I'm not going to be discriminated against.' I think that's the most important thing.

Since leaving the PSNI in 2008, Thompson has worked with Invest NI, the state agency that encourages foreign investment into the North. During the course of his work, he has identified the shifting trends within his own community, as well as the growth of the all-island economy and its benefits for businesspeople in the North. He suggested that a referendum should be held in the latter part of this decade and that the process of unification could happen between 2030 and 2035. The 2021 census, he said, will be a further catalyst for movement and will concentrate minds for people in the unionist population on the possibility of a united Ireland, sooner rather than later. He said:

> You now have a de facto border in the Irish Sea, and that has made the penny drop for some unionists who feel they are going to be abandoned. The unionist people always maintain that they don't trust the British government and yet keep on going back and trusting them. How many times do they have to keep going through this process before they realise that the interests of Northern Ireland aren't the interests of the south of England?

Business and farming people, from his experience of six years working for Invest NI, will ultimately decide what is in their best financial and economic interest and that of their children when it comes to living under new constitutional arrangements. For unity to happen, he argued, it is up to an Irish government to sell it, something that has never been done:

> de Valera said, 'You're going to join us,' and that was it. He never asked what would the unionist and people with British identity want? He could play it well politically, and the same with Charles Haughey and others. They promised they were going to be the people to bring unity about, but in practice it suited them politically not to have Northern Ireland. Fianna Fáil formed 9 out of 10 governments until recent decades and they wouldn't have

been able to do that in a single Irish state. It is a new ball game when all these Northern votes come in and what way they're going to break.

One of the more powerful symbols of unionism over the decades is the massive parliament building at Stormont, with the statue of Lord Edward Carson – a unionist, born in Dublin, who opposed the partition of his country – dominating its long avenue. Thompson said:

> Sure, why does the Dáil always have to sit in Dublin? Why couldn't they bring it on the road or move a second chamber up to Stormont or something? It will probably horrify some people but why not? You've got a building there and you might as well put it to some good use.

The risk of loyalist resentment fuelling their return to the violence of the past is a matter with which Dr Dermot Walsh, a former professor of law at the universities of Kent and Limerick and a leading expert in policing and criminal justice, has been familiar for many years. Born in Whitehead, close to Carrickfergus in east Antrim, Walsh grew up as a Catholic and nationalist in a small Protestant and loyalist town, starting secondary school just as the Troubles broke out in 1969. At interview with this author, Walsh recalled:

> I went to a Catholic grammar school in Belfast [St Malachy's], which meant getting the train at 11 years of age and then walking through the volatile interface between the loyalist Tiger's Bay and the republican New Lodge Road area every day. Coping with burning barricades, riots, bomb explosions, the sound of gun shots and being the target of attack was a regular occurrence.
> On the train, we were heavily outnumbered by pupils going to 'Protestant' grammar schools, most notably the Belfast Royal Academy. There was very little interaction between us. They

portrayed an innate, almost instinctive, righteousness and superiority, which tended to reinforce our experience of being second-class citizens. Unlike them, we were conscious of the risks of openly expressing our sense of identity or how we felt about politics and conflict. We were expected to be submissive, even invisible.

The Troubles did not impact dramatically on life in Whitehead. Yes, some of the few Catholic business premises were bombed, and there were a few Troubles-related murders. On the whole, however, there was no constant or widespread violence against Catholics in Whitehead. Presumably, that was because it was a 90 per cent Protestant and loyalist town of about 2,000 people. There wasn't a big enough Catholic or Irish nationalist minority for us to be seen as a threat, and in fact, many of the Catholics in Whitehead would have been pro-British and acceptably submissive to the majority narrative anyway.

But there was a small number of us who identified as being Irish and Catholic, and we did not always display the submissiveness expected of us. That marked us out as targets for attack from time to time, but it never really took the form of anything more serious than street-fighting among youths.

Walsh graduated with a law degree from Queen's and was called to the Bar of Northern Ireland in the early 1980s. At the same time, however, he was diverted into academia and research on the operation of the emergency legislation in Northern Ireland and, in particular, human rights abuses perpetrated by the RUC and British Army. He then took up a lectureship in law at University College Cork, where he taught for 10 years. He returned to the North with his family in the early 1990s to take up a senior lectureship in the University of Ulster at Jordanstown. A disturbing incident occurred at their home in Whitehead, where they were living at the time:

One Saturday night, I was at home with my wife and my brother having a few drinks and she noticed through the blinds a car behaving suspiciously in the immediate vicinity just after midnight. As she watched, the car came back around again, and a hooded man got out and headed in the direction of our bungalow. As he came into our driveway heading for the front door, he put his hand inside his jacket. She panicked and moved the blinds as she felt we were about to be attacked. Realising that he had been seen, the man turned abruptly, and went back down the road where the car came along, picked him up and drove off at speed down the avenue.

The incident coincided with Walsh being offered a chair in law at the University of Limerick. Much to the relief of his wife, who is from Cork, he accepted the position and in 1996 they moved South where he continued to teach and write on policing and criminal justice. His research on Bloody Sunday, published on the 25th anniversary of the massacre, helped to pave the way for the establishment of the second tribunal of inquiry, which went on to exonerate the victims of that day.

In 1998, Walsh published a ground-breaking study on the legal and constitutional status of the Irish police. This was followed by a major text on human rights and policing in Ireland. Both were in-depth, detailed examinations of all aspects of policing in the Republic, critically assessing how or to what extent they did or did not live up to basic human rights standards. He was one of the few independent media commentators raising the issue of police abuse, malpractice and indiscipline in the years before the scale of criminality within the Gardaí was exposed at the Morris tribunal of inquiry into police wrongdoing in Donegal in the early 2000s.

During our discussion in the summer of 2020, Walsh said that:

> a united Ireland would not necessarily entail the whole island being policed by the Garda Síochána or some other form of Dublin-

based force. In fact, it would open up an attractive opportunity for bringing policing closer to the communities they serve across all 32 counties.

An important distinction can be drawn between what some academics refer to as 'high policing' and 'low policing'. The former encompasses political policing, anti-terrorist policing, organised crime policing of major criminal networks and gangs and so on. It relies heavily on the gathering and analysis of intelligence and the cultivation of informers. It extends beyond criminal activities to reach perceived threats to the established political and economic orders. If not rendered subject to effective oversight, 'high policing' will present a potent threat to transparency, human rights, accountability and democratic legitimacy in policing.

'Low policing' by comparison refers largely to community-based policing; the policing that most of us engage with on a daily basis. Its primary focus is on crimes against the person and property, public order, anti-social behaviour, emergencies and threats to personal and community safety. It is identified with policing by consent. Done well, it makes a vital contribution to a peaceful and orderly society in which the needs and rights of all are served on the basis of equality and respect.

Critically, the delivery of 'high' and 'low' policing does not have to be squeezed into a single organisational straitjacket. Indeed, there are very sound reasons for keeping them separate. In Ireland, unlike most other democratic jurisdictions, however, we have made the cardinal error of combining both within the same, 'civil' police organisation. The Garda, for example, has always provided the domestic state security service, as well as the civil policing service. For most of its existence, the old RUC effectively combined both as well. To my mind, this is seriously damaging to transparency, democratic legitimacy, accountability and policing by consent. Under the mantle of the familiar everyday police service, lurks the 'eyes and ears' of a self-interested political establishment keeping the law-abiding community under constant surveillance.

There is no justification for this peculiar approach to the delivery of policing. While there will always be a degree of overlap between them, community civil policing and state security policing can and should be delivered through distinctly separate organisations. The former lends itself to local community-based policing services, while the latter is appropriate to a single centralised national police and security service. Adopting that sensible division in Ireland would be a positive advance on current policing structures, North and South. It would also make a positive contribution to a harmonious united Ireland in that it would avoid the frictions that could otherwise be generated in loyalist parts of the North if local policing was seen to be delivered by a national police force controlled from Dublin.

In practical terms, what this would entail on the ground is the establishment of distinct civil policing services in each of the main cities across the island; and the same for individual counties or combinations of counties. These police bodies would be rooted in their communities and would provide the broad range of civil policing services to meet the needs of those communities and the state as a whole. In addition, there would be a single national police organisation with the lead responsibility for dealing with counter-terrorism, major organised crime gangs, systemic threats to the stability of the state and international police co-operation.

The concept of locally based police forces along these lines has always been a core feature of police organisation in England, the US and many other comparable jurisdictions. It was also a familiar feature of Irish policing before partition. Local police forces proliferated since the early nineteenth century and several cities had their own police forces separate from the RIC.

Sensible adaptation of the concept today could enhance police-community identity and relations across the island as a whole. Critically, it could also help ease fears in those loyalist communities where political resistance to a united Ireland runs deep. They would get reassurance from having their everyday policing needs met by a police service that they can identify with. In some of these communities, that would even be an advance on their current situation. In other words, policing doesn't have to be an obstacle to developing a united Ireland.

Walsh suggested that the recent and growing friction and tension between the PSNI and loyalist working class is, to some extent, a consequence of the Patten reforms on policing that emerged from the GFA. Former government minister, and the last British governor of Hong Kong, Chris Patten proposed a root and branch reform of the RUC, which resulted in the departure of many officers, including some who had an unhealthily close relationship with, or sympathy for, illegal loyalist organisations. The recruitment of more Catholics and the political decision by SF to endorse the new policing service has weakened the bonds between the loyalist and unionist community and 'their' police force.

The Protestant community 'of all shades and classes', Walsh said, had identified the RUC and the B Specials as their police force:

> Not only was it drawn almost exclusively from them, but it was seen as their first line of armed defence against the perceived threat to their hegemony from the Irish/Catholic minority within and from the Irish state on the other side of the border. There was no scope for conflict or tension between any section of the Protestant community and their police.

Walsh is also conscious of the long history of penetration and control exercised by sinister forces:

Having been born and grown up in the heart of loyalist Ulster, I have long been familiar with the manner and extent to which the unionist hostility to the Irish nationalist community penetrated to the core of policing. Despite Patten and the peace agreement, I am not confident that that has been eradicated. There continue to be examples of operational decision-making that, at least on the surface, evoke reminders of a unionist police force hostile to the needs and rights of the Irish nationalist community.

He cited as an example the investigation by the PSNI and Durham police into filmmakers Trevor Birney and Barry McCaffrey. In 2017, the two journalists made the acclaimed documentary *No Stone Unturned*, which looked into the UVF attack on a bar in Loughinisland, County Down during the soccer World Cup in 1994, in which six Catholics were shot and killed. The documentary exposed the key role played by a UVF member and RUC police informant in the killings and the disappearance of key evidence following the attack.

Instead of being seen to go after those identified as responsible for the attack, in 2019 the PSNI arrested Birney and McCaffrey and seized documents and other material from their homes and office over allegations that a Police Ombudsman document had been stolen. The two journalists won a High Court action against the PSNI, challenging the actions in enforcing a warrant to seize material, and were awarded £875,000 (€966,000) in damages.

Walsh observed how, during the dirty war with armed republicans, the dark hand of British security was believed to have co-operated with elements within loyalist organisations in the killing of many nationalists, including prominent solicitors Pat Finucane and Rosemary Nelson. During our discussion, he said that the single biggest change during his lifetime has been the manner in which the confidence of the Catholic and nationalist community has grown, not only in west Belfast but in loyalist-dominated parts of the North:

The one thing that has changed fundamentally here in my lifetime is the confidence of the Irish community. They have taken responsibility and leadership and are much more assertive about their identity and place. They have thrown off the second-class citizenship to which they were consigned following partition. Even in parts of Ballymena, a traditional loyalist heartland, the open expression of Irish identity is not uncommon. When I was a teenager that was unthinkable. It would have been very quickly and aggressively suppressed.

The growing confidence of the nationalist community is reflected in his own profession, with the number of young lawyers in Belfast exceeding those from a traditional unionist background:

People like Pat Finucane blazed the trail by being seen to take a prominent stand in using the law to challenge the abuses of the political and security establishments; even to the point where it cost him his life. He inspired many others to become lawyers, motivated primarily by the desire to make a difference for victims of oppression and discrimination.

Walsh has also noted the trend for solicitors and barristers from Belfast taking cases on behalf of clients challenging injustice through the courts in Dublin and across the South. While this can be seen as a positive contribution towards the development of an all-island legal profession, the competition has not always been welcomed in the profession south of the border. It also flags up an important difference between the two jurisdictions that could prove as challenging as policing for the transition to a united Ireland. That difference is the Constitution. Unlike the North, the South has a written Constitution. It has a fundamental impact on law-making, legal principle and the administration of justice. How should that be developed? As Walsh asked during our interview:

Do you extend it to the North? Do you modify it? Do you develop it? Or do you try and operate two systems? There is now a strong familiarity with, and attachment to, the 1937 Constitution, not just among lawyers but also among society generally in the South. The Constitution has already undergone some radical amendments quite smoothly in recent years to meet the perceived needs of the polity there. People and legal practitioners in the South will have to be persuaded that it needs further change, not just to meet the rapidly changing environment of the 21st century, but also to accommodate the needs of unification. It must also be borne in mind that engaging with a written Constitution, including its entrenched Bill of Rights, will be a new experience and challenge for most lawyers in the North.

Developing the 1937 Constitution to cope with the demands of unification would also present an interesting challenge for the judicial systems and judges North and South of the border. It helps that both stem from a common legal tradition and many of the judges engage regularly with each other and have deep mutual professional respect. It does not follow, however, that they will be on the same page on how the challenges of unification could and should be met. As with policing, there are diverse options, ranging from the maintenance of two co-operative systems through to complete integration. Even more than policing, however, the shape of any appropriate solution will depend heavily on other key aspects of unification arrangements.

While the legal profession has attracted a new generation of solicitors and barristers from the nationalist community, the judiciary in the North has also undergone a major transformation over the past two decades.

Siobhan Keegan, the first female chief justice in the history of the North was appointed in 2020. Both she and her predecessor, Declan Morgan, had a Catholic and nationalist upbringing, and both have played key roles in developing more effective and independent judicial investigations into legacy cases from the conflict through the Coroners' Courts. Justice Keegan was the coroner in the inquest of 10 of the people killed during a sustained attack by the British Army Parachute Regiment in August 1971 on the people of Ballymurphy, west Belfast. In May 2021, 50 years after the massacre, Keegan delivered her devastating findings to the survivors and relatives of the victims at the International Convention Centre in Belfast.

Those killed were unarmed and 'were entirely innocent of any wrongdoings on the day in question,' the judge said to loud applause; 9 of the 10 shootings were attributed to the Parachute Regiment and the use of lethal force by soldiers was not justified. 'They were all innocent people. This was a tragedy for all the families,' said Keegan, as reported in the *Irish News* in May 2021. 'The army had a duty to protect lives and minimise harm, and the use of force was clearly disproportionate.' She said there was no evidence to suggest any of the deceased were linked to the IRA.

During his final months as Lord Chief Justice for the North, Declan Morgan led the hostile reaction to the decision by the British government to introduce legislation under the UK Internal Market Bill that would breach the Withdrawal Agreement agreed with the EU in late 2019. Northern Ireland Secretary Brandon Lewis first raised the prospect in September 2020 when he spoke about his government planning to break international law in a 'very specific and limited way'. (UK Parliament TV, 8 September, 2020)

The UK Internal Market Bill provided ministers with the power to decide unilaterally how the NI protocol would be implemented once the Brexit transition period was completed at the end of the year. The move revived tensions with the Irish government and the EU over the Irish border and prompted a warning by President of the European Commission Ursula von der Leyen about the importance of Britain sticking to the legally binding treaty as it had agreed. '*Pacta sunt servanda*,' (agreements must be kept), von der Leyen was quoted by *Reuters* as having said, in relation to a fundamental principle of international law.

Morgan, as well as former Conservative Party prime ministers, John Major and Theresa May, condemned any action that could 'undermine trust in the system of the administration of justice', as reported in *Irish Legal News* in September 2020. More ominously for Boris Johnson and his colleagues, US Speaker of the House Nancy Pelosi added her voice when she warned, 'If the UK violates that international treaty and Brexit undermines the Good Friday accord, there will be absolutely no chance of a US–UK trade agreement passing the Congress. The Good Friday Agreement is treasured by the American people and will be proudly defended in the United States Congress.'

With a US presidential election due in less than two months, Pelosi's intervention signalled that there would be a radical departure in policy towards the UK if Donald Trump was replaced by the Democratic Party candidate, Joe Biden. The Internal Market Bill also rang alarm bells in the devolved administrations in Scotland and Wales due to the renewed powers it transferred to government ministers to make strategic decisions concerning the UK as a whole. Under the devolution settlement, these unilateral decisions were disallowed and the latest proposals were described as a Tory power grab by the SNP and by former Labour leader Ed Miliband, among others, in Westminster.

Following a late-night phone call with Johnson, Taoiseach Micheál Martin told RTÉ's *Morning Ireland* that 'trust has been eroded but he [Johnson] made it clear to me that the UK was fully committed to meeting the obligations of protecting the single market and fluidity of trade North and South.' But Martin's faith in Johnson's commitment was clearly undermined by the British prime minister's plans to override parts of the Withdrawal Agreement. Martin went on to say that:

> The stakes are higher now because of the British action. The publication of the bill signals an attempt by the UK government to

essentially break its commitment entered into [in] an international agreement and that is very serious. It's very worrying news for everybody and in my view makes no sense and I've consistently said this to the British Prime Minister. I think the European Union leadership will be very concerned in how negotiations go from here.

11

THE SHARED ISLAND UNIT

As he contemplated the prospect of a breakdown in the Brexit talks, Martin's own political future was called into question by a Red C opinion poll held just weeks into his first term as Taoiseach: FF took just 25 per cent, compared to FG at 35 per cent and SF at 27 per cent. Martin's personal ratings had also dropped by five points. In response, Éamon Ó Cuív, an open critic of the Taoiseach, called for him to be replaced and commented on Twitter that it 'looks like my prediction of there being two large parties but FF not being one of them is coming to pass. The threat is existential. FF won't survive if we persist with the myth that the decline is simply due to external factors and not the party's direction.'

Internal bickering over the disappointing results for the party in the February 2020 election and the subsequent refusal of the leadership to engage in government formation discussions with SF did not diminish Martin's very public and outright hostility to the now main opposition party over its relationship to the IRA and its role in the armed conflict in the North over 30 years. For many nationalists in the North, and not a few in his own party, FF policy and Martin's focus were determined by the electoral threat posed by SF and the prospect of it becoming the dominant political force on the island following a successful referendum for unity, which Martin was accused of seeking to postpone for as long as possible.

In his online address to the MacGill school in late October 2020, Martin made an unrestrained assault on SF, accusing unelected people in the party of organising 'behind the scenes' a 'political funeral' to mark the death of Bobby Storey in Belfast in June. He claimed that there was a decision to defy public health guidelines in order to 'make a very clear political statement around the war as they'd call it'. He said that 'people were summoned from the length and breadth of the country to attend to make a statement.' In response to questions, Martin declined to envisage any future alliance with SF in government until he was satisfied that it was run by elected representatives: 'I have never been satisfied to this day that has been the case with the modern Sinn Féin party,' he said while insisting that FF was 'committed to a united Ireland; that has always been its position.' He accepted that the thrust of the Shared Island initiative was to promote co-operation between North and South rather than to press for unification and that his 'noble objective' was to:

> say to all persuasions on this island, how do we share this island?
>
> We have done research on Northern Ireland ourselves as a political party over the last number of years. We have identified a very strong middle ground in Northern Ireland, that want to get things done for them, that want to create a future.

The formal launch of the Shared Island Unit (SIU) in late October 2020 provided more details on the range of its government-financed research and practical support for all-island co-operation and development. The SIU was to commission expertise from existing state bodies to deepen the comparative analysis of the economies and health systems, North and South. It envisaged the participation of the social partners, including employers and trade unions, in an organised forum to discuss the development of an all-island economy and intensified co-operation between both jurisdictions. Announcing the financial details of the initiative at the launch, Martin said that the government would make €500 million available 'for the next five years' to research ways of 'deepening North–South co-operation' and building a 'shared island agenda'. He named Aingeal O'Donoghue – a former civil servant in the Department of Foreign Affairs – as head of the unit, assisted by principal officer Eoghan Duffy, with up to five other staff to be appointed. The key areas of focus would be the all-island economy, an all-island climate strategy, investing in the north-west and border regions and commissioning research to 'support the building of consensus around a shared future on the island'.

He confirmed that the SIU would work in co-operation with the ESRI on commissioning the 'comprehensive research programme', particularly focusing on the economy, health and education on the island, and with the National Economic and Social Council which, he said, had already completed a scoping report.

The government was also committed, Martin said, to supporting cross-border, capital projects, including the long-awaited completion of the A5 motorway from Monaghan to Derry, the Narrow Water Bridge across Carlingford Lough and the upgrading to a higher speed rail connection between Dublin and Belfast. The plan also envisaged the development of a new university in the north-west, linking colleges in Letterkenny and Derry, as well as increased co-operation in existing cross-border health initiatives. The announcement was not particularly ground breaking, given that many of the funding proposals had already been mooted or, in the case of the A5 motorway, abandoned in 2011 during the financial crisis. Martin's speech to an online audience of stakeholders also raised speculation among FF members as to whether the Taoiseach was distancing himself from the traditional commitment of his party to a united Ireland.

During his speech he said he wished to

> probe some of the simplistic narratives about what we have all come through, which have emerged on both sides of the

border. The persistence of identity politics, where a position on constitutional identity is judged to be of primary importance, hindering productive discussion about policy priorities or good governance, is a challenge that we must also recognise.

In his comments to the media following the launch at Dublin Castle, Martin said that his priority was to focus on the GFA instead of on territory or a border poll. When asked if he had abandoned a united Ireland, the Taoiseach replied, as reported in the *Irish Examiner*, 'It depends what you mean by a united Ireland.' Asserting his belief in the GFA, he insisted 'it's not territorial for me'. He made it clear that he would not be seeking a referendum on unity during the current term of government. Arguing that the immediate priority was to increase co-operation across the border in areas such as infrastructure, tourism, business and cultural projects, he said, 'My focus is on building, on strengthening shared relationships on the island.'

While there was a positive response within the party to the Shared Island initiative, former minister and Laois Offaly TD, Barry Cowen, reiterated the core FF principle of a united Ireland and called for a referendum in 2028, the 30th anniversary of the GFA. 'Fianna Fáil must and will still abide by our aims to peacefully secure the unity and independence of Ireland as a Republic and carry out the democratic programme of first Dáil,' Cowen said, as reported in the *Irish Times* in October 2020.

The Taoiseach's remarks prompted a hostile reaction from the DUP, which accused Martin of interference in the affairs of Northern Ireland. UUP leader Steve Aiken said his party would not be engaging with the Shared Island discussions unless an 's' was added to make them about shared islands. Addressing her party ard fheis on the same day as the Taoiseach's speech, SF leader Mary Lou McDonald noted that it was disappointing that:

Micheál Martin failed to address Irish unity today.

No longer is the goal of a united Ireland seen as an aspiration. It is seen as a common-sense proposition and necessary for the future prosperity of everyone who calls this island home. Of course, preparations and discussions about what a united Ireland should look like must include the unionist community as equals – it must be a process for them as it is for anybody else.

However, it's a mistake to think we can unify the people of this island while retaining the division that the border has cemented for generations. It certainly won't be achieved by pushing back against a referendum on Irish unity.

SDLP leader Colum Eastwood was quoted on the Derry Daily website as saying:

> Our view has long been that those of us who want to see constitutional change have a responsibility to engage in a positive and respectful conversation with all of our neighbours. But we also have to demonstrate the benefits of co-operation and the potential we have to fundamentally reshape the lives of those we represent for the better. (*derrydaily.net*, 22 October 2020)

Not all unionists adopted a negative response, however. Peter Robinson used his column in the *News Letter* on 23 October 2020 to propose a new think tank to promote the union, as a more productive response: 'Success at a border poll will be down to a steady and consistent espousal of the real value of the United Kingdom membership, not a three-week splash'.

Picking up the argument, former UUP communications director and commentator Alex Kane noted in an article for the *Irish Times* that, in his SIU launch speech, Martin had made it clear that a border poll was not on his agenda for five years. Kane warned that unionists could not afford to sit back and wait. Acknowledging the growing strength of SF across the island and the resurgence of civic nationalism in the form of Ireland's Future, he warned that unionism was in danger of being left behind:

> Right now – and I don't think it's just down to Brexit and demographics – all of nationalism and republicanism seem to be on the same page. Sinn Féin continues to promote the 'unity project' above and beyond all else and is strong on both sides of the Border.
>
> A new form of civic nationalism has been organising and campaigning across Northern Ireland, pushing the case for a united Ireland. And Martin has pushed the issue up the agenda after last week's speech. Interestingly, in a response to a question afterwards he said: 'The Government has said that for the next five years a border poll is not on our agenda ... I've made it very clear it's not on our agenda for the next five years.'
>
> Robinson knows that five years is but a blink in politics. He knows, too, that in five years it might be Mary Lou McDonald who is taoiseach. Any unionist who thinks that a border poll can't or won't happen is deluding themselves. All of nationalism is working on the basis that the poll is more likely than not. Key players within nationalism are preparing for that poll and making the case for unity every day and from every available platform. Unionists must do the same for the union.

Joining the rising tide of nationalist voices was Jim O'Callaghan, the emerging favourite as successor to Martin. In a none too subtle, but polite, rejection of Martin's speech days earlier, O'Callaghan made a call for preparations to begin for a border poll and argued that it was incumbent on nationalists and republicans to put forward a vision for a united Ireland. In an interview with blogger Mick Fealty of Slugger O'Toole, O'Callaghan said that FF and the SDLP should collaborate in preparing for a border poll and put forward a constitution for a new

Ireland. He also said that he would like to see a merger of the parties following their current partnership as 'a couple engaged for years'.

In the interview, O'Callaghan put forward a contrasting set of priorities to his party leader, without making any overt criticism of Martin. Indeed, he claimed that the Taoiseach was not 'shying away' from a referendum and shared his goal for the reunification of the two jurisdictions. However, his own emphasis was on preparing for a border poll which, he said, 'is going to happen':

> It will be for the secretary of state to decide, but we can't simply wait around. My fear is that a border poll would end up the same as the Brexit poll, which was chaotic. Each side and various other sides should present their views on the preferable constitutional position. Let's debate it, let's prepare for it and let's vote on it and let's move on from it.

At a virtual meeting with IF in early November, Martin was pressed again to prepare for constitutional change. The Taoiseach was accompanied by Aingeal O'Donoghue and Eoghan Duffy, and the discussion was more constructive and less hostile than the meeting a year earlier between IF and the FF leader, according to those present. During their discussion, Niall Murphy and Professor Colin Harvey questioned the recent statement by the Taoiseach, which suggested that he was not pursuing constitutional change. According to Murphy in the *Irish Times* on 7 November 2020, the IF delegation:

> impressed upon the Taoiseach that to say constitutional change is simply off the table is the wrong approach for him to take. The North has been forced out of the EU against the will of its citizens, and we watch as a shambolic government in Westminster plots a delusional political future in the international wilderness.
>
> The requirement for planning and preparation and specifically for the establishment of an all-island citizens' assembly is

something the Taoiseach must implement as a matter of urgency. We outlined to the Taoiseach that there is a significant section of the population in the North that support re-entry to the EU via a unity referendum. The voices of these people must be heard and respected. We also made clear that we are living in a time when leading unionist political figures are saying unionism must prepare. He too must prepare the Irish people and nation for potential constitutional change.

Ten days later, the group reported a constructive meeting with the SF leadership, including Mary Lou McDonald, Michelle O'Neill and TDs Pearse Doherty and Matt Carthy. At the discussion, the IF delegation said it planned to exhaust the boundaries and limits of the SIU and to extend its campaign for a unity referendum to the diaspora in Britain, the US and beyond.

Within weeks of the SIU launch, SF published the discussion document, 'Economic Benefits of a United Ireland'. At the launch, finance spokesperson Pearse Doherty explained the growing disparity in per capita income and in living standards between North and South as evidence of the failure of the NI economy and how the subvention from the UK showed 'that it can no longer survive without fiscal transfers'.

The document posits that after removing the cost of pensions owed to NI workers by the British state, and the annual contribution of £1 billion by the North towards the cost of the security forces, the subvention comes down from the estimated and regularly-cited figure of between £9 billion and £10 billion to between £3 billion and £6 billion. This, Doherty summarised in his speech, amounts to between 1.3 and 3 per cent of modified gross national income of the economy in the South. He said:

Irish unity would allow for co-ordinated investment and development; something the border region has been missing for a century. Irish unity would utilise economies of scale, allowing one economy to develop rather than having two economies compete. The current trajectory of the all-island economy attests to these opportunities ...

In 2018, sales between the North and Britain fell by 9 per cent; while in the same year, the North's total exports to other markets exceeded exports to Britain.

He pointed to the growth in cross-border trade between the North and South to £7 billion each year:

Again, this is not to minimise the importance of Britain as a trading neighbour; but to highlight the growing importance of the all-island economy and the evolution of trading relationships. The greatest threat to trade, north and south, is of course Britain's damaging decision to leave the European Union. ... Irish unity would secure our place as an open, outward-looking, progressive island at the heart of Europe. ... The role of the EU would be even more central in the event of Irish unity.

As nationalists and republicans continued to push the case for a united Ireland, notwithstanding the disagreements on the timing of unity referendums, the threats posed by Covid-19 and Brexit continued to dominate public affairs on the island in the final months of 2020.

A second wave of Covid-19 across the country, with case numbers surging in both jurisdictions, led once again to sharp differences between the medical experts and politicians. By the end of October, reported deaths from the virus since the start of the pandemic in the South totalled 1,915, while the number of coronavirus infections had reached 62,002. In the North, the death toll was 700 with 39,116 cases recorded, a figure described by Dr Gabriel Scally in the *Irish Times* as 'shocking and disappointing'.

Once again, Scally warned about the failure to adopt an all-island strategy for confronting the virus and called for an external review by the NI executive to examine why the effort to control it wasn't working. The Executive, he told the newspaper in mid-November, 'should urgently review what their arrangements are for the control of the pandemic in Northern Ireland because at the moment, it certainly isn't working.' Dr Scally argued that 'if there had been a unified approach, North and South, that had a well-thought-out strategy, the situation would be entirely different.' An all-island plan should have been adopted from the early stages of the pandemic and as soon as the memorandum of understanding was signed by the Dublin and Belfast health ministers in June. It was the only way, he argued, to deal with the high number of Covid-19 cases along the border:

> Certainly, I can see no harmonisation that has taken place as a result and very limited, if any, integrated working, whereas we should have had an agreed approach across the whole island. I am very disappointed that the memorandum of understanding between North and South hasn't resulted in integrated action, an integrated approach, an integrated strategy.

Scally called for an emergency summit between politicians from Dublin and Stormont to 'sit in a room and hammer out an agreement about how we're going to control this virus.' He added that:

> we're paying the price for the failure, and particularly the border counties are paying the price for that.
>
> The Irish border has always been porous and people have always moved across it. It's 310 miles of the most permeable border in Europe, probably … which is why it has always been a nonsense to have different approaches to responding to the virus between Northern Ireland and the Republic.

Although the population was older in the North, Scally suspected the reason the death rate was significantly higher there than south of the border was due to the slow pace of its testing and tracing system:

> If it takes someone three days to get a test and five days to get the answer to that test, by that time other contacts will have developed the illness and also be infecting people. The whole thing is dependent on being fast. If you are slow, you are ineffective.

He described as scandalous that the opportunity to tackle the virus was not properly taken during the summer when deaths and cases were very low, and claimed that the failure to restrict incoming travel to the island with 'some managed isolation on the ports and airports' had contributed to the spread of the virus: 'At that stage, the numbers were so small that they could have been got down to zero quite easily on the island. But there was no chance of that happening because cases were being introduced by people arriving from abroad'.

And while delays in testing and tracing were hampering efforts to deal with the virus in the North, there was criticism south of the border about the failure to scale up capacity.

Dr Mary Horgan, president of the Royal College of Physicians of Ireland and consultant at Cork University Hospital, earlier added her voice to those calling for a strengthening of the testing and tracing capacity in the South and a revitalisation of the public health and hospital infrastructure in a sustainable way. In an article for the *Irish Times* on 27 October 2020, Horgan called, in particular, for more detailed analysis of the data on the spread of Covid-19 to understand 'how, where and why people get infected' and 'to link this to real-time data that shows how this impacts on the regional hospitals in terms of admissions'. She said:

> Early assessment of those who require hospitalisation, using the interventions such as steroids for those who are severely or critically ill, saves lives. Forensically analysing this data can define

Ireland's vulnerable population, to access real-time data on Covid-19-related hospital and ICU admissions to inform our restriction levels, to provide data on where clusters happen so that chains of transmission can be broken.

This data-based approach is how we can manage outbreaks in a rapid, agile and focused way in the months ahead and ensure that we can continue to provide access to other vital health services. The public needs to feel safe to be able to attend hospitals for treatment for strokes, cancers and other illnesses that are as much of a risk to many people as Covid-19. Remember, Covid-19 is only a part of what our health service is treating.

With public finances stretched, the numbers on pandemic payments beginning to rise and the normally busy pre-Christmas spending period looming, some senior politicians and civil servants on both sides of the border were pushing against the health and scientific advice. The deficit in the South's finances of over €9 billion by the end of September 2020, compared to a surplus of €38 billion over the previous year, was stressing senior government officials, and battle lines were being drawn between those seeking to defend the economy over the public health priorities of chief medical officer, Dr Tony Holohan and the NPHET team.

Leo Varadkar very publicly criticised Holohan and his colleagues for the sudden manner in which the Level 5 restrictions were announced in October when he reminded them that it was up to the government to make policy. As he pointedly told Claire Byrne on RTÉ:

I have confidence in NPHET to dispense public health advice. That's what they do. They don't advise the public, they advise the government and the government decides.

One thing that needs to be borne in mind is that these are very good people – 40 of them – but all coming from medical or scientific or civil service backgrounds. None of those people, for example, would have faced being on the Pandemic Unemployment Payment yesterday. None of them would have to tell somebody that they were losing their job and none of them would have to shutter a business for the last time.

As a six-week lockdown was coming to its end in late November, NPHET's critics at the highest levels of government, and in the retail and hospitality businesses desperate to re-open for December, grew more agitated. A row erupted over international travel after Holohan advised of the substantial risks unless strict testing and quarantining measures were imposed on arrivals. Many countries across Europe, including Britain, experienced an even greater surge of Covid-19 deaths and infections and the pandemic reached one million cases in the US. This led to warnings that the usual Christmas homecoming of tens of thousands from across the globe into Ireland was clearly unsustainable.

Senior government figure Martin Fraser and his counterpart in the Department of Public Expenditure and Reform, Robert Watt, were dragged into the fray as the media was privately briefed on the deepening tensions between the scientists and the politicians. One report, clearly inspired by senior political sources and without irony, blamed NPHET for spinning against its political masters. It described how senior civil servants 'went mental' in their criticism of the doctors and scientists who, they claimed, were involved in an organised media campaign to challenge ambitious, and perhaps risky, government plans for lifting the Covid-19 restrictions and opening the economy in the run-up to Christmas. As Pat Leahy reported in the *Irish Times*:

People in Government believe this is a careful and deliberate strategy by the public health experts to push the Government towards a more restrictive and cautious reopening. Holohan is central to the team's operation and that's why the Government pushback has been personally directed at him. He is, say people who have worked with him, forceful and focused; they also say he is reluctant to take no for an answer.

'He's like Hizbullah, there's no negotiating with him,' laughs one official, who speaks highly of him.

During the winter 2020 lockdown, the Taoiseach confirmed more than once that the government intended to exit Level 5 restrictions on 1 December, while 'taking into account' the advice from NPHET. He told RTÉ's News at One, 'The fact that we are doing well gives us flexibility … I want a meaningful Christmas; we can't be at Level 5 forever.'

The government advised against people travelling home from the US, Britain and other countries across Europe due to their high infection rates, but Martin and Varadkar were pushing for a greater relaxation of restrictions than the health experts were prepared to recommend.

NPHET warned of a fragile situation and that a rapid reduction of restrictions to Level 3 could quickly reverse the downward trajectory of the disease. The *Irish Times* reported that:

> if restrictions are eased now to a similar extent but more rapidly than in the summer, from a higher baseline force of infection, in winter and over the Christmas period a third wave of disease will ensue much more quickly and with greater mortality than the second. NPHET is concerned that the disease trajectory could once again turn quite quickly.

In the North, the divisions were less evident between the government and the medical advisers than between the parties in the power-sharing executive at Stormont. In mid-November, the DUP used the contentious mechanism of a cross-community vote to veto proposals by health minister and UUP member Robert Swann, for an extension to the Tier 4 restrictions already in place. Eventually, a one-week extension was agreed by the DUP, UUP and Alliance and the UUP, despite SF arguing that it was inadequate, and a partial reopening of hospitality and other services was allowed in advance of the relaxation in the South in early December.

Covid-19 had stretched the capacity of the Health and Social Care (HSC) – Northern Ireland's publicly funded healthcare system and part of the UK's overall NHS – which was now facing lengthy and mounting waiting lists and a severe backlog in diagnosis and treatments for a range of medical conditions that made it the worst-performing health service across the UK. By late November, 327,000 people – or one in six of the North's population – were waiting on a first appointment with a consultant, with 155,000 of those delayed access for more than a year. As with the situation south of the border, people were forced to wait for up to three, and even five, years for basic cataract, hip or knee surgery, unless they availed of private and costly medical care.

In a scathing analysis of the HSC, Brian Feeney wrote in the *Irish News* how, in England – with a population of about 55 million in November 2019 – just 1,398 people were waiting more than 52 weeks for their first outpatient appointment. In comparison, the referral-to-treatment time in the North registered 108,000 people waiting for their first appointment in a population of 1.9 million. Waiting lists were similarly atrocious in the South, with 612,083 people waiting to see a consultant for the first time in September 2020 in a population of almost 5 million. Echoing criticisms made of the HSE across the border, Feeney wrote of the HSC:

> There is a vast bureaucracy with various superfluous layers of management and tedious managerialism with managers, who know zero about medicine, directing clinical staff around and allocating beds. There are too many trusts and too much contrived artificial competition.
>
> Perhaps more important, HSC has failed to manage hospital staff. That's polite language for saying they have consistently failed to employ enough nurses and doctors. Preferring to throw money at agency staff. At present there are at least 2,500 too few nurses

who are run ragged by increasing demands. If you haven't the staff, you can't carry out procedures.

Feeney said that, despite the recommendations of the Bengoa report and:

> the promise made in the New Decade Same Approach con job of, all together now, 'a new action plan on waiting times', the real problem is the secretive, rigid, irreformable HSC. Never mind hospitals and GP surgeries, any minister hoping to make progress needs to dismantle the HSC and completely restructure it beginning at the top.

The Covid-19 crisis contributed to the extension of waiting lists, North and South. Many urgent cancer and other treatments were not carried out, and ICU capacity came close to breakdown during the first two surges in infections, but the health services continued to function across the island.

A shortage of beds, nurses and doctors, an over-reliance on agency staff and a lack of consultants in key areas, including public health, were also blamed for the waiting list crisis in the South.

In both jurisdictions, however, it was evident that some of the fundamental weapons against the spread of Covid-19 – including rapid and widespread testing, well-resourced contact tracing, controls on movement and effective quarantining arrangements for international travellers – had either not been deployed or not quickly or sufficiently enough across the country. The warnings of an inevitable third wave were largely ignored in the rush for a 'meaningful' Christmas.

12

THE AMERICAN CONNECTION

The election of Irish American Joe Biden as US president in the 2020 November election presaged a change in the relationships between Washington, London and Dublin that would profoundly influence the growing debate about unification and the benefits and timing of a referendum. It also directly influenced the strategy of the British government as the Brexit negotiations were reaching their December climax and the end of the transition period agreed a year previously.

In the wake of US election, the Johnson government withdrew its controversial Internal Market Bill, which had threatened to derail the Brexit negotiations. Within days of Biden's victory, his key adviser, senior US congressman Richie Neal, gave an interview to journalist Martina Devlin for an IF online event, during which he spoke of his Irish background – his mother hailed from Kerry and his father from County Down – and stated that he was hopeful of a united Ireland within his lifetime. In his early seventies, the influential congressman is also chair of the Friends of Ireland, a US organisation that supports initiatives for peace and reconciliation in Northern Ireland. During the Clinton years, he had successfully lobbied for a re-balancing of the longstanding and special relationship between the US and UK administrations. Neal and his colleagues believed that a more balanced view was required in relation to 'the issue of Ireland and, in particular, to the North of Ireland. … We succeeded I think in having great influence on Bill Clinton, who levelled it up as we might say.'

Neal believes the Biden administration shares the same enthusiasm for engagement on Ireland and of the importance of protecting the success achieved during Clinton's time in brokering the Good Friday Agreement: 'I've talked to them and they have my enthusiasm. We understand that America is a guarantor of the Good Friday Agreement. George Mitchell is a close friend of mine, he was an honest broker. Bill Clinton took great pains to make sure that all sides were included.'

Neal said that, during his recent visits to the North and in engagements with senior British politicians, he and the Democratic leader of the House of Representatives, Nancy Pelosi, insisted that there will not be a post-Brexit trade deal between the US and the UK if there is any dilution of the GFA, particularly in relation to the border:

I made it clear, as speaker Pelosi did with me. We travelled to the border, we made it clear to the Brexiteers … that there would be no bilateral trade agreement with the United States if the Good Friday Agreement was disturbed. That border, symbolically, politically and substantively, had to be abolished. And that's our bottom line as it relates to a trade agreement with the UK.

More than 30 years ago I was on a delegation visit with the speaker of the house Tom Foley. As we travelled from Donegal to Derry the bus was stopped, it was an armed encampment. British soldiers mounted the bus with night vision, heavy armaments and they searched that bus from top to bottom and the speaker of the house was part of the entourage. When I visited the border with speaker Pelosi not long ago, my phone pinged as I crossed from Donegal to Derry. I think that's a pretty good description of the success we've had.

In Neal's view, the current debate around Irish unity should result in unification, with the agreement of those of the unionist tradition. As he told Devlin during the interview, he regards former DUP leader Peter Robinson as a friend and one who is open to the idea of an agreed Ireland:

> We hope that convincing people of both traditions, that economically, politically and again substantively, that [it] makes the most sense for everybody … Peter Robinson over the last couple of years has said really encouraging things. I do regard him as a friend now. I think that when people you disagree with do the right thing, we all need to say so. Robinson has certainly argued for what could become an agreed upon Ireland and that means hopefully eventually the six counties joining the Republic.
>
> I think again one of the lessons that was learned from the Troubles, even though this was an 800-year dispute, or at least a 300-year dispute, the 30 years of violence [took place] in an area the size of the state of Connecticut. There were 30,000 British soldiers in that geographic area. I've not met or heard of anybody who would ever suggest that we should go back to those bad old days … [For many years] the argument was that the North was the most prosperous part of the island. I don't think there's anybody that would make that argument any longer.

Asked by Devlin whether he thought he would see a united Ireland in his lifetime, Neal replied:

> I'm hopeful.
>
> I think it would have to come about according to the Good Friday Agreement and that would be based upon a democratic vote that would take place and I think an energetic effort to convince the unionist tradition that they have nothing to fear about living in the Republic of Ireland, a modern, prosperous nation. I think

threatening them or trying to bomb them into a united Ireland, as John Hume used to say, won't work.

I don't anticipate that there would be any other route other than a referendum question. It would not be seen as hostile or threatening to the unionist tradition as well as the recognition that living in a unified nation would in many ways best represent their fortunes.

Certainly, in his first public comments on Ireland just weeks after the election, President Biden had foreshadowed Neal's sentiments when he told reporters in his hometown of Wilmington, Delaware that he did not wish to see a 'guarded border' on the island after Brexit. As reported on RTÉ News on 25 November 2020, Biden also revealed that, since his election victory, he had talked to Boris Johnson, Emmanuel Macron and Micheál Martin: 'We do not want a guarded border. We want to make sure. We have worked too hard to get Ireland worked out. ... The idea of having the border North and South once again being closed – it's just not right. We have got to keep the border open.'

During the campaign, Biden had repeated the warnings by Nancy Pelosi and Richie Neal that any threat to the Good Friday Agreement would jeopardise a future trade agreement between the US and the UK. If the British government was under any illusions about the intentions of the new administration regarding Ireland, and indeed its wider foreign policy objectives in contrast to those of his more isolationist and Brexit-supporting predecessor, Donald Trump, his comments in Delaware made them transparent.

Biden's appointments of Jake Sullivan as national security adviser, Jen O'Malley Dillon as deputy chief of staff and Carmel Martin as member of the domestic policy council, as well as other Irish Americans to senior posts across his team, confirmed that the administration would reflect the new president's leanings towards his ancestral roots. The former vice-president of Irish American Democrats, John McCarthy, was appointed as a senior White House adviser, while Amanda Sloat, a graduate of Queen's University Belfast, was named as a senior director of foreign affairs at the National Security Council. Biden also appointed Marty Walsh, an Irish American former trade union leader and Boston mayor, as secretary of state for labour, a key position in devising strategy for post-pandemic recovery and the return to work of millions of Americans. Walsh was among those who signed the IF letter to the Taoiseach in November 2019.

Raised in a traditional Irish-Catholic family in Scranton, Pennsylvania and with family origins in County Mayo and County Louth, Biden has been a frequent visitor to Ireland over many decades and supported efforts to resolve the conflict in the North from his earliest years in Congress. As a young senator from Delaware, he was a founding member of the Friends of Ireland, along with Ted Kennedy and Tip O'Neill, in the early 1980s. He was also a sponsor of the effort in the Senate to establish the International Fund for Ireland, which was designed to underpin the Anglo-Irish Agreement of November 1985. Biden maintained a life-long interest in human rights issues in the North, promoted the peace negotiations and was a staunch defender of the GFA and North–South co-operation since the historic deal was ratified in 1998.

Biden's accession to the White House was recognised immediately in Dublin as crucial to the government's chances of securing a Brexit outcome that was more favourable, or at least less threatening, than the prospect of a 'hard deal' as negotiations between the UK and EU reached the end game. Senior government officials described the Biden factor as a 'double lock' for Ireland in its efforts to ensure there would be no hard border and that trade with the UK and NI would continue with the minimum of bureaucratic and economic disruption.

After four years of negotiations, in late December 2020, the EU and UK confirmed an agreement on trade and security that maintained the NI protocol, keeping the North in the EU single market and customs union. The 'least bad' version of Brexit, as it was described by Micheál

Martin in the *Irish Examiner*, allowed for the continued flow of goods, including agri-food products, from Ireland into the UK without tariffs or quotas. The introduction of customs controls would potentially mean additional costs and delays in the transport of goods from the island into the UK and across the land bridge to the EU. Those working in Irish fishing industry faced a significant loss of income when the deal included a 25 per cent cut to the €650 million in fish that EU-registered boats caught in British waters each year. The Withdrawal Agreement, signed on Christmas Eve, ensured that there would be no hard border, customs or other obstacle to building an all-island economy. The protocol allowed the North to trade freely with both the EU as part of the single market and with the UK, although customs checks on the Irish Sea would still be required to ensure that certain animal and food products complied with EU regulations before passing through ports in Larne, Belfast and Warrenpoint. The reality was dawning that the strategy of unionism, and particularly of the DUP, to achieve a hard Brexit, and the reintroduction of a guarded land border on the island, had backfired spectacularly. The trade deal was signed just days before unionists were to mark the centenary of the foundation of the state of NI in 1921 and nationalists the 100 years of enforced partition.

Alex Kane predicted in the *Irish Times* on 30 December 2020 that the 100 year 'celebration' of the union would be ignored by nationalists across the island, and that it would be:

> difficult for unionism: a difficulty heaped upon it by Boris Johnson, the man cheered at a DUP conference when he pledged to save the North from semi-colonial status, then was later propped up by the DUP when he became prime minister. Yet it is Johnson who has shifted the North from its 'place apart' status into the much more precarious position of becoming the constitutional equivalent of a granny flat.

The North is now, arguably, in a weaker constitutional position than at any time since 1921, pushed there by the actions of the very man in whom the DUP invested so much trust. The DUP's problem – which is a problem for all of unionism – has been noticed by nationalists and republicans in the North, as well as by the Irish Government. That explains why the SDLP, Sinn Féin and prominent voices within civic nationalism and academia in the North have refused to participate in the Centenary Forum to mark the formation of Northern Ireland.

Kane claimed that their absence was rooted in a conviction among nationalists that the UK was 'hurtling towards inevitable dissolution, starting with Scotland', coupled with a belief that:

> the Northern Irish wing of the union is doomed precisely because the Northern Ireland protocol has placed the North outside the constitutional ambit of Great Britain.
>
> Civic nationalism in the North, along with Sinn Féin and the SDLP, is focusing a lot of attention on unity right now. And while the Irish Government doesn't have the issue at the top of its agenda, I think it would be remarkably complacent of unionism to assume that work isn't being done in the background. My assumption, for what it's worth, is that the Irish Government is now proceeding on the basis that a combination of circumstances will make the demand for a poll irresistible ... The five years mentioned by Martin, along with Mary Lou McDonald's recent claim of Irish unity by 2030, should represent breathing space for unionists: time to think about a common approach and strategy and prepare a coherent, united pro-union case for when the Border poll comes.

His view was echoed in a spate of articles and across various media, North and South, and in the UK. Many speculated on the future of the union now that the transition period had ended and Britain was finally liberated from the shackles of the EU and as the centenary year dawned in the North.

13

THE ARINS PROJECT

Early in January 2021, Brendan O'Leary marked the official launch of the ARINS (Analysing and Researching Ireland North and South) project with a detailed and timely reflection on the prospect of a unity referendum. In an article for the *Irish Times*, O'Leary suggested that unionists were now in a political minority and fast becoming an electoral minority in the North, while the union now depended on:

> the consent of cultural Catholics, whose opinions on that union are more volatile and averse than those held among those of Protestant heritage. ...
>
> Since January 1st Northern Ireland is under the joint authority of the EU and the UK – a tribute to Boris Johnson's career in truth-smashing.
>
> To address rational fears, Northern Ireland has been re-engineered in a remarkable improvisation. It is now a double 'federacy' or an annex to two different unions. The Belfast Agreement 'in all its parts' is now protected in two treaties: the one Ireland and the UK ratified in 1999, and the 2019 Protocol on Ireland and Northern Ireland agreed between the UK and the EU

that has just taken effect. ...

Northern Ireland remains within the EU's single market for goods, and, for practical purposes, in its customs union, but without European political institutions. Unless Stormont decides otherwise in 2024, the government of Ireland will have more influence on economic regulations affecting Northern Ireland than the Westminster parliament. ...

To resume full citizenship of the European confederation, many northerners have taken out Irish passports. Up to half the population have them, while the number taking out UK passports has slid. Later, they may support Irish unity to return to the European Union – not to Pearse's, Cosgrave's, or de Valera's Ireland.

O'Leary went on to ask whether people in the North could enjoy the best of both worlds promised by the Withdrawal Agreement by having access to both the UK and EU trading blocs or whether they would polarise between two conflicting options:

'Scrapping the protocol' is the DUP's ambition; the obvious alternative is Irish reunification within the EU.

Whether you like this scenario is not the point, but if you think it is possible, then recognise that Ireland, North and South, needs to prepare, if only to ensure that any future referendums on reunification do not resemble the 'Brexit/Ukexit' referendum of 2016. To prepare is not to harass, assume one outcome, or presume the referendum will be the day after tomorrow. Preparation can be open, peaceful and pluralist, ensuring multiple voices are heard, and available to constant correction.

Not to prepare is to take the ostrich as the paragon of political virtue.

In his view, the South was the 'most obliged to prepare properly because, under the Belfast Agreement, the initiation of a Northern referendum on unification rests with the UK secretary of state; Dublin has no veto and could be taken by surprise.' Arguing that voters must be given an 'informed and properly clarified choice, not a choice between the status quo and rivalrous descriptions of paradise' in a future referendum, he wrote that legislators in the Dáil would have to offer a precise model of unification or:

> a detailed constitutional process that would follow affirmative votes for unification. ...
>
> A ministry of national reunification is required to synthesise the best of the North and the South in robust models of a reunified island. It must engage unionists, nationalists and others – the latter and 'soft nationalists' will be the pivotal voters in the North. It must organise citizens' assemblies, and it will need to oversee a united Ireland transition fund, to be launched after the pandemic is controlled. (O'Leary, *Irish Times*, 11 January 2021)

O'Leary's contribution was accompanied by analysis from Dr Peter Shirlow, also a founding member of the ARINS project, and a pro-union voice who claimed that there was no evidence that the necessary conditions for a border poll were close.

Instead, in his article for the *Irish Times*, Shirlow claimed that the most recent polling and other data suggested that the majority in the North wished to remain in the UK although 'the desire for Irish unification has grown, but not significantly, since 1998'. He said that those promoting unity among the nationalist population:

> typically present the 26 counties as Nirvana and the Wee 6 as a hapless place due to its links with perfidious Albion. Unionists respond that 15 per cent of southerners live in poverty, that rural Ireland has been abandoned, and like to remind us that two-thirds of the southern population do not have access to free healthcare. ...

Within political unionism we find a limited space that promotes and persuades for the union. And yet, across the aisle, there is no serious blueprint setting out what a united Ireland would be.

Instead, he suggested, that:

the structures of the Good Friday Agreement, the Northern Ireland Protocol and the new Shared Island Unit of the Department of the Taoiseach are the points through which to build and sustain an interdependence that will not be bogged down by wearied conjecture and sectarian head-counting.

The protocol entails a policy of enhanced all-island relationships that will build economic, cultural and political opportunity. The protocol and its promotion of greater North–South co-operation, combined with Northern Ireland being within the EU customs code and UK customs territory, can frame critical all-island connectivity.

Shirlow criticised the binary approach to the issue, which he claimed:

relies on and propagates the skewed idea that there are two economies on the island, as defined by the Border. In fact, there are several – among them Dublin, Belfast, the southwest, and the 'left behind'.

There is an immediate case for building an Atlantic corridor linking Derry and Limerick. The furthering of linkages between North and South through culture, environment and tourism can also raise the levels of mutual dependence and assist in the avoidance of conflict.

For those who are pro-union, greater North–South connection can render the Border so invisible that the desire for unification will abate. For those who are pro-unity, greater interdependence can re-establish connections cast asunder by partition. Interdependence is the antidote to the politics of immiserating dissonance that have crippled Northern Ireland for so long.

Shirlow's views reflected the small but growing appetite among middle-class unionists for a middle way of 'interdependence' between the united Ireland and the pro-union positions, while postponing for the foreseeable future the prospect of the referendum envisaged under the GFA.

Meanwhile, Gavin Robinson, a leading figure in the internally riven DUP, warned his unionist colleagues to prepare for a border poll. On 18 January, the *Irish News* reported that the east Belfast MP echoed the views of former leader Peter Robinson that unionists should not ignore the North's constitutional future: 'Peter is absolutely right, not only about how we should think about these things: how we should engage in wider discussions within unionism how we position ourselves, and how fundamentally we advance the cause of the union through thought and argument.'

Welcoming his remarks, Brian Feeney said in the same article that they were an acknowledgement that unionism needed to appeal beyond its traditional religious support which no longer guarantees a majority. In reference to the outcome of the UK election in December 2019, Feeney said:

> These remarks are not just about preparing for a border poll – it's also a recognition that thousands of middle-class unionists have deserted the DUP for Alliance, exemplified by the shock victory (for Alliance) in North Down and the 17 per cent drop in the DUP share of the vote in Lagan Valley.

For those within unionism who feared that any mention of a discussion on Irish unity would effectively mean a concession to its possibility, the intervention of the former UK chancellor of the exchequer, George Osborne, in the debate added insult to injury. Osborne wrote in the *London Evening Standard*, of which he is the editor, that the DUP were the authors of their own Brexit misfortune and that the North was already 'heading for the exit door' of Britain:

> By unleashing English nationalism, Brexit has made the future of the UK the central political issue of the coming decade. Northern Ireland is already heading for the exit door. By remaining in the EU single market, it is for all economic intents and purposes now slowly becoming part of a united Ireland. Its prosperity now depends on its relationship with Dublin (and Brussels), not London. The politics will follow. ...
>
> Northern Irish unionists always feared the mainland was not sufficiently committed to their cause. Now their short-sighted support for Brexit (and unbelievably stupid decision to torpedo Theresa May's deal that avoided separate Irish arrangements) has made those fears a reality. It pains me to report that most here and abroad will not care.

A member of the Conservative government led by David Cameron that called the Brexit referendum in 2016, Osborne said that the outcome had effectively placed a question over the survival of Britain itself. While most English people would not shed a tear for the North of Ireland, losing Scotland to independence would be a disaster and could, he added, finally put an end to Britain's position as a leading world power. In advance of elections in Scotland in May 2021, it was widely acknowledged that Nicola Sturgeon and the SNP would emerge victorious and push for a second independence referendum. Osborne suggested that it would be a mistake for the British prime minister to allow this to happen.

An opinion poll by LucidTalk, published in the *Sunday Times* in late January 2021, showed that just over half of those surveyed in the North supported a referendum within five years. It found that 47 per cent of respondents in Northern Ireland wished to remain in the UK, with 42 per cent in favour of a united Ireland and 11 per cent undecided. Asked if they support a referendum on a united Ireland within the next five years:

> Some 50.7 per cent said there should be a vote on whether Northern Ireland remained in the UK at some point before 2025, while 44.4 per cent said there should not, and 5 per cent did not know. When the 'don't knows' are taken out, 53.3 per cent were in favour of holding a border poll.

Another LucidTalk poll for the BBC *Spotlight* programme on 20 April 2021 showed that 37 per cent of respondents supported a border poll within five years and another 29 per cent 'at some point after five years'.

In the South, the response to the wave of speculation and analysis about eventual unity following the Brexit deal included an unrestrained attack on nationalist proponents of a referendum, and IF in particular, by *Sunday Independent* columnist, Eoghan Harris. On 3 January 2021, Harris described 'Northern bourgeois nationalist pressure groups like Ireland's Future' as offering 'a more sophisticated united Ireland agenda' than SF. In response, the IF chairperson, Frances Black, wrote:

> Our group promotes the need for referendums in both parts of the island under the terms of the Good Friday Agreement as the means by which to effect constitutional change. We are not a political party and are not affiliated to any political party.
>
> Ireland's Future notes that any move to new constitutional arrangements requires serious thought, consideration and planning. We believe that the requisite planning for these potential changes must be broad, inclusive, detailed and comprehensive.
>
> Ireland's Future has lobbied the Government on the issue of the establishment of an all-island citizens' assembly as a forum to enable discussion on future constitutional change. We encourage discussion on all salient issues pertaining to Irish reunification including economic modelling, and human, cultural, and political

rights/protections relevant to any prospective new constitutional arrangements on the island. (*Sunday Independent*, 10 January 2021)

In subsequent commentary, Harris went on to attack other supporters of the campaign, including Colin Harvey, in a continuing effort to tarnish its work as its influence grew.

Four days after Black's reply, Belfast-based columnist Newton Emerson argued in the *Irish Times* that the IF campaign had initially prioritised a border poll before the restoration of the Stormont institutions in early 2020 'above compromise and delivery within Northern Ireland' and claimed that support for its demands:

> can hardly have increased since, as so much of it was premised on a no-deal Brexit and the absence of devolution ...
>
> Throughout Stormont's collapse, Sinn Féin outsourced much of its messaging to the Ireland's Future campaign, perhaps best known in the Republic for its 'civic nationalist' letters to taoisigh.
>
> The party endorsed and heavily promoted Ireland's Future, which at its height advocated giving up on power-sharing and Northern Ireland altogether, proclaiming unionist intransigence to be insurmountable. That message was heard repeatedly at a major conference the campaign organised in Belfast in January 2019, also attended by representatives of the SDLP and the Irish government.

In a letter of response in the same newspaper, Niall Murphy dismissed the allegation that IF was connected to Sinn Féin: 'This statement is untrue, not backed up by any evidence and damaging to our organisation which has remained deliberately unaligned with political interests ... Ireland's Future is not connected with Sinn Féin or any other political party. Nor do we lobby on behalf of political parties.'

14

DISCUSSION, DEBATE AND DEMOCRACY

A dramatic surge in Covid-19 cases across the island in early January 2021 led to over 1,000 deaths and more than 100,000 cases during the month in the South. It was attributed to a new and more infectious variant than previously experienced, first identified in Kent in the UK in late December.

The meaningful Christmas, as envisaged by Micheál Martin when he announced the lowering of restrictions, had turned into a nightmare as the new variant spread rapidly through the population, facilitated by the numbers returning from the UK for the holiday season. The crisis was compounded by the return to Ireland of large numbers of Brazilians, many working in the meat industry, who had made their way home for the annual festivities in their country, which was grappling with its own vicious variant of Covid-19 and a government in denial of its impact. By the end of January 2021, TheJournal.ie reported that the total number of deaths in Ireland from Covid-19 had reached 3,292, with case numbers of 195,303.

In the North, the Kent variant had spread even more rapidly, with NISRA reporting more than 4,500 cases in one week at the end of January and 2,355 Covid-19 related deaths since the start of the pandemic. Hospitals were operating at 95 per cent capacity and public health specialists were warning again that the failure to resource an effective testing and tracing system a year after the pandemic began was in part responsible for otherwise avoidable Covid-19 fatalities.

Once more, Gabriel Scally reminded people that across the globe over two million people had died from what he described in an *Irish News* article as 'this eminently preventable disease'. The variation in deaths between countries and regions, he argued, confirmed that a failure to track and curb the spread of the disease and to prevent its importation from abroad led to 'agonisingly high' and unnecessary deaths.

> The death toll on the island of Ireland, with more than 3000 deaths in the Republic of Ireland and over 2000 in Northern Ireland, far exceeds the death toll from the Troubles or the combined total of deaths in the Irish War of Independence and the Civil War. With appropriate action at the very earliest stage of the pandemic, the vast majority of those Covid-19 deaths would have been avoided.

The dry statistics were shocking but the case studies of those who died in various settings, from the many in their older years to infants who suffered fatal respiratory complications from the virus, were even more harrowing.

Scally blamed the Department of Health in the South for its failure to:

> modernise and adequately resource the public health system and recognise the public health doctors and their leaders, the directors of public health around the country, as equals to their colleagues in clinical medicine. There was masterly inaction from the department, despite the explicit advice it received about severe public health deficits over the past 15 years.

A year since the World Health Organization had designated the Covid-19 outbreak as a 'public health emergency of international concern', Professor Scally wrote, there was still no effective Find, Test,

Trace, Isolate and Support system (FTTIS) in place in relation to both jurisdictions on the island:

> A good strategy for Ireland might consist of, first, strong and rigorously observed societal measures to get the new cases down to tiny numbers. Second, an effective FTTIS and rapid outbreak management system that is well-resourced and locally well-connected. And, third, mandatory public health measures at borders that will prevent reintroduction of the virus, and particularly new variants.

The Covid-19 crisis and Brexit collided when the EU announced in January 2021 that it planned to invoke Article 16 of the NI Protocol it had agreed with the UK in order to prevent any shipments of the AstraZeneca vaccine through the 'backdoor' to Britain. Article 16 permitted either party to the Protocol to take special safeguard measures in exceptional circumstances if it believed that the terms of the deal were about to be broken. The threat was in response to an alleged infringement of the guarantee by the makers of AstraZeneca to honour its supply commitments to the EU and to prevent any transfer of the vaccine to third countries outside the bloc.

While the EU quickly withdrew its threat following urgent appeals by the Taoiseach to commission president Ursula von der Leyen and his warning of the dangers the row posed to North–South and Anglo-Irish relations, it provided fresh ammunition for the unionists over the perceived danger of the protocol to the status of Northern Ireland. In a *Guardian* article at the end of January, DUP leader and First Minister Arlene Foster was quoted as describing the EU action as an 'absolutely incredible act of hostility towards those of us in Northern Ireland'. She also complained that the disruption of trade flows between the North and Britain caused by the protocol were already causing difficulties for hauliers and were causing tension within the North:

We've been asking the PM to deal with the flow problems and indeed, since January 1st, we've been trying to manage along with the government the many, many difficulties that have arisen between Great Britain and Northern Ireland and there are actions he could take immediately … There is great unrest and great tension within the community here in Northern Ireland so this protocol that was meant to bring about peace and harmony … is doing quite the reverse. The protocol is unworkable, let's be very clear about that, and we need to see it replaced because otherwise there is [sic] going to be real difficulties here in Northern Ireland.

The *Irish Times* reported that SF deputy First Minister Michelle O'Neill described the EU response to the vaccine row with Britain as 'clearly unwise, ill-judged and totally unnecessary' and called for 'cool heads' to prevail. However, marking the cards of the DUP on the issue, O'Neill said that the protocol, 'while imperfect', must remain in place.

Unionists were promised that the protocol could be reviewed in 2024 and removed by a majority vote at Stormont, but this was of little consolation to them given their declining representation in the Assembly. Clearly, the protocol, just like Covid-19, was not going away anytime soon. DUP ministers delayed the introduction of infrastructure required for checks at entry points in the North for goods coming from the UK and some loyalists used graffiti to threaten those employed to implement them. The head of Mid and East Antrim Council, Ann Donaghy, said that some staff at the port of Larne had been removed from duty after graffiti threatening them appeared in the area. The PSNI later reported that there was no evidence of a genuine threat.

Firms exporting foodstuffs and other goods from Britain to supermarkets across the North experienced delays due to the new regulations and paperwork required, but the expectation was that these teething problems would be overcome in time. Business groups in manufacturing and other sectors unaffected by the protocol urged their members to recognise the value of having the best of both worlds, with access to both UK and EU markets, offered by the Brexit deal.

The EU action was seized upon by Jim Allister of the Traditional Unionist Voice (TUV) and loyalist flags activist and social media campaigner, Jamie Bryson, who were breathing down the political necks of the DUP. In turn, the DUP was changing its views on Brexit and the protocol with every wind. After her close party ally and MP for Lagan Valley, Jeffrey Donaldson, sought clarification of the protocol's arrangements to make it more acceptable, Arlene Foster called for it to be scrapped altogether. Clearly, she was feeling the heat from party colleagues who had for months been privately discussing a future without her as leader (RTÉ *Six One News*, 3 February 2021).

Among Foster's chief rivals was Edwin Poots, who had overseen preparations for the implementation of the protocol in his capacity as agriculture minister. Poots was among those now adopting a harder line in complete contradiction to his expressed views eight months previously. In a June 2020 letter to UK Secretary of State for Environment, Food and Rural Affairs George Eustice, obtained by the *Financial Times*, Poots described alignment with EU rules on food and agricultural products as a 'key ask' in reducing the impact of the Irish Sea border: 'This could be achieved, for example, by dynamic alignment with relevant parts of the EU acquis [the body of common laws, rights and obligations to which EU member states are bound] and the UK joining the common veterinary area [as in the Swiss/EU arrangement],' Poots wrote. He insisted that his demands 'must be met' in order to avoid 'unacceptable burdens' on Northern Ireland's population. Poots was forced to step aside from his position for medical treatment in early February but made his now harsher attitude to the protocol very clear before his departure. The DUP announced a five-point plan that involved disrupting engagement in North-South dialogue on matters relating to the protocol, opposing protocol-related bills, laws and other measures in Westminster and the Northern Ireland Assembly, and launching an e-petition to demonstrate the 'strength of feeling' citizens have in relation to the protocol.

The UUP which, so far, had failed to capitalise politically on the external difficulties and internal squabbles of the DUP, set out a six-point plan to mitigate the impact of the dreaded protocol. These included an extension of the grace period of three months before the proposed phytosanitary arrangements and other checks put in place, and a UK government taskforce to identify a permanent solution by the end of the derogation period. It sought new legislation that would make it an offence 'to prohibit the use of our territory (NI) for the export of goods to the EU that are not compliant with EU regulations and standards, as required to maintain the integrity of the single market.' In the same paper, the UUP called for an all-islands body 'within the existing North/South and East/West structures' of the GFA to 'resolve the issues with onward supply and EU Customs Officials at NI ports and other Irish Sea and airports.'

The Covid-19-inspired protocol controversy came against the background of disastrous polling for the DUP, continued internal rumblings against Foster's leadership and open dissent by MPs, including Sammy Wilson and Ian Paisley Jr, as well as predictions that SF would become the largest party in the North following assembly elections in May 2022.

Thrown into the mix was a statement by the Loyalist Communities Council (LCC), made up of representatives of the UDA, the UVF, the Red Hand Commando (RHC) and other paramilitary and illegal organisations, who warned that their identity was under threat from the protocol. In early February, LCC Chair David Campbell warned that unionist anger at the protocol could lead to a return to violence, although he hoped that the days of loyalist fighting were over. 'We live in an imperfect society and one fights in different ways', Campbell told the BBC's *Nolan Show*, adding that 'if it comes to the bit where we have to fight physically to maintain our freedoms within the UK, so be it.'

A former chair of the UUP and adviser to its former leader, David Trimble, Campbell recalled how the party had been displaced by the DUP because of mistakes it had made, including its role in framing the GFA. Explaining his comments after he was subjected to intense criticism from Arlene Foster and others, Campbell was quoted in the *Irish News* as saying that he had made his remarks 'in the context of fighting against freedoms being removed by a tyrant like Adolf Hitler or Stalin, certainly not in reference to Brexit. …That has to be a political fight, a fight based on common sense'.

Accepting that 'there is no place for violent activity', Campbell called for leadership from the DUP and gave notice to Foster that her political future was in question: 'If the protocol isn't improved upon how can they continue? …The pressure from the ground up will become too great and the first minister's position will be untenable,' he said.

Campbell again reminded people that the rise of the DUP at the expense of the UUP was due to a 'tipping point' in unionist opinion following the 1998 peace agreement. 'I can see similarities and if they [DUP] don't learn from our mistakes they await the same fate. Whether my old party can step up I don't know,' he said

Either way, Campbell said, the LCC 'would be monitoring the situation to ensure that there would be no actual or perceived diminution in Northern Ireland's constitutional position'.

Images of a large group of masked UVF supporters parading through the streets in east Belfast added to the general impression of loyalist mobilisation against the hated protocol, while the continued graffiti and other reported threats to workers in the port were followed by the temporary lifting of the customs checks. The disarray within unionism, however, continued to deepen, while the existential danger to the union itself was highlighted by those who were already unhappy with Foster and with the Brexit deal that they had so strongly promoted only months earlier. Unionist instability was also playing out against the background of the growing calls for a border poll, not least from the US where the installation of Joe Biden as president was seen a significant boost for those Irish Americans who had long campaigned for Irish unity.

As tensions mounted in the run-up to the annual St Patrick's Day celebrations in Washington, senior politicians involved in the negotiation of the GFA intervened in the debate surrounding the protocol and a referendum on Irish unity. Former Taoiseach Bertie Ahern suggested that the appropriate time to hold one would be in 2028, on the thirtieth anniversary of the Agreement. The conditions for a referendum would require that the institutions set up by the GFA, including the NI Executive 'were stable for a prolonged period – we haven't had that, ever since the agreement, in 23 years', Ahern said. He wrote in the *Irish Times* that nationalists were entitled to a referendum under the terms of the GFA, but that the 'conditions have to be fulfilled' and they were not yet in place. Ahern continued:

> It was an absolute understanding to bring republicans and nationalists on side, that somewhere in the future would be a poll. ...That aspiration has to be there and it has to be fulfilled. I don't think it is for now.
>
> I understand within loyalism, within loyalist groups, [there is] a huge dislike to [sic] the protocol and particularly the border down the Irish Sea. ... There is [sic] some anxieties and we have to watch that.

A LucidTalk poll in late January 2021 signalled a leakage of support from the DUP to the TUV and Alliance. This, along with the rumblings about the protocol, caused some leading unionists to suggest that the GFA should be scrapped and a hard border reinstated on the island. This was the logic expressed by Jamie Bryson who argued in the *Unionist Voice* newsletter and on social media platforms that the root of all unionist problems lay in the GFA.

It was no great surprise that leading DUP figures, who had never supported the Agreement, echoed these remarks as they detected the growing support among the party membership for Jim Allister's hard-line position. The GFA had not been acceptable to the DUP until its leader, Ian Paisley, agreed to power-sharing with Martin McGuinness and SF in 2007, having displaced the UUP and David Trimble as the main voice within unionism.

Trimble, a Tory member of the House of Lords, entered the protocol row with a claim that it was a breach of the GFA and its promise that the constitutional position of the North would not be altered without the consent of a majority of its people. He made an impassioned plea in the *Irish Times* for the issue to be quickly addressed as, he warned, 'the unintended, but unquestionably escalating tensions created by the Northern Ireland protocol represent a real and present danger to the lives of people living in Northern Ireland.'

Trimble described how supermarket shelves were empty, and that:

> customs declarations are required for personal online purchases from Britain for everything from clothes to ink cartridges [while] horticultural trade by retailers and personal orders worth hundreds of millions of pounds every year have virtually stopped.
>
> Petty rules have been enforced by European Union inspectors who oversee the work of UK officials at Northern Ireland ports – to the extent that used machinery has been turned away if there is soil in the treads of the tyres. Some businesses have been waiting weeks for supplies of parts. ...
>
> This false mantra of protecting the Belfast Agreement and keeping the peace in Northern Ireland has become the shield behind which the EU, the Irish government, nationalist parties in Northern Ireland, UK politicians, and even US president Joe Biden hide behind when challenged about the damage to democracy and the economy in Northern Ireland as a result of the protocol. ...

But rather than the protocol protecting the Belfast Agreement, the fact is it is pulling it apart. I fear that tensions are once again starting to rise. We have already seen the threats to inspectors at ports in Northern Ireland. The democratic mandate of the Stormont parliament has been called into question. People's livelihoods and the economy of Northern Ireland are reeling from the protocol's pettifoggery.

Trimble claimed that there was a real potential for those, within the loyalist and unionist community, 'who engaged in past violence to take action again into their own hands'.

Peter Robinson, who stepped down from his position as DUP leader and first minister in early 2016, wrote in the *News Letter* in February 2021 that unionists faced two options:

> learning to live with the new arrangements or collapsing Stormont's power-sharing institutions. …
>
> One lesson learned after decades of dealing with governments is that they don't yield unless life has become uncomfortable. At present only the pandemic is suppressing the outpouring of frustration and the protests that accompany that dissatisfaction.

In reference to some calls for a restoration of the land border on the island as an alternative to the protocol, Robinson said:

> How infuriating it is to hear people, some of whom should know better, recite the mantra that a land border on the island of Ireland would have been a breach of the Belfast Agreement. Naturally, they ignore the equally valid truth that a border in the Irish Sea is contrary to the spirit of the agreement.

Robinson also asserted in the article that extending the grace period before the full implementation of the protocol would not 'soothe the tension within unionism'. He wrote, 'If there is the stomach for defiance then, in truth, you cannot try to ditch the protocol and administer it at the same time. Is the scrapping of the protocol more important than the continued operation of the Assembly?'. He then acknowledged that an outbreak of violence over the protocol would 'would be hugely damaging'.

His comments were welcomed by Jim Allister, who insisted that 'preserving our Britishness and the integrity of the UK should matter more to unionist politicians than Stormont, if operating the protocol is its price. Now, is the time to act in defence of the union.'

As Allister, along with the leaders of the DUP and UUP, prepared to mount a legal challenge to the protocol on the grounds that it was a breach of the Act of Union – the legislation enacted in 1801 which confirms British sovereignty over NI – nationalists and others across the island wondered where the campaign against the protocol might lead.

Gerry Adams, writing for the Belfast Media Group in February 2021, said that the dire warnings by Trimble, Robinson and other unionists over the protocol were echoes of the past:

> Warnings of violence by unionists to get their own way have been a regular feature of Irish political life going back to the nineteenth century. Sectarian pogroms, the use of the Orange Card by unionist and Tory politicians, discrimination in jobs and housing, the gerrymandering of elections, state collusion with death squads, have all been part and parcel of unionist strategy when faced with anything that could be construed as a threat to their domination.

Citing comments by DUP MP Sammy Wilson, that the 'real danger is that frustration and anger will be challenged through violence against easily identified targets', Adams replied:

> Operation Fear needs [to be] challenged ... Mr Wilson needs to explain who these 'easily identified targets' are. ... If they are easily

identified, surely he can let the rest of us know who he means
… He could also let us know who will be doing the challenging
through violence he is predicting. If he has information about
this, has he alerted the PSNI?

Mr Wilson wasn't alone. A former member of David Trimble's
negotiating team during the Good Friday Agreement talks, David
Campbell, who is now the Chair of the Loyalist Communities
Council, has claimed: 'If it comes to the bit where we have to
fight physically to maintain our freedoms within the UK, so be
it'. Again, this begs questions. For example, who is the 'we' Mr
Campbell is talking about? Would he elaborate? And who will they
fight physically against? The English government? The European
Union? The rest of us?

Brexit is a child of the DUP. They were repeatedly warned that
it would be bad for the North and bad for the economy. When
the Department of the Economy published a report in July 2019
warning of 40,000 possible job losses as a result of Brexit, Jeffrey
Donaldson said he could live with that. It would, he claimed, have
a short-term impact on the North's economy, but that this could
be mitigated.

Adams took issue with Trimble's claim that the voice of the majority
unionist community was being ignored in relation to the protocol. He
reminded Trimble that it was the consent of the majority of the people of
NI that would determine the outcome of a unity referendum under the
terms of the GFA. He wrote:

Since the foundation of the Northern state in 1921 until the Good
Friday Agreement there was a unionist veto. It was often referred
to as the 'consent principle' but it was only unionist consent that
was involved. This was a negative mechanism that encouraged
unionist intransigence and a lack of engagement with the rest
of us.

However, the Good Friday Agreement is quite clear – the status of the North depends on 'the consent of a majority of the people' and not on the consent of the majority of the unionist people … Mr. Trimble should know this – he negotiated it in the Good Friday Agreement.

As debate raged in the North, the response in Dublin was to express concern and hope that the EU and British government could quickly iron out the technical difficulties with the implementation of the protocol. After EU Vice-President Maroš Šefčovič and UK minister Michael Gove met to discuss the matter at the EU–UK Joint Committee on the implementation of the Brexit agreement in early February 2021, the EU negotiators rejected calls to abandon the protocol. In the words of French politician Michel Barnier – who led the Brexit negotiations for the EU – at the European Business Summit on 11 February, 'the difficulties on the island of Ireland are caused by Brexit, not by the protocol. The protocol is the solution'.

Irish Times columnist Fintan O'Toole explained that the 'protocol helps to keep the peace process afloat.' On 16 February 2021, O'Toole wrote:

> The EU's threat of a sudden and unilateral suspension of the protocol was both stupid and outrageous. It undid in hours what the EU had managed to do over the years since 2016, which was to establish itself, in contrast to the Brexiteers, as a responsible actor in relation to Northern Ireland.
>
> Reprehensible as this was, there is one thing that has to be borne in mind: it didn't happen. It took about nine hours from word of the plan first emerging for the EU to drop it entirely. The EU was wrong-headed. It was not pig-headed.
>
> But let's not forget that Boris Johnson was playing this reckless game weeks before the EU's ridiculous démarche. On January 13th,

he told the House of Commons that 'we will have no hesitation in invoking Article 16'…

This is a proxy war. There are some real difficulties with the operation of the protocol, but they are perfectly capable of being dealt with by competent officials acting with goodwill and applying common sense. Northern Ireland has had enough of real wars; it doesn't need to be the battleground for proxy ones.

Under continuing pressure from unionists and loyalists, including a DUP online petition calling for the triggering of Article 16 of the protocol in order to secure unfettered trade between Britain and the North, the Johnson government decided to extend the grace period on checks until October.

The unilateral move in early March provoked a threat of legal action by the EU against what it said was 'the second time the UK had sought to breach international law in relation to the special arrangements put in place for the North'. The first time was the Internal Markets Bill, which the UK government introduced in September 2020 in an effort to delay any checks on goods moving into NI from Britain, a proposal it was soon, and embarrassingly, forced to withdraw.

The Covid-19 crisis in the US prevented the traditional handover of the bowl of shamrock by the Taoiseach to President Biden during the 2021 St Patrick's Day celebrations in Washington but did not deter the unity debate and the protocol row from crossing the Atlantic. The *Irish Times* reported that, in advance of their online meeting on 17 March, a group of US senators submitted a resolution expressing support for the full implementation of the GFA 'to support peace on the island of Ireland'.

The cross-party motion, proposed by Democrat Bob Menendez, the chair of the Senate Foreign Relations Committee, and Susan Collins, a Republican senator from Maine, cautioned that the introduction of 'barriers, checkpoints or personnel on the island of Ireland would threaten the successes of the Good Friday Agreement'. It insisted, as earlier proposed by Nancy Pelosi and endorsed by President Biden, that any new trade agreement between the US and the UK should take into account that the conditions of the Belfast Agreement are met. If there was any doubt or confusion about the damaging implications of British interference with the NI protocol, Foreign Minister Simon Coveney and EU Vice-President Maroš Šefčovič were also in Washington to brief the Friends of Ireland group of senators and congressmen during the week. As part of the St Patrick's Day celebrations, Arlene Foster and Michelle O'Neill also spoke to President Biden and Vice President Kamala Harris by conference call.

SF, meanwhile, made its objective of a united Ireland loud and clear. The party enjoyed considerable support in the US, and with Biden as president, its position was stronger than ever. SF and its US supporters recognised that Biden and his team were deeply invested in the resolution of the Irish conflict and that the seeds planted through intensive lobbying work – done over many years by Adams and by US party representatives Rita O'Hare and her successor Ciaran Quinn – were about to bear fruit. The party also worked with trade unions and business groups in the US, which in turn provided finance to the party.

In the two decades since the GFA was signed, SF leaders constantly reminded their friends in high places in Washington that Conservative Party governments, along with the UUP and DUP, had consistently blocked all efforts to work the peace settlement. Since 2007, when the St Andrews Agreement cleared the way for the power-sharing executive headed by Paisley and McGuinness, commitments on policing, legacy issues such as the killings of nationalists by the security forces, and other basic equality and language rights, had been stalled. Now, the party argued, the democratic right to hold a referendum on unity, as envisaged in the GFA, was being denied.

The US-based Friends of Sinn Féin raised the considerable funds to place several expensive advertisements in leading US broadsheets to promote their message to Irish America. As St Patrick's Day approached, the ads featured in the *New York Times* and the *Washington Post*, as well as the *Irish Echo* and *Irish Voice* newspapers based in New York. The message called on the Irish government to promote, and plan for, Irish unity, and on the British government to set a date for a referendum, as promised in the GFA. The half-page message said:

> A new Ireland is emerging, and more and more people are looking beyond the divisions of the past. A new Ireland that is seeking to undo the damage of the undemocratic partition of Ireland 100 years ago and the recent British imposed Brexit. The Good Friday Agreement provides for a referendum on Irish unity. It is for the people to determine their future. The choice is clear. A united Ireland and membership of the European Union. Or a divided island at the mercy of the British government.

Among the arguments pressed by SF on its audience across the US was that, unless a date was set, there would be no urgency on the governments to make the detailed and painstaking costed preparations required to ensure that voters would have at least an outline of what a post-referendum island might look like. Also implicit in the call was the claim that governments and other parties, in Britain and Ireland, would obstruct and delay any constitutional change if it did not suit their interests, and were well experienced in using any and every political or other method to do so.

The St Patrick's Day online meeting between the Taoiseach and President Biden yielded a typically neutral joint statement and called for the 'good faith implementation of international agreements designed to address the unique circumstances on the island of Ireland' and 'preserving the hard-won gains of the peace process' but it must have been clear to the British observers, including Foreign Secretary Dominic Rabb who was in Washington, which way the US administration was leaning in the row over the NI protocol.

Martin told an audience of Irish Americans that he did not consider it appropriate to call for a unity referendum, arguing that it would serve only to increase differences rather than reconcile them. 'I think it is divisive and puts people back into the trenches too early,' he said in comments that could only have served to confuse those US supporters of the GFA who were of the view that a democratic vote on unity was its key concession to Irish nationalists and republicans. Within days, Martin faced criticism at home when he voiced similar objections to a border poll, pushing the prospect even further down the road than his predecessor, Bertie Ahern.

Invited onto a special edition of the weekly televised *Claire Byrne Show* on RTÉ, the Taoiseach, Tánaiste Leo Varadkar, Mary Lou McDonald and DUP MP Gregory Campbell were questioned on 'What a united Ireland might look like' in the event of a referendum in favour of unity. While there was a degree of unanimity among the three party leaders in the South on the need to prepare for referendums and the questions it would pose to voters, there was predictable disagreement on when it should take place, with Martin seeming to dismiss any poll for at least a couple of decades. McDonald argued for the setting of a date as soon as possible in order to prepare for a referendum in five years, while Varadkar suggested that it was more important to ensure it was done properly than early. Campbell rejected any suggestion of a referendum and implied that the sooner a hard border was reimposed on the island, the better. This and other comments from Campbell provoked an angry response from commentator and lawyer Joe Brolly who railed at the racist and homophobic nature of the DUP before he was shut down by the host and prevented from finishing his point. Brolly, a popular GAA pundit from a republican family in Derry, asserted that the outlook of the DUP was a short-term fantasy:

> What we've seen with Arlene [Foster], Gregory Campbell and Ian Paisley Jr is this short-termism all the time. You see them

chuckling and guffawing when people are trying to have a serious discussion. Just like we saw Gregory tonight, laughing at the Irish language, laughing at Gaelic sports, the homophobia, the racism, all those things.

Brolly got a chance to explain himself in his *Sunday Independent* newspaper column some days later, when he said that he intended to:

> go on and make the point that only when we honestly call this out, can we solve the Northern problem. If you took the sectarians, homophobes and racists out of the DUP, there would be hardly anybody left, so Gregory Campbell must have been bewildered that I was cut off by RTÉ.

Brolly went on to call for a civic forum 'that gives a voice to the highly educated and decent Northern Protestant constituency that has been drowned out by the DUP – the one Andrew Trimble referred to on Monday night.' A former Irish rugby international from a unionist background, Trimble said on the *Claire Byrne Show* that he welcomed the discussion on an all-island future if it was inclusive of those who identified as British. He said he looked forward to a fusion between those who see themselves as Northern Irish, Irish and British on the island.

In the same article, Brolly wrote that the British wanted 'out' of the North and their departure was 'inevitable'. He believed that an organised transition to a united Ireland could involve the retention of Stormont and Protestants continuing to have the same rights as they have now, including the right to UK citizenship and a UK passport.

> The first step might be a two-state solution. Stormont might remain but it would no longer be a political kindergarten overseen by the British. Both states would be in the EU … With the UK gone, there would be no point in triumphalism. Short-termism would be replaced by the dull nuts and bolts of long-term

problem solving. Progressive, well-educated Protestant voices would emerge.

In her column of 29 March 2021, *Irish Times* journalist Una Mullally focused on what she described as the 'stasis of Micheál Martin' on the show, which, she said, 'is not just an issue for Fianna Fáil – in many ways, his leadership is a manifestation of their contemporary irrelevance as a party.'

Describing how Varadkar and McDonald 'did us all a favour by discussing the issues around Irish unity in a mature, measured, respectful and hugely encouraging manner, during which they were often on the same page,' Mullally accused Martin of dithering and for failing to use the opportunity to deliver 'any big ideas, big aspirations, big vision'. She wrote:

> What was most profound was that where McDonald and Varadkar spoke a lot about the future, Martin spoke primarily about the past. He talked about his brand of republicanism à la Wolfe Tone, whom I'm sure would only be punching the air at the very mention of 'common agendas like an all-island research hub'. …
>
> That the leader of the country would arrive to a studio to discuss such an important issue and dither through, is simply not good enough. Deflating, demoralising, uninspiring, disconnected, and putting forth arguments for paralysis as opposed to action, is not where new generations in this country are at. Not only that, but such stasis is dangerous; the future of our island is not just another can to kick down the road.

The apparent reluctance of the leader of Fianna Fáil to envisage a unity referendum within five, ten or even thirty years, came as something of a shock to many of his own party supporters. His appearance was followed just days later with a speech from his party colleague and leadership rival, Jim O'Callaghan, who, in considerable detail, set out his road map to a referendum and the prospects for constitutional change.

In a lengthy paper delivered to Sidney Sussex College, Cambridge, where he had studied law as a post-graduate student in the 1990s, O'Callaghan spoke to the political, economic and legal consequences of Irish reunification. Assuming that the British secretary of state would likely call a border poll within a decade, after discussions between the UK and Irish governments, it would make practical sense that both would co-operate in the preparatory work required.

Given the difficulties in engaging with the unionist parties in framing the nature, economics and laws of a united Ireland and the guarantees for those of a British identity that it would be recognised and respected, a huge responsibility would rest on civic groups to 'propose, discuss and debate what this new country would look like', in advance of the unity referendums, O'Callaghan said.

In his view, a new Ireland would require a new constitution. The debate for a new Ireland 'must encompass the political fault lines that exist between people in each jurisdiction including conservatives and liberals, right- and left-wing economic views, supporters and opponents of the EU, new Irish people and those whose roots are of the island, workers and employers, unionist/loyalist and nationalist/republican and neither'.

O'Callaghan anticipated that unionists would garner some 11.3 per cent of the vote in a national election in a united Ireland compared to 1.1 per cent in Britain, based on the most recent counts for the Dáil and Westminster, and thus would have more influence in government formation. He envisaged a bicameral system of government with an Assembly/Dáil sitting in Dublin and a Senate in Belfast. He proposed that a certain number of cabinet seats should be reserved for unionists.

The flag, anthem and emblems of the state would be agreed after broad consultation among the parties and through a forum such as a citizens' assembly. Two national languages, English and Irish, he suggested, would be recognised while the new country would become part of the EU and operate in the eurozone.

'Neutrality may become a more complex and contentious issue

because unionism may wish to avoid neutrality and support the British state in its conflicts,' he said. 'However, it appears inevitable that the majority of political representatives at present will support the new state adopting a position of neutrality in international affairs.'

O'Callaghan recommended the retention of the PSNI as one of the regional forces of An Garda Síochána, each operating under a national policing authority.

A practising barrister, O'Callaghan asserted that the judicial arm of government 'will cause the least difficulty'. He proposed the continued operation of 'different laws on both sides of the [present] border until, over time, the new legislature passes laws that operate for all of the new territory.'

On economic unification, O'Callaghan dismissed the focus on the amount of the annual UK subvention to the North as 'strangely defeatist'. He said, 'Northern Ireland should not be doomed to forever be a relatively poor region of a wealthy country, forever subsidised by taxpayers in wealthier parts of Great Britain.' The subvention, he said, could be phased out during the 10-to-15-year transition period, or longer in the case of public service pension liabilities incurred by the UK exchequer prior to unification. The EU should provide regional development funding and the same, attractive corporation tax rate should apply across the island.

'Harnessing the strength of the whole island would help make these six counties a more prosperous region of a prosperous country,' he said.

High-speed rail links between Dublin and Belfast and to other cities, developing the all-island energy market, promoting renewable energy and attracting inward investment to the North, in particular, would raise productivity and foster new, innovative, ventures.

The European Convention of Human Rights would form the basis for the legal protections for all those living in the new Ireland, while a new constitution would protect the rights, cultures and traditions of minorities, including the religious and cultural freedoms of those with a British identity. People from NI, and those born there in the future, would be entitled to maintain and claim British citizenship, he said.

O'Callaghan concluded his speech by saying that the people of Northern Ireland would decide its future status in a referendum that 'will be vigorously contested and professionally argued', while there will also be a requirement in the South to approve any new constitutional arrangement. 'Resolving the problems caused by the partition of Ireland and aspiring to the cherished aim of reunification,' he said, 'are legitimate political issues that should be decided by discussion, debate and democracy.'

Among the first to welcome O'Callaghan's contribution was Ireland's Future, whose recently appointed chief executive Gerry Carlile said on Belfastmedia.com that it confirmed that:

> The conversation on constitutional change and a new Ireland now forms part of everyday discussion.
>
> There is a growing momentum around the requirement for preparation and planning. Ireland's Future encourages the Government in Dublin to establish an all-island Citizens' Assembly or National Forum that can begin to formalise the outworkings of what Irish unity will entail for the people of this island north and south.
>
> Ireland's Future particularly agrees with Jim O'Callaghan TD when he states that, 'irrespective of what the new country requires or permits, nothing will diminish the traditions and culture of unionism. Its strength lies in its people. Its home is in Ulster. Its future rests in improving the quality of life for all the people on the island of Ireland within the European Union and in close harmony with the three other nations [of the UK].' Ireland's Future urges our friends and neighbours from a unionist and British background to get involved in the planning process and to play their part in shaping the future as we move on a trajectory towards referendums on both parts of the island.

The timing of the referendums was also raised by SDLP leader Colum Eastwood who warned that, while he expected a unity vote within 10 years, it was possible that the British government might go earlier while the unionists still had the numbers to win it. He told the *Sunday Business Post* on 14 March 2021:

> There is still a possibility that the British government would call a referendum early to support unionism because they think that unionists have the numbers right now. That's where nationalism has to be careful what it asks for. ...
>
> We have to be clear that it will be a united Ireland, and a new Ireland that will celebrate and very much involve the British tradition and the Good Friday Agreement will remain and all the protections within it.

He agreed, however, that nationalists should not be expected to refrain from calling for a referendum because of unionist or loyalist sensitivities.

Influential journalist Justine McCarthy used her weekly column with the *Sunday Times* to rail at the hypocrisy of politicians who accused SF, Ireland's Future and others of sectarianism for calling for a referendum and a united Ireland. Citing a recent poll of voters in the South by public relations firm, Edelman, which found that 52 per cent were in favour of a united Ireland, with 30 percent undecided, McCarthy said that it:

> will take years of debate and planning before any referendum with a chance of success could be held. ...
>
> It will be 23 years this Easter since the signing of the agreement that brought a semblance of normality to Northern Ireland. An entire generation has been born and come of age since then. Unionist parties have lost their electoral majority. Sinn Féin has strengthened its all-island presence, being the main nationalist party in the north and the lead opposition party in the south.

Pointing to the initiative by Liverpool University's Institute of Irish Studies in early March to launch an online platform for 'pro-unity and pro-union voices to debate the future of the island of Ireland and the UK', McCarthy suggested that 'this state keeps its head firmly stuck in sand that is shifting all around. ...The ruling parties' constant refrain that they don't want to scare off unionists is wearing thin. Might their real concern be that they don't want to scare off their own electorate?'

15

TURF WARS AND PROTESTS

I n late March 2021, the Public Prosecution Service (PPS) announced that, having considered all the evidence and advice from senior counsel, there was 'no reasonable prospect of conviction in respect of any of the reported individuals' in relation to the funeral of Bobby Storey in June 2020. The evidence confirmed that the organisers of the funeral had engaged with the PSNI in advance about the funeral arrangements and that there was a large degree of confusion around conflicting and changing Covid-19 regulations at the time.

The decision not to prosecute leading SF politicians who attended was condemned by First Minister Arlene Foster, who called on Simon Byrne, the chief constable of the PSNI, to resign. This unprecedented demand by the first minister was followed by claims of two-tier policing against the loyalist community. The tensions surrounding the protocol and the wider talk of constitutional change undoubtedly contributed to the outbreak of loyalist violence on the streets of Belfast and in some towns across the North, which erupted in early April. The PPS decision not to prosecute leading republicans over their attendance at the funeral added another spark to the flame. In some loyalist areas, there were sustained attacks on police officers and vehicles during riots that took place in the days and nights leading up to the 23rd anniversary of the GFA on 10 April. Riots, involving mainly working-class teenagers, erupted across the North, including at the interfaces with nationalist areas in west Belfast, Derry, Carrickfergus and Coleraine.

For several nights just before Easter, there were confrontations with the police, with householders protecting their wheelie bins, preventing pavement slabs from being used as weapons. The most serious clashes took place on the peace line at Lanark Way, on the Shankill Road in Belfast, where young loyalists, some wearing black hoods and balaclavas, sought to entice nationalist youths on the Springfield Road to join in battle. Lines of people in the nationalist community faced abuse after they blocked angry youths from engaging with the loyalist attackers during the days and nights of rioting in west and north Belfast. Dozens of police officers were injured during the violence and cars and a bus were also set alight. One teenager was badly burnt by a petrol bomb which ignited his clothing as he was throwing another one at police. Older men associated with the UVF and UDA were identified encouraging and assisting the young loyalists to prepare petrol bombs.

According to Shankill Road community worker Eileen Weir, who spoke to journalist Susan McKay in the *Irish Times* in the days following the disturbances, the riots were organised through social media. 'These young people out throwing fire-works and petrol bombs don't know what they are doing,' said Weir. 'This is antisocial behaviour organised on Facebook and social media.' She blamed the 'disgraceful' language of unionist political leaders which, she said, was 'putting people on edge'. Weir accused DUP politicians of making incendiary comments: Sammy Wilson had threatened 'guerrilla war' on the protocol if it was not abandoned. His colleague at Westminster, Ian Paisley Jr, claimed that the Brexit protocol was to blame for the violence and that the decision by the PPS not to prosecute anyone for the breach of regulations surrounding the funeral of Bobby Storey in June 2020, was, he was quoted in the *Belfast Telegraph* as saying, 'the straw that broke the camel's back'.

In March 2021, LCC chair David Campbell announced that its members, the illegal UDA, UVF and RHC paramilitary groups, had withdrawn support for the Belfast Agreement over the protocol and warned that people should not 'underestimate the strength of feeling on this issue right across the unionist family'. While insisting that protests should be 'democratic and peaceful', Campbell said that emotions were similar to those felt by unionists about the 1985 Anglo-Irish Agreement.

On 9 April, the LCC declared in the *Belfast Telegraph* that none of its associated organisations 'have been involved either directly or indirectly in the violence witnessed in recent days'. However, it also appeared to claim some influence over events when it successfully called for protests to be called off following the death of Prince Philip, the husband of Queen Elizabeth.

As historian Diarmaid Ferriter noted in an article for the *Irish Times*, unionist leaders have a long record of 'falling back on a self-image of persecution' which is being 'wildly exaggerated' as representative of half the population of the North. Ferriter wrote:

> Following the Brexit referendum in 2016, DUP leader Arlene Foster decried the suggestion that it might damage the 1998 Belfast Agreement as 'outrageous commentary'. It was nothing of the sort. The current DUP tactic of politicising policing issues – not helped by the arrogant and recklessly irresponsible organisation of the Bobby Storey funeral by republicans – and of criticising the recourse to violence while readily feeding loyalists a narrative of victimhood, is dangerously foolish and self-defeating. It makes a mockery of the idea that Northern Ireland during its centenary can strike a mature, inclusive pose.
>
> Foster has been quick in the past to approvingly cite the assessments of the Police Service of Northern Ireland (PSNI) in relation to the IRA when it suited her political purpose; it is now,

however, politically convenient for her to call for the resignation of the PSNI Chief Constable Simon Byrne.

Foster also sought to blame the Irish government for colluding with the imposition of the protocol and refused to nominate a unionist minister to attend a meeting of the NSMC in mid-April, which was intended to discuss the improvement of rail and other cross-border transport projects. Despite hardening her position and receiving an assurance, for what it was worth, from Boris Johnson that there would be no referendum on unity 'for a very, very long time to come' – as broadcast on BBC *Spotlight* on 20 April 2021 – the first minister was forced out of office after an internal party coup involving some of those most responsible for inflaming unionist and loyalist opinion against the protocol, the police and the GFA.

On the nationalist side of the interface with the Shankill Road, senior SF member and community leader Sean 'Spike' Murray spent several nights trying to stop young nationalists from taking on the loyalist rioters and was subjected to severe abuse for doing so. A former IRA prisoner, Murray had also attended Storey's funeral and, in his view, there had been 'a bit of opportunism' in the criticism of SF deputy First Minister Michelle O'Neill, following her attendance and her breach of Covid regulations after she was photographed standing close to two mourners. 'Michelle had done a great job dealing with the Covid-19 crisis and here was an attempt to criticise her,' said Murray. 'It didn't work because the other political parties were giving her praise for the work that she was doing.'

The decision by the PPS not to prosecute anyone over their attendance did not surprise him as the organisers had met with senior PSNI officers in advance of the funeral and had agreed on the arrangements to ensure compliance with Covid-19 regulations. 'There were a number of meetings between our people and PSNI senior command, as would happen ... regarding any sort of big event, including sporting occasions,'

Murray said. He confirmed that appeals had been made for people to watch the service online. Thousands did, but thousands more joined the cortege and lined the streets of west Belfast for the funeral.

Murray described the scenes at the Lanark Way interface in the aftermath of the PPS decision:

> We had protests at the interface for three days. The police didn't adopt the right tactics on the first couple of nights. Part of the problem was a lot of their people who have the experience have now left the force. The community activists on our side have what is known as an interface strategy. This is meant to apply certain operational policies from a policing perspective. Senior police hadn't a clue what we were talking [about] because they weren't part of those discussions when it was agreed a number of years ago. We took some abuse, I can tell you.

Murray also engaged with community workers on the Shankill who were just as shocked at the sudden eruption of rioting. High unemployment and poor educational standards, as well as a criminal drug culture, are a fact of life in both communities, he said, and more co-operation and work are required to provide hope and opportunities for young people:

> The real challenge is how to improve conditions and life opportunities for young people. The problem for the youth service providers is that they bring them into education courses, including basic English, vocational and other skills but there's no employment at the end of that. It's soul destroying for some of these kids. ...
>
> In many loyalist working-class areas, there's no community infrastructure whatsoever. It is the same culture in some parts of the nationalist community. They're not encouraged by their families to stay in education. A lot of kids who were in education

lose focus and come out of the system because of drugs. They're not getting a learning environment in the family home and it is difficult to create it outside. It's a mirror reflection in the loyalist community which is why we're saying to them we should be working together more closely on these issues.

However, co-operation across the community has been weakened by the crisis within political unionism and loyalism. Murray, along with Gerry Adams, met with loyalist leaders following the Easter riots to try to ensure they would not be repeated during the marching season. However, he said it is unclear whether the traditional political forces are as influential over the new generation of young loyalists: 'Myself and Gerry Adams met with senior loyalists in June. We outlined the common issues of concern, on social deprivation. We planned two further meetings and they cancelled both.'

Other loyalists, including Jamie Bryson, are making inroads into the former strongholds of the UVF in east Belfast as unionism becomes more fractured, although Murray did not believe there is as large a stomach for confrontation as some have suggested, in either community.

It has not got gained any real traction. There's no stomach for confrontation. We've been through this for so many years and young people are more interested in other things. We were out on the streets physically stopping our kids from fighting loyalists and we took abuse for it at Easter. You haven't got the same level of leadership in the loyalist community because they are that fractured. I think that makes it more dangerous. You've got a turf war between former UVF factions in east Belfast. The UDA has broken down into fiefdoms on a geographical basis. The east Belfast UVF is now just a criminal gang. Some sections of the UDA are heavily involved in drugs as well.

The unity of the LCC is also under strain with some loyalist leaders unhappy with the inflammatory comments of its chair, David Campbell, and are threatening to leave the coalition, he said. Murray has engaged with loyalist community activists on a range of initiatives over the years, notwithstanding the current difficulties which are amplified by the debate over the unity referendum.

> There has been a lot of change since the Good Friday Agreement, including demographic change, the growth of Sinn Féin North and South, especially in the South, while the whole debate about a united Ireland is going mainstream. Brexit has energised that debate.
>
> We have to spell out a version of what we mean by a new Ireland, what type of education system, what type of a health and welfare system will we have, all the basics in life. We're going to have to be able to answer those questions, and to sit down with unionists to try and reassure them regarding their sense of Britishness.
>
> I've had some very good conversations with people like Glenn Bradley but there aren't many Glenn Bradleys out there. A lot of pro-union people are afraid of having that conversation because they think, if they have, they are on a slippery slope to a united Ireland. I have worked well with [NIA's] Tommy Winstone and other former loyalist prisoners, but once you hit the constitutional question it's like they get lock jaw. They don't want to discuss it.
>
> You talk to some loyalist people and they can't get around the fact that their forefathers were opposed to Home Rule and had a very strong link to the monarchy but who now feel let down and shafted by the British government. I think sometimes they're just in a quandary, about who they are loyal to and who's loyal to them.
>
> This is where I think an organisation like Ireland's Future could play a major role reaching out to people like that and having

that discussion. If it's coming from Sinn Féin, they're not going to listen to it, they close their ears, but if it's coming from others it can work.

Martin O'Brien is director of the Belfast-based Social Change Initiative, and former senior vice-president with Atlantic Philanthropies (AP), which financed the work of NIA and other projects aimed at empowering teenagers through education across both communities in the North. O'Brien has worked on peacebuilding and human rights for over 40 years. As part of its human rights strand, AP also promoted the reintegration of loyalist and republican ex-prisoners and facilitated dialogue between them. O'Brien was also involved in supporting the work of reducing tensions and preventing violence at the most volatile interfaces. He spoke to this author about the attempts community leaders, on both sides of the divide, made to de-escalate the Easter 2021 rioting in west Belfast:

> Many of the people who were organising those human chains would have engaged with AP over the years. These groups are doing their best and people like Debbie Watters, Sean Murray and others in the loyalist and republican communities play a very significant role in trying to bring a bit of calm and a bit of reason in the loyalist community.
>
> Now, you have a bus being driven by Jim Allister and Jamie Bryson and a lot of people are getting on to that bus. Others are trying to dissuade people from getting on but they're doing it very quietly. It seems to me they're afraid that they are going to be replaced by younger, more militant people. That, in a way, is the story of unionism.
>
> Just look at this discussion on the protocol. Which prominent unionist is saying, 'Look, lads, there's an inevitability about this; this protocol isn't going anywhere. There are things that are wrong

with it, but we have to work through it'? None of them are saying that. It seems to me that there's a real failure to face up to reality.

O'Brien pointed to a recent article by Bryson in the *Unionist Voice* where the GFA was identified as the root cause of all unionist woes, a view shared by Allister and which is gaining support across the unionist community. O'Brien contended that the reversion to blaming a peace settlement that was agreed by a solid majority of people in the North, is irrational. He referred to a book, *How Britain Ends*, by Scottish journalist Gavin Esler, which has a section about English nationalism. These people, Esler said, are suffering from a kind of melancholia about the loss of Empire and that it's like a mental illness, he recalled.

For O'Brien, Esler's description hit close to home:

> Everything he [Esler] writes about the English Defence League you could ascribe to loyalism and that is, in part, what we're dealing with. There is a level of irrationality with all of this because the truth of the matter is that the Good Friday Agreement is the best friend of unionists and loyalists. It basically says that, 'In the future, if things change, your identity and rights have to be respected.' That part of the Agreement is underexposed it seems to me.
>
> Everybody's fixated on the border poll but, regardless of the outcome, you have to be treated fairly and whoever is in charge has to respect your identity. It's in the international agreement between the two governments. So why decide to bring down the Good Friday Agreement?

Concerned that the more reasonable voices within loyalism, and indeed unionism, are often reluctant to say anything in public that could expose them to criticism from the 'seemingly more radical groups', O'Brien submits that, 'A very small group of quite extreme people, are saying what should be done and they're setting the agenda very effectively.'

O'Brien feels that the current discussion of a future island is too often reduced to the binary options of staying within the UK or joining a unitary 32-county state:

> The Good Friday Agreement doesn't really help us in that regard because it does present those binary options, when in fact there is a range of things that you can do around federalism. Mad as it might seem, if you talk to loyalists or unionists around the border counties you hear farmers asking, 'Well, are we going to lose our land?' Kids at the bonfire are saying, 'We're not going to be able to have our bonfires any more.' Both of those are far from likely but yet they are fears that are played on.

He has also observed that unionists are fearful of losing their majority in the Stormont assembly and SF becoming the larger party, a fear that has pushed the DUP, in particular, to the right and a more hard-line position against the protocol than it might otherwise have taken.

The debate on a unity referendum, said O'Brien, has added another focus to unionist anxieties:

> Sinn Féin and people interested in moving this debate [on a united Ireland] forward are not in control of what other people say and do. But they are in control of what they do themselves. What are they doing to convince people who don't think a united Ireland is a good idea? That to me is where this is going to be won or lost.

Supporting the development of deliberative processes, citizens' assemblies and preferendums – referendums in which voters are offered choices between several options – could be very helpful, O'Brien has suggested:

> Having an effective independent media which engages fully in the effort to explain, inform, question and educate is a key requirement especially when it comes to hugely significant choices and debates.

There is also an obvious need for more community engagement and education around both developing proposals and engaging in their substance.

O'Brien argued that there is also a continuing need to support community-based peacebuilding:

> The Belfast/Good Friday Agreement provides the bedrock for a sustainable peace but the important process of explaining it to a new generation and monitoring its implementation remains. Over the period since Brexit, we have seen threats of violence, street protests and the political use of the spectre of violence. However, less visible has been the tireless effort by many community activists, on all sides of our community, to prevent the escalation of violence. Their work needs to be recognised and acknowledged, but also supported through timely and flexible funding for local initiatives.

16

UNWELCOME GUESTS OF THE NATION

A rlene Foster's decision, announced in late April 2021, to step down as party leader and first minister followed months of internal rumblings against her leadership led by the traditionalist Free Presbyterian wing of the party. Agriculture minister Edwin Poots quickly emerged as the main contender to replace her. Recently returned to his post after medical treatment, Poots enjoyed the support of the evangelical faction of the party. His ally and fellow MLA for Lagan Valley, Paul Givan, was first to support his candidacy. Poots's main rival for the position, Jeffrey Donaldson, was completely out-manoeuvred by the coup planners. Donaldson was politically close to Foster and together they deserted the UUP to join the DUP in 2004. While there are no more than 10,000 members of the tiny Free Presbyterian Church founded by the Reverend Ian Paisley, over one-third of the DUP MLAs, and more than half its councillors, are members. Poots and his evangelical colleagues were long opposed to gay rights, marriage equality and abortion rights. As a creationist, Poots held to a belief that the Earth is 4,000 years old.

The successful heave against Foster followed her decision to abstain on a UUP motion in the assembly to ban gay conversion therapy, which outraged the fundamentalists. Poots had previously supported bans on gay men donating blood or gay couples adopting children. During the early months of the Covid-19 crisis, he claimed that Catholics were super spreaders of the virus citing inaccurate figures of case numbers in different areas of the North.

Despite his hard-line, conservative views, including a scepticism about climate change, Poots supported efforts to restore power-sharing with SF after the collapse of the executive in early 2017. He subsequently led the DUP team in negotiations with senior SF members Conor Murphy and Stephen McGlade. He promoted an all-island health initiative for congenital cardiac care for children. After boasting about his intentions to block legislation on the Irish language, Poots subsequently agreed to it as part of the New Decade, New Approach agreement that restored the executive in early 2020, but then obstructed its implementation. In mid-May, he defeated Donaldson in the leadership contest by 19 votes to 17 by the DUP's 8 Westminster MPs and 28 members of the assembly, a result that reflected its continuing and deep divisions. With only a few hundred active members, the party was already losing voters to the more socially liberal Alliance and the choice of Poots was unlikely to arrest this fall in support among unionists.

At the same time came a change of leadership in the UUP following the resignation of Steven Aiken. His replacement was Doug Beattie, a former British army officer who had suggested in some media interviews that he wanted the party to move towards the centre in order to recover voters drifting to Alliance. Beattie proposed the assembly motion to ban gay conversion therapy which had contributed to Foster's political defenestration. The change of leaders in both parties served to underline the existential crisis of unionism as it celebrated the centenary of the NI state.

The victory of the Scottish National Party (SNP) in May elections and the promise by its leader, Nicola Sturgeon, that she would legislate for a second independence referendum added to the fragility of the pro-union advocates in the North. Within weeks of his narrow victory, Poots was removed as DUP leader following a revolt by the party's executive over his agreement with SF to resume power-sharing. He resigned as party leader after he nominated Paul Givan as first minister of a new executive against the wishes of the party's ruling body. Poots was replaced by Donaldson, who was the only candidate to put himself forward and who used his first public statement as leader, as *RTÉ News* reported on 26 June, to accuse the Irish government of 'cheerleading' for the protocol and ignoring the concerns of unionists. Following his 'coronation' in late June, Donaldson said:

> The Irish government and the Irish prime minister have made clear that they want to protect the peace process, they want to protect political stability in Northern Ireland. But the Irish government has to step away from being a cheerleader for one part of the community. If the Irish government is genuine about the peace process, is genuine about protecting political stability in Northern Ireland, then they too need to listen to unionist concerns.
>
> It's not just London, Dublin also needs to understand that if we're going to move forward and have co-operation, if they're intent on harming our relationship with Great Britain, they cannot expect that it will be business as usual on the North–South relationship.

He announced that he would seek to secure a 'coalition for the union'. This would be an annual UK-wide 'conference on the union' involving civic and political society, business and academics in order to promote 'pro-union ideas, research and relationships'; a 'unionist convention' to build 'practical and strategic unity'; and 'a new pro-union campaigning group' that would work alongside the unionist political parties. He did not explain how he would convince the British government to scrap the NI protocol. He also allowed the Stormont executive to continue in operation and continued the agreement made by Poots with SF on the appointment of Givan as first minister. In exchange for accepting the first minister's nomination, SF received a commitment from the British government that it would enact Irish language legislation in the autumn.

Concerns over a fresh escalation of street violence during the annual Twelfth of July celebrations were heightened when nationalist residents of the New Lodge area in north Belfast complained about the risk to their homes from a massive bonfire in the adjoining Tiger's Bay area and attacks on their community by those building it. They also criticised the decision of the PSNI not to move on the intelligence they had about the UDA in north Belfast gathering weapons and petrol bombs in advance of the Twelfth, or to assist contractors to remove dangerous and illegal bonfires.

Infrastructure Minister Nichola Mallon of the SDLP and SF Communities Minister Deirdre Hargey unsuccessfully sought a court order to force the PSNI to remove the bonfire, while unionist politicians insisted it was a legitimate expression of their culture. Donaldson, Beattie and Jim Allister of the TUV visited the bonfire in the days leading up to the Twelfth in an unprecedented show of support by the leaders of political unionism. Jamie Bryson represented the Tiger's Bay Bonfire Group in discussions with Mallon over the controversial pyre. The bonfire was lit and the night ended without violence.

Among the casualties of the loyalist campaign against the protocol during the summer was the first fully integrated Irish preschool, which was forced to relocate from Braniel Primary School in east Belfast because of a social media hate campaign. Naíscoil na Seolta was due to open its doors for the first time in September 2021 with 16 children from across the communities in the traditionally unionist area. Among those involved in setting up the preschool was Linda Ervine, who said that an alternative site would be secured for the project. The parents and teachers involved decided to move venue following anonymous threats made against them and their children on social media.

In an early indication that Beattie would entice more moderate unionists into the UUP fold, Ian Marshall announced his decision to join the UUP in late July. It was a development that 'soft' unionists hoped might herald a more open approach by the party to all-island engagement under its new leadership. Marshall said in the *Irish Times* that he intended to run for an assembly seat in the next election and called on unionists to accept that, 'We have a protocol that is here to stay.' He acknowledged that it was causing disruption and cost to some business but said that it also had advantages: 'There can be opportunities here for business and trade. It goes back to the pre-Brexit situation when we had all this access before, but we forfeited that,' he said.

Meanwhile, the political and diplomatic efforts of the Irish government were focused on leveraging US and EU support for its position on the protocol in advance of the G7 summit of world leaders in London in June. Accepting that the protocol was causing problems for business and trade with the UK, Simon Coveney insisted that the solution was to be found in repairing the practical difficulties rather than removing it and endangering the single market. Coveney used the opportunity of a stop over at Shannon Airport by US Secretary of State Antony Blinken and National Security Advisor Jake Sullivan to explain to the senior White House officials how the NI protocol was being undermined by British ministers, despite their having agreed to it in an international treaty. On 25 May 2021, the Irish foreign minister spent two hours with Sullivan, who has family roots in County Cork, discussing a range of issues – including the ongoing Middle East crisis and Iran – but their bland statement in relation to the North understated the significance of the meeting. According to a report in the *Sunday Times*, 'Mr Sullivan and Foreign Minister Coveney reaffirmed their commitment to protecting the gains of the Good Friday Agreement for all communities in Northern Ireland.' Sullivan, it said, 'spoke with Coveney for two hours, focusing heavily on the Northern Ireland protocol and leadership change across unionism'.

However, it later emerged that the Shannon Airport encounter would form the basis for an unusual and dramatic intervention by a US diplomat in London. On 3 June, the US chargé d'affaires in Britain, Yael Lempert, delivered a diplomatic message, or démarche, to Brexit minister David Frost, which expressed the inceasing concern of her government over the protocol stalemate. According to the official British government minutes of the meeting, quoted by the *Times* newspaper, 'Lempert said the US was increasingly concerned about the stalemate on implementing the protocol. This was undermining the trust of our two main allies. The US strongly urged the UK to achieve a negotiated settlement.' Lempert told Frost and John Bew, foreign policy adviser to Boris Johnson, that if Britain agreed to a veterinary deal that meant following EU agri-food rules, Biden would ensure that the matter 'wouldn't negatively affect the chances of reaching a US–UK free trade deal.' She also asked how the US could be helpful in brokering a deal with the EU over the protocol.

Following the publication of the exchange, Coveney confirmed that the US intervention was a direct consequence of his discussion with Sullivan in Shannon Airport when he asked the secretary of state to assist with the resolution of the standoff between the UK and the EU. 'We asked him to and then we followed that up with a note on the meeting to give a very clear Irish perspective on what we thought the points of tension are and how we can move beyond them,' Coveney told RTÉ's *Prime Time*. 'And I think that was received well'.

Following the G7 summit, and the implicit threat of economic sanction from the US and the EU, Frost appeared to soften his language on the protocol which he had previously described as unsustainable.

The EU's offer of a veterinary agreement to eliminate 80 per cent of the checks on the Irish Sea border and to extend the grace period for the introduction of the protocol was now under consideration by the British. A spokesman for Boris Johnson acknowledged that the prime minister was focused on finding 'radical and urgent solutions within the protocol'. Frost had spent weeks assuring unionist politicians and Tory supporters of Brexit that he would get rid of the protocol, including at meetings attended by the LCC. Among those who criticised his engagement with representatives of illegal organisations was the North's justice minister Naomi Long, who also condemned a warning by the LCC that Irish government ministers were unwelcome in the North while the protocol remained in place.

Although the Northern Ireland Office privately briefed that Frost was meeting paramilitary groups in order to get them to keep a lid on street violence in loyalist areas during the marching season, the nationalist parties and Alliance were incensed. They were particularly angered when the LCC issued a statement in early May that it had met with Frost and Secretary of State Brandon Lewis at a time when the LCC was telling Irish government ministers they were not welcome north of the border.

It was perhaps no surprise then, given LCC's 'veiled threat' to Irish government ministers and officials – as Naomi Long described it in the *Irish News* – that LCC chairman David Campbell stood down from the board of the peace-building, cross-community and cross-border charity Co-operation Ireland. Over decades, the charity had received hundreds of thousands of euro in support from Irish government funds through the Department of Foreign Affairs, including for projects in communities controlled by the loyalist paramilitaries. On the board of the charity with Campbell were a number of politicians, including former Taoiseach John Bruton; its vice-chair, former foreign minister Charlie Flanagan; former DUP leader Peter Robinson; and former SDLP MP Margaret Ritchie; as well as former Irish rugby international Trevor Ringland. Peter Sheridan, chief executive of the charity since 2008, was previously an assistant chief constable of the RUC and PSNI and a member of the NI Equality Commission. The joint patrons of Co-operation Ireland are President Michael D. Higgins and Queen Elizabeth II.

Its chair, Dr Christopher Moran – a property tycoon, DUP supporter, Brexiteer and Tory party donor – had been a front row guest at the DUP's conference when it was addressed by Boris Johnson in November 2018. Indeed, at the beginning of his rousing speech, Johnson thanked Moran for arranging his invitation to the event. That same weekend, however, Moran was the subject of a media investigation by the *Sunday Times*, which revealed that a London apartment block he owned was being used for prostitution. The newspaper reported:

> More than 100 prostitutes were operating out of flats at Chelsea Cloisters, a Sloane Avenue apartment building owned by Dr Moran, where the rent for two-bedroom flats can cost more than £2,500 per month. Scotland Yard is now examining evidence provided by the newspaper before deciding whether to investigate. There is no suggestion that Dr Moran is involved in any illegal activity.

A legal representative told the *Sunday Times* that Dr Moran had not tolerated prostitution at the building or profited from it in any way. The newspaper also claimed that the prime minister, Theresa May, was under pressure to return the £290,000 Moran is said to have donated to her party. The revelations were embarrassing to the DUP and to Johnson, but it turned a spotlight on the make-up and political connections of a leading charity supported by the two governments. More sinister and damaging to the charity, however, was the role of a board member in making threats, however veiled, to one of its key funders.

In response to the threat, Varadkar was quoted in the *Irish Independent* as saying that he did not think the LCC decided 'who's welcome in Northern Ireland and who isn't,' and that 'Irish government ministers will continue to travel to Northern Ireland to engage with people from all backgrounds'. In mid-June 2021, Varadkar told the Fine Gael ard fheis that he believed that a united Ireland could happen in his lifetime. This was in sharp contrast to remarks by the Taoiseach Micheál Martin who, on an episode of BBC's *Spotlight* marking the centenary of Northern Ireland, had referred to the next century when speaking of the prospects of a united Ireland.

In his leader's address at the online party conference, Varadkar said that 'the views of unionists must be acknowledged, understood and respected but no one group can have a veto on Ireland's future.'

He rejected the 'crude vision espoused by Sinn Féin', which was, he said, 'a cold form of republicanism, socialist, narrow nationalism, protectionist, anti-British, euro-critical, ourselves alone, 50 per cent plus one and nobody else is needed.' Instead, he said that:

> Unification must not be the annexation of Northern Ireland. It means something more, a new state designed together, a new constitution and one that reflects the diversity of a bi-national or multi-national state in which almost a million people are British. Like the new South Africa, a rainbow nation, not just orange and green.
>
> We have to be willing to consider all that we'd be willing to change – new titles, shared symbols, how devolution in the North would fit into the new arrangements, a new Senate to strengthen the representation of minorities, the role and status of our languages, a new and closer relationship with the United Kingdom.

He went on to say that, until it was clear how a united Ireland would work, holding a border poll would be premature. Arguing that Fine Gael had 'a duty to engage with each other and others to find answers these questions', he suggested it consider organising a branch for party members and activities in the North. Varadkar dismissed criticism of his speech from Brandon Lewis over his 'united Ireland' remarks after the secretary of state urged politicians to 'to dial down the rhetoric, particularly at this time of year'. In response, Varadkar told *RTÉ News* that:

> It was the wrong time during the three years of Brexit because of those negotiations. It was the wrong time this week because of the difficulties the DUP was having. It'll be the wrong time for

the next few months because of negotiations around the protocol and the marching season. It'll be the wrong time next year because we're running into the assembly elections and it'll be the wrong time after that. For those people, including some in my own party, who are uncomfortable talking about unification, they will always be uncomfortable.

Varadkar used the ard fheis to promote his nationalist credentials in advance of a by-election in Dublin South Bay in early July, not least because at that time it was believed that the main challenge to his party would come from SF. Instead, the Tánaiste's favoured party candidate, James Geoghegan, was beaten into second place by Labour senator Ivana Bacik in a significant blow to Fine Gael and Varadkar. Fianna Fáil was even more damaged by the dismal performance of its standard bearer, Deirdre Conroy, who won less than 5 per cent of the vote. Sinn Féin candidate Lynn Boylan, a senator and former MEP for Dublin, came in third with over 16 per cent of the vote. The result prompted another wave of criticism of Martin's leadership from disillusioned backbenchers and party members and, although a likely contender for Martin's job, Jim O'Callaghan was also implicated in the disastrous result as director of elections for Conroy's campaign.

In the wake of the party's weak performance, a number of FF backbenchers led by Marc MacSharry, a consistent and outspoken critic of the leader, sought to mount a challenge to Martin. The Sligo TD claimed to have the support of a significant number of Oireachtas party members, whom he said had signed a petition calling on the Taoiseach to resign as party leader. However, MacSharry said, O'Callaghan had declined to participate and, instead opted to await a more timely opportunity, which put an end to the heave.

Martin did not avoid another damaging blow when one of his most vocal media supporters, columnist Eoghan Harris, had his contract with the *Sunday Independent* terminated. The paper's management and owners, Mediahuis, discovered that Harris was contributing to a Twitter account that had been routinely, and anonymously, criticising journalists and other public figures for over a year. Following complaints to Twitter over the handle @barbarapym2, the social media company suspended the account, which it said was in breach of its rules on platform manipulation, and eight others linked to the Barbara Pym account.

The account, named after a dead English novelist, had directed its attacks on journalists and other public figures deemed to be 'soft' on SF. Among those subjected to attack on Twitter were Aoife Grace Moore, a Derry-born reporter with the *Irish Examiner*; Paul Larkin, a former producer with RTÉ and the BBC; and Seán Murray, a Belfast filmmaker (and son of Sean 'Spike' Murray), who had recently directed *Unquiet Graves*, a documentary exposing the activities of the notorious loyalist Glenanne Gang. International lawyer Francine Cunningham, the Strabane-born wife of Peter Vandermeersch, the publisher of the newspaper, was also the subject of abuse in a tweet on an account called @northernwhig. The tweet, according to *Village Magazine*, suggested that she had nationalist tendencies and, remarkably, described her as 'the ex-wife of Frank Connolly', although we have never met, less still married.

Niall Murphy and his Belfast firm KRW Law represented a number of those abused by Harris on the various Twitter accounts, including Larkin, Derry rights activist Emma DeSouza and Denzil McDaniel. Murphy also advised IF members Martina Devlin, a long-time journalist with *Independent Newspapers*, and Colin Harvey, who were also the subject of adverse comment by Harris.

It appeared that Harris had grown ever more agitated and reckless as the debate over a unity referendum gained momentum and as the vote for SF reached unprecedented levels in the South. He argued that the surge in nationalism would destroy democratic values, and he promoted Micheál Martin, a fellow Cork man, as the political leader most capable of protecting his imagined citadel against the barbarian hordes from the North, led by SF and IF.

Contrary to the accusation by Harris that it was ignoring the wishes and sensibilities of unionism, IF organised a successful and widely-viewed video production featuring a number of prominent members of the Protestant community as part of its efforts to further discussion on Irish unity. The webinar, entitled *New Ireland – Warm House for All*, was hosted by broadcaster and journalist Andrea Catherwood in February 2021, and featured independent MLA Trevor Lunn; Ireland's first female Baptist minister Rev. Karen Sethuraman; trade unionist Mark Langhammer; as well as Denzil McDaniel and Glenn Bradley. It reflected the effort and capacity of the movement to attract those of a non-nationalist background into its orbit. None of the participants came from a Catholic/nationalist background but all were open to the debate on a united Ireland.

IF also produced a detailed economic analysis on the benefits of a united Ireland which estimated, with up-to-date figures provided by the ESRI and others, the real level of the British subvention to NI at less than half the claimed £10 billion per annum. It also set out the advantage people in the South enjoyed in income, wealth and life expectancy compared with those living across the border. In early July 2021, the economic report was presented to 50 prominent members of the business community at a Chatham House Rules event in Belfast, which was addressed by Niall Murphy and Rev. Sethuraman. Among those present were a number of businesspeople from unionist backgrounds.

In June, Professor John Doyle of DCU produced, in a contribution to the ARINS project, an important, peer-reviewed study on the subvention. His study found that the real cost of the UK subvention to the North, calculated at £9.4 billion in 2019, could be less than £3 billion when liabilities incurred by the British state are removed. He found that pension payments in 2019 to retired workers in the North amounted to £3.4 billion, a political obligation that would remain on the UK exchequer after a united Ireland is agreed, just as it continues to pay pensions to those in the South who previously worked in Britain.

In reality, he accepted, the pensions issue would have to be negotiated between the British and Irish governments, following a vote for unity. Some £2.4 billion of the subvention related to the annual payments by the North towards the UK national debt but, according to Doyle, this is more of an accounting exercise as no contribution has been made from NI finances towards UK debt liability for several decades. In his conclusion to the 2021 report, Doyle said, 'The cost of the subvention objectively – in terms of what is relevant to the debate about Irish unity – is no more than £2–£3 billion'.

Any discussion on the cost of unity would also have to consider the benefits, including from corporation tax, that would accrue to the Irish exchequer from an all-island economy as well as other amounts that might be negotiated with Britain as part of its disengagement from Ireland. The role of the EU, which had continued to fund peace and other cross-border projects since Brexit, was the subject of much conjecture given that, post-reunification, it would be in the EU's interests to protect and advance the interests of Ireland as a single economic entity within its common trade area as well as securing the external border on its north-west Atlantic seaboard.

17

EUROPEAN VALUES AND DEFENCE

D utchman Carlo Trojan, before he became secretary general of the European Commission in May 1997, had been responsible for administering the EU's Northern Ireland peace fund, via a series of PEACE programmes, of €240 million. Trojan was EU representative on the International Fund for Ireland for many years and promoted the PEACE programme as a 'bottom-up process' with extensive cross-border and cross-community initiatives. The ultimate European, Trojan speaks five languages, was born in Italy and is married to a Dane. He was also central to the EU response to German reunification and assisted with the unsuccessful effort to achieve unity in Cyprus before its accession to the European Community.

In discussion with this author, Trojan said his impression is that, in recent years, the Conservative Party was more concerned with winning the votes of the DUP at Westminster than in the people of Northern Ireland. He shared the view of Emmanuel Macron that it would be better if Ireland was a single state within the EU. 'No European politician would dare to say that loudly because that would be interference in domestic British affairs,' he said. 'But obviously, things would be much more simple and easier if the whole island of Ireland was one entity within the EU.'

It could take a decade before the conditions for Irish unity have matured, Trojan argued, yet the discussion about a new Ireland has some similarities with the merger of east and west Germany in 1990 when the new united country was entitled to automatic membership of the EU on reunification. It has already been agreed that a united Ireland would be guaranteed membership of the EU without the requirement of an accession process or treaty. Trojan explained:

> Once a referendum has passed in Northern Ireland and in the Irish Republic, then NI becomes automatically part of the Irish Republic. As it becomes automatically part of the Irish Republic, it also automatically becomes part of the European Union. The laws of the Irish Republic by definition have to be compatible with the European Union laws so the end result is very comparable with what happened with German reunification.

Trojan said that the transition will be easier for Ireland as there will already be an all-island economy, not least arising from the fact that NI, under the protocol, remains part of the EU customs and trade area. 'If this is developing more and more into an all-island economy with Northern Ireland as part of the internal market and the custom union, you will see more and more divergence between Northern Ireland and the rest of the United Kingdom,' he said.

Trojan said he could see further divergence down the road between the EU and Britain in the fields of environmental and food policy, and in worker's rights and employment protection rules, for example. He pointed out that, as the North stays part of the internal market, it will have to abide by both existing and future rules of the internal market. While German reunification was an effective takeover by the west of the east, there was also an enormous transfer of money, not least as a consequence of the prior decision to set one-to-one parity between the West German Deutschmark and the East German Ostmark. As Trojan said:

West Germany is still paying the costs of unification. If you look at the all-island economy, what is very important is to have more and more cross-border entities and projects. That is already taking shape in Ireland. You see that in agri-business where you have a lot of cross-border co-operation. You have to also allow some time for the political process in Northern Ireland to develop and especially better cross-community co-operation. As a matter of fact, that should start very much in the field of education. It takes some time to have unification both in the hearts and minds of people and, for different reasons [than Germany], the same applies in the case of Northern Ireland.

The decision by the Irish government to guarantee the funding to ensure that students from the North can still avail of the Erasmus programme after the Withdrawal Agreement was, in his view, 'very wise'. The programme provides for financial support from the Irish government to enable students to study in other EU countries. 'The same was true for East Germany,' said Trojan, 'because young people were able to study in other countries, to get to know other young people. This was hugely important.'

It was also notable, he said, that the British made concessions to allow Gibraltar to remain part of the customs union and the single market late in the negotiations on the Withdrawal Agreement in December 2020. 'It's comparable to Northern Ireland,' he argued. 'Gibraltar will be part of the customs union and the single market and there will be a special regime for protecting the external border. I was quite pleased when I saw there was an agreement between Spain and the UK that has taken years and years to come to.'

In time, he said, the development of the all-island economy, with the support of the EU and the US government will open the way for an agreed all-island solution. 'It will come,' Trojan said, but, in his view, the Irish government and other promoters of Irish unity should be cautious and make full use of the support they enjoy across the EU, particularly in the European Parliament, to achieve their goal.

In 2000, David O'Sullivan, a former career diplomat who also served as EU ambassador to the US, became Trojan's successor as secretary general of the European Commission. O'Sullivan agrees that the decision of the Council of Ministers in 2017 to allow a unified Ireland to immediately have membership of the EU was significant. At interview with this author, he said:

> It was a very clever move by Enda Kenny in the aftermath of the Brexit referendum to get recognition from the EU that the reunification of Ireland would not need to be considered as the accession of a new country. There's no accession process; there's no joining or waiting time.

O'Sullivan asserted that a unity referendum will only be truly successful if a sufficient minority of unionists and a large majority of nationalists and non-aligned people support it. Those most opposed would have to be willing to accept the outcome, however reluctantly. In his view, that requires creating a narrative which assuages the worst fears of the unionist community:

> How do you get to a point where you have persuaded a sufficient minority of unionists? Because of course you will, almost by definition, never persuade them all. More importantly, you have to win over a large majority of nationalists. There is a substantial body of middle-class nationalists who look at the subsidy coming from Westminster, who look at the NHS and who say, 'We like the South and the idea of a united Ireland, but we think we're better off as we are. Our hearts might say united Ireland but our pockets say we should stick with the UK.'
>
> The other moving part is what happens to Scotland. It is very clear that if ever the Scots were to vote for independence, it would

be a big game-changer, because the question then is what union are the unionists attached to anymore? Particularly given the affinity between Northern Ireland and Scotland for all the obvious reasons.

Those who run the EU administration tend to be generally supportive of the principle of Irish unification, not least as it would make life a lot easier for them after Brexit, O'Sullivan said. The difficulties surrounding the implementation of the NI protocol highlighted the conundrum that results from a UK that is no longer in the EU, an Ireland that remains a member and the imperative of not setting up a land border between them, he said. O'Sullivan and his former colleagues at senior levels of the EU have nothing but the highest praise for Michel Barnier in dealing with the 'complete nightmare' of the protocol and the general situation regarding Ireland during the negotiations on the Withdrawal Agreement. O'Sullivan said:

> Talk about trying to square the circle. People sometimes forget, however, that Barnier was in charge of regional policy in the commission under [European Commission President Romano] Prodi when I was secretary general back in 2000, and he was responsible for the EU-funded PEACE Programme. He travelled many times to Northern Ireland and he was deeply impressed by what he saw. He said to me once, 'Europe has to get in behind this, this is what Europe is about. This peace and reconciliation is an amazing thing that's happened in Ireland. We have to be 100 per cent behind them.'
>
> He didn't just discover Northern Ireland and the Good Friday Agreement at the moment of doing Brexit. It was in his DNA and he immediately thought that, whatever else happens, we have to preserve the peace process and we have to avoid a hard border because he had witnessed the dismantling of the border. He was

there for all of that. The idea of the EU as its own peace project drives support for the GFA, including possible future unification, provided that it is done constitutionally and democratically.

It is important to remember that the British government has to agree to holding the poll and to agree – which they logically would because of the Good Friday Agreement – to abide by its outcome. Anything that smacks of secession or not following the constitutional rules would cause problems for a number of EU member states, particularly the Spanish with the Catalan situation.

There would, in O'Sullivan's view, be additional financial support from the EU to assist with the reunification project after a referendum, although 'probably not nearly enough to compensate for the massive transfers you see coming from London at the moment'. He said:

> I know that people speculate that London would continue to pay some money for a transitional period and probably they would. But I don't know how much or for how long. The other question is, what does it take to give comfort to the unionists who will still look to the UK? To what extent would the new arrangements perpetuate the protocol with Northern Ireland as part of both the EU and the UK markets, or to what extent there would be a willingness to say, 'OK, the reunited country is an independent country, a full member of the EU and therefore no particular special commercial arrangement is needed with the UK other than that prevailing for the EU as a whole?'

The answers to these questions depend, he argued, largely on how things evolve over the next five or ten years:

> One of the ironies of what is happening now will be to reduce slowly over time the economic ties between Northern Ireland and GB and increase North–South economic ties on the island of

Ireland. This is not the result of a nationalist plot. It is simply the logical consequence of Brexit. Ironic since the DUP, for example, was fully behind Brexit.

O'Sullivan believes that the Irish government has been wise in talking about a shared island, cross-border co-operation and investment in infrastructure rather than about unity as an objective in itself:

> Stuff like that will just slowly tilt the focus in the North more towards the all-island economy and a bit less towards the East–West relationship. However, relations with Britain will remain very strong. Let's be clear, that's not going to go away … All my instincts from 40 years of doing European work tell me *softly, softly, catchee monkey*. Jean Monet's concept about 'creating de facto solidarity' is key. You create links, invest in infrastructure, cultivate economic and commercial ties, and people just start to think in all-Ireland terms. Not politically, you're not forcing them to salute the tricolour instead of the Union Jack. You're just saying that this makes life better for all of us. The more successful the Irish economy and society looks, the more attractive some form of unification becomes. This is why I believe that now is not the moment to be emphasising unification. The unionist community is feeling threatened by the protocol. We should resolve the real problems which implementing the protocol creates and then focus on making all these new arrangements work so that people can see that they are not directly connected to the constitutional issue. The constitutional debate will evolve naturally in due course.

He went on to say that 'detailed planning will be required, in advance of any future border poll,' and people should know, at least in general terms, what kind of a united Ireland they are voting for in advance of a referendum:

You can't just ask people, 'Are you in favour of a united Ireland or not?' It is like asking, 'Do you want to leave the EU?', as the UK did. Lots of people voted to leave in the UK on the assumption that they could keep all the benefits and lose the bits that they didn't like. It is slowly dawning on them that Brexit does come with real economic costs.

There would have to be at least the outline of a project on the table, that this is the united Ireland that you'd be voting for, although there may be variants that could be discussed afterwards. You will probably need some kind of constitutional convention to thrash out the details, but you'd certainly need a fairly well-developed blueprint of what kind of Ireland you're talking about, and that people would be voting for. The challenge is to find a way to involve the unionist community in that conversation since to ask them to speculate even very hypothetically about unification is to ask them to consider what for many of them would be their worst nightmare. This needs, above all, time. It cannot be rushed.

On the global implications of Brexit, O'Sullivan and his former colleagues in the Commission are very concerned by the refusal of the UK, a nuclear power and permanent member of the UN security council, to rule out a formal security agreement with the EU. A united Ireland would raise questions about the security of the island and its relationship to NATO, he said. In the event of a European conflict with Russia, the western flank of Ireland would become vulnerable if there is no security arrangement with other countries. He said:

> I'm not saying a united Ireland would have to join NATO but what would be its relationship to NATO? At present I don't think anyone cares whether we're in NATO or not. But if you had a united Ireland and there was a suggestion that Northern Ireland was then leaving NATO, I think people would certainly ask questions.

For example, who is going to be responsible for looking after the security of this reunited Ireland and what kind of arrangements would there be if situations arose where it is necessary to protect its airspace or territorial waters? I don't think anyone has given it a lot of thought.

Notwithstanding these issues, there is what O'Sullivan calls a 'commonplace assumption' in the European capitals that Irish unification is now quite likely to happen, even though he frequently has to remind people in Brussels and across the EU that there is a significant number of people in the North who think of themselves as British. O'Sullivan explained:

> There is an implicit assumption that the historical trend is a future vote for reunification, not least because of demographic shifts, and that Brexit has made that much more likely. However, they also believe that it is up to the Irish to figure out how to make this happen in a peaceful and constitutional manner.

O'Sullivan described how devastated so many British colleagues who have worked for decades in the EU are at the Brexit outcome, many of whom also foresee an end to the British union with Northern Ireland in the not-too-distant future:

> Many British people I know fear that Brexit will weaken the solidity of the ties holding the four parts of the UK together. There are very few people in the UK who have any great commitment to the union with Northern Ireland. Many regard it as a burden and as a sort of legacy issue now. I think if there were a vote [in NI to leave] in the morning, people in the UK would frankly be relieved in many ways. There are a few diehard unionists in the Conservative Party who might be shocked, but the cynical way Boris Johnson basically threw the DUP under a bus is reflective

of the true feelings. There is zero attachment to Northern Ireland and many people in the UK that I talk to are working on the assumption that reunification is pretty much inevitable. It's just a question of when and how. We in Ireland, of course, know that it is nothing like as simple [as] that.

Tom Clonan is a security consultant who was previously a captain in the Irish Defence Forces and served in the Lebanon, Bosnia and other conflict zones. In 2000, as a serving officer, Clonan completed a PhD in Dublin City University. His doctoral thesis focused on women in the military and revealed shockingly high levels of sexual violence, sexual assault and rape within the Irish Defence Forces. Despite receiving criticism and reprisal from senior military figures for his 'whistleblowing', Clonan's findings were completely vindicated following an independent government inquiry from 2001 to 2003 entitled the 'Study Review Group'.

Clonan has also campaigned ceaselessly on behalf of disabled children, including for his son Eoghan, who suffers from a rare neuromuscular disease. Clonan is a frequent critic of the failure of the health service to cater for children with severe disabilities. He is a supporter of Ireland's military neutrality, which he believes should be retained after the reunification of the country. He was concerned that there has been little or no debate or preparation by the defence forces for its future in a united Ireland. During an interview with this author, Clonan said:

> There seems to be an unwillingness on the part of the government parties to talk about what is going to happen next but whether we like it or not, we are looking at an all-island future coming down the tracks. There is no plan, no discussion and I think that is very remiss. One of the most valuable things we have is our neutral status. Along with our diaspora, it gives us great credibility in the world. There is a lot of instability at present and there are probably going to be regional and major conventional conflicts within our lifetime.

Clonan sees the Irish experience of conflict and the prospect of constitutional change as more comparable to the Balkans than to the reunification of east and west Germany:

> We are more like ... Bosnia with the potential for major instability and, possibly, fairly awful violence. There are people in the government who think we only have to extend this 26-county republic out to 32 counties and everybody would be happy with that. I don't think nationalists want our current situation, with a badly run economy and health service. I don't think any unionists would want to be a part of this three-ring circus. They would want their heads examined.
>
> But if we reach out to all traditions and talk to each other I think there could be something really wonderful that would combine the benefits of the European Union and some special relationship with whatever is left in Britain after Boris and the boys. I certainly believe it is important to sustain our neutral status at all costs. That is really important in a very volatile world.

Ireland has significantly underspent on defence compared to the EU average. There is also a major recruitment issue and a shortage of key skillsets across the different forces of the navy, army and air corps. Clonan argued:

> We have a number of ships tied up that can't go to sea. The Irish Fisheries Board has had to request the EU to send coastal patrol vessels to patrol our territorial waters for the first time in the history of the state. In the air, the Royal Air Force (RAF) provides security and air cover for Ireland. The Air Corps can no longer train its own pilots, who are being sent to Australia to learn how to fly planes. Helicopter pilots are going to the US army aviation centre in Fort Rucker in Alabama to train. An organisation that doesn't have the capacity to replicate its own skillset is an organisation that is on its

last legs. The army is also under serious pressure with personnel shortage and a lack of gender balance and diversity. It does not reflect society as it is. Our position is so weak that we can't really call ourselves neutral as we are so dependent on the RAF and other states. We are Europe's weakest link in defence and security.

On the domestic front, Clonan identified the challenges posed by dissident republicans and the groups emerging from within the loyalist community that no longer appear to be under the control of the LCC:

The LCC don't seem to have a handle any more and there is a very intimate linkage in the North between organised crime and both dissident republicans and dissident loyalists. The first group are mobilising republican rhetoric to prevent the normalisation of policing.

The South now has the same homicide rate per head of population as the rest of the EU, but we have one of the highest homicide rates by firearms in Europe. They are 5 times those of Britain and that is directly connected to organised crime gangs and their links with former paramilitaries.

Unfortunately, Brexit has re-energised identity politics. We were all Europeans, but now you're either Irish or you're British and it is an absolute disaster. The PSNI has said on the record that they believe that one of the outcomes of Brexit is an increased security problem within Northern Ireland. There has been a weird absence of discussion about what we need to plan for in relation to security. There is also a fetish in the media in the South with demonising Sinn Féin. There has been little or no discussion of the threat caused by the DUP and the rhetoric and the language that they are using in relation to the protocol.

There is absolute obsession with hammering Sinn Féin, and anybody who says they would like to talk about a referendum or a border poll is immediately shut down. Not only is there no discussion of what we need to do next but when anybody seeks to discuss it, they are accused of being somehow subversive. Micheál Martin said this isn't the right time to discuss a referendum. In my view, this is absolutely the right time. All the lights are flashing on the dashboard.

The UN global strategy on terrorism asserts that there is going to be an inextricable link between terrorism and organised crime all around the world, whether it is Islamic State, or what is left now of Al-Qaeda, or in the Maghreb or the Philippines. There is always a crossover with people smuggling, sex trafficking, narcotics, and Ireland is no different.

Across Europe we have a rise of ethno-nationalism. In Hungary, they have mobilised against refugees and asylum seekers. There are none in Hungary as they just pass through but people there believe it is a threat. All it takes is for someone to just keep using this rhetoric. I know that we have a tendency to look at ourselves in isolation as being exceptional, but narco-terrorism and the rise of ethno-nationalism identity politics are happening more broadly.

I think the English and the Tories have absolutely no interest whatsoever in holding on to Northern Ireland. They just want to get rid of it. Then it will be our problem and how do we cope with it and manage it? There has been no discussion around a design for the future. I don't know what is happening in health or in social protection or education but certainly in defence there is no discussion. I don't see any preparation on the policing side either.

18

INTEGRATING IS A GOOD WORD

Many of the leading cultural talents in Ireland – actors, musicians, poets and visual artists – have voiced their support for unity, and more than a few have signed the IF petition calling for a citizens' assembly and on the Irish government to prepare for a referendum in the coming years. Their vision is not for the absorption of the North into the existing order but for an island based on equality and that protects and nurtures Irish culture.

Actors Adrian Dunbar and James Nesbitt are among those born in the North who have supported the call for unity and have expressed their views on what a united Ireland might look like in the future. Dunbar, who has won plaudits for his leading role in the British television series, *Line of Duty*, has performed major roles on stage and screen in Ireland and Britain for decades. Nesbitt has appeared over recent years in several popular films and television series, as well as the Netflix produced crime thriller, *Close Up*. Asked by the *Irish Times* how they would envisage Ireland 100 years from now, the two actors were certain it would be reunited and were optimistic about the new Ireland. Dunbar said:

> In 100 years and much less I expect Ireland to be unified and at peace with herself. Irish unification and freedom after hundreds

of years is in our DNA, it is in effect a big part of who we have become to ourselves and the world. ... I am leaning towards a federal or provincial approach to unification. The cities of Cork and Galway are both at exciting stages of development and primed for regional assemblies. Belfast would of course run Ulster from Stormont and perhaps with the Leinster regional base in Kilkenny; Dublin would remain the focus of all our ire.

I believe that Fine Gael and Fianna Fáil will have merged and Sinn Féin will be the main party if they adhere to forward-thinking ideas. At the moment, I think they are the only party that has a chance of delivering the Republic promised by Connolly, Clarke, Mac Diarmada and Pearse. The Green Party however will be power brokers and voting for them now seems appropriate. ...

By the way, if we get our provincial republic, we in Ulster will want Donegal, Cavan and Monaghan back. I look forward to a time when we can travel again from Virginia [in Cavan] to Ballycastle [in Antrim] without leaving Ulster.

Nesbitt, meanwhile, referred to 'generosity and humour' as indispensable parts of Irish culture and character and sees a future beyond unionism and nationalism a century from now:

Certainly, I would hope that the essential charm, generosity and humour of the Irish people will still be a huge part of what it means to be Irish. That is what I would want to greet me when I return on my white charger.

What will be different will be the politics and the structure. After the 'great debate' of the 2020s and 2030s the words 'unionism' and 'nationalism' will have disappeared from discourse, to be replaced with a sense of togetherness and of unity of the people. Not only on this island, but across a new commonwealth of nations sharing common goals and created by agreement rather than by coercion or imperialism.

We will have had almost 70 years of peace and harmony and cultural, social and economic growth in an Ireland that is a key partner in that new commonwealth of nations. ...

It is perhaps worth looking to a type of federal Ireland loosely based on the historic provinces – each with its own leadership team within the wider context. ...

I genuinely think it can happen if we are prepared to have that prolonged debate about what we want to look like as a people and how we want to develop and grow.

Nesbitt did not see the rationality of two separate soccer teams on the small island and recognised how other sports played on an all-island basis have equalled the best of much bigger nations.

Stephen Rea, one of the finest and best-known Irish actors on the local and international stage, is also from the North and has been an active promoter of Irish unity for decades. During the long period of broadcast censorship of SF in Britain, Rea performed the voice of Gerry Adams on the BBC. Born in Belfast, Rea, along with Brian Friel and Seamus Deane, helped to found the Field Day theatre and publishing collective in 1980, as a cultural response to the political crisis and conflict. He was married to former IRA volunteer, the late Dolours Price, with whom he raised two children. Rea's riveting performance in David Ireland's play *Cyprus Avenue*, about a Belfast loyalist who is convinced his new-born grandchild is Gerry Adams, enjoyed a hugely positive reaction after runs in Belfast, Dublin and London before Covid-19 struck. Rea was involved in the civil rights campaign and was also in Belfast during the street violence of the late '60s after the arrival of British troops in the North and the introduction of internment in 1971. Rea argued that the political struggle for Irish independence has always been integrated with cultural expression. He told this author:

I had gone to London to be an actor, but I used to come home a lot. And then all sorts of people were interned. They were ordinary, like Michael Farrell [student leader and founder of People's Democracy]. They picked them up because these people wanted an intelligent reaction to the injustices. It was an awful, traumatic time but it was inevitable.

If you set up a deliberately sectarian state, eventually it will come to something. We were long-haired demonstrators, just hanging out. I was in Derry a couple of days before and then I was on the Falls Road in Belfast. We were just lending support and then we got fired at like everybody else. A few of my mates who were with me were in the IRA within a short space of time because it seemed to be the only option.

I understand the state was founded in violence, it had been tainted in violence and I understand why people thought that they could dismantle it with violence. The Easter Rising would not have been successful had it not been a violent rising. Everything had been so entrenched, the whole British thing. My experience was that they [Irish republicans] weren't the first to be violent. They were responding to violence.

We are also talking about the collision points between activism and art. What I find so upsetting about the refusal to celebrate Pearse, McDonagh, Connolly and McDermott and the rest of them was that they were all involved in the arts. They saw the point of it all and they had the imagination. They weren't just violent people or even violent people.

I'm not baptised in any religion. I come from a long line of Agnostics. I remember asking my grandfather [a Protestant] if he'd signed the [Ulster] Covenant. I just wondered what his politics were. He said, 'A lot of bloody nonsense,' and in a sort of way, cleared the path for me.

Rea is sceptical about the recent attachment of FG to Irish unity:

A partitioned island makes no sense. The waste of energy in maintaining it could be used for other things. The British government is always going to stand by the unionists. They hate them but they're going to use them to get one over on Sinn Féin. I think Fine Gael has only grabbed the unity thing because it's another way of taking the momentum out of the sails of the Shinners. I don't believe for a moment they believe in it.

I think it's time to create a new world. I know I'm an idealist, but people should have all the things that they need. Homelessness has always been an issue in the South and I think, 'Can you imagine the hell of not having somewhere to put your children at night?'

In 1980, Rea approached Brian Friel, with a view to using theatre to explore the history and context of the conflict. Among the early plays they produced was *Translations*, first performed in Derry's Guildhall, which examined the manner in which the British colonists attempted to erase the Irish language and brought it, as author Seán O'Faoláin once said, to the brink of destruction. Rea said:

My first instinct when I started Field Day was that I went to Friel and asked him to be a partner. It was one of those miraculous things. He was actually working on *Translations* at the time. That sort of gave it real cultural power, the context of that play. He understood the deliberate destruction of the language as part of the violence of colonialism, in the same way as the Gaelic League was formed at the turn of the twentieth century as a response to the enforcement of British culture.

We were taking new plays that normally would just have been seen in Dublin. It was very community-based and very exciting to open a play in Derry and have people come up to you and say,

'I've never been in a theatre in my life before and I thought it was wonderful.' So it wasn't that we were proselytising, it was just that the people needed to hear what we were on about.

Rea has watched the rise in confidence of the nationalist people of the North, culturally and politically, as unionism has been shrinking politically and demographically:

> The truth is, the confidence of the nationalist people is growing and it should grow. Look what the unionists got away with for 100 years. There was never any referendum about partition. They just were allowed do it and do it the way they wanted. Even people who were part of that system now admit that it was shocking how they treated the Catholics and got away with it.
>
> That's what ends up with women like Dolours [Price] being destroyed because of the courage they had in resisting it. I was there when the whole thing turned, when the loyalists came down Bombay Street, in Belfast and started burning houses and shooting at people. That's when the IRA decided to get guns out.

In his view, the worst fears of unionism and loyalism – their ultimate betrayal by the British – will soon be confirmed. Rea knows very few decent English people who see the logic of their involvement in the North. He said that his friends and colleagues in theatre and film:

> look at me with kind of dazed eyes trying to get me to give them some rationality. They see people the likes of [DUP MP] Gregory Campbell who are living so far in the past.
>
> The British government should say to the unionists, 'Look it's gone on long enough. You've had the place for 100 years. It's more of a mess now than it ever was.' They should admit that, 'This kind of partition hasn't worked in India, it hasn't worked in Cyprus. We've made a balls of it, wherever we've been.'

Rea does not believe it will be a big step for businesspeople, the artistic community, the wider Protestant and non-affiliated community to reach an accommodation with those from a Catholic and nationalist background, although he is concerned that, out of ignorance and fear, some loyalists will engage in sectarian attacks. Many younger people in the North, however, feel and want to remain European and that is now part of the attraction of a united Ireland, he said, and unionism will have to adapt to the wishes of a new generation:

> Unionists can't actually bring themselves to say that they were responsible for a lot of the ills that Catholics had to put up with, and that they were put in place to maintain that situation. That's pretty difficult to say if you've spent your life marching on the Twelfth, but it doesn't matter whether you're a Catholic or a Protestant anymore. It's only a tribal definition that is no longer relevant.

Meanwhile, Rea continued during our discussion, in the South there is a growing population of new Irish who have 'embraced the originality of Irish culture, that it is all about music and dance and humour. They love it.' He said that the NI protocol, which maintains unobstructed access to the EU for cultural workers in the North, is important for the film industry:

> It may be a kind of utopian thing, but I think Europe is great … it makes such sense to work this protocol as it means people in the North are being protected and they're being given privileges that Scotland hasn't got for instance.
>
> The British have to get over their imperial past and their withdrawal from the EU was part of their refusal to do that. I don't know how or if they can, in a nice paternal or maternal way, say to their children, the loyalists, 'Look, we've had enough of this, go on out and play with those nice boys out there.' I don't know what

the structures for Irish unity might be, but I imagine there would have to be a slow filtering away of partition. It's already largely gone from when I was a kid.

But there also has to be change of mind in the South because those who run the place are as possessive of the status quo as the British and unionists are in the North. The nationalist drive for independence from Britain is not living in the past, it's moving forward. It's time to be firm about it and say, 'Look, we're all going to be part of the same organism.' You have to do it by steps. You can't suddenly say, 'OK, all the pillar boxes are going to be green.' But everything they used as the basis of fear, like 'Home Rule is Rome Rule', is not the case any more. In the South, we have far more liberal laws, which are not imposed from Westminster but decided upon democratically. It's a huge change that you wouldn't have even imagined a while ago and we just have to keep that going.

In her 1985 poem 'Caesarean Section in a Belfast Street', Paula Meehan recalls the birth of a child whose mother has just been killed in an IRA bomb attack in the city. Her words captured the brutality of the war in the North and the crushing of the most basic human instinct: to give life.

> You were dragged into history
> By a soldier's bloody hands. He cursed history
> That soldier agent of your miracle birth
> Among the sirens and screams and ghosts of the past
> That shattered the silence of her womb.

(Meehan, 1985)

Born in Dublin, Meehan has told the story of contemporary Ireland through her poems, many of them exploring the oppression of working-class women in a society that long treated them as second-class citizens, or the 'slaves of slaves' as James Connolly once described. Her description of the tragic circumstances of a birth on the street was her reaction to a newspaper caption over the story, 'Snatched from Death'. Meehan explained to me:

> It is a long, complicated poem, a sestina. A bomb goes off and the pregnant woman actually dies but they manage to save the near-term baby. I've written about the hunger strikes, too, in early books; my collections that haven't been republished. It's not that I wouldn't have believed that they're useful or valuable in some way, but they're just not as achieved as the poems that came afterwards. Later work is more centred on how oppression of women especially, but for working-class people generally, is systemic.
>
> Those early poems that I wrote out of 'the Troubles' would have been made at a time I was most trying to find a language for this kind of unbelievable stuff that was happening on our small island. I was striving to avoid it becoming just, you know, guff. There's an awful lot of that written: standing up and shouting your head off, the literary equivalent of 'The Men Behind the Wire' [the Wolfe Tones' song]. The tragedies unfolding in the North were not venal. To make poems that could carry the charge of those Troubles was not a venal thing. I think the poets were trying, and largely succeeding, to negotiate the territory without any agenda except to make the best possible poems.

Her friend, the late Seamus Heaney, perhaps best expressed for Meehan the challenge faced by the poet in writing about their closest friends and community. 'I have friends in the North from every stripe of sanity and lunacy, from all over,' she said. 'Heaney definitely drew a line in the sand and basically what he said was, which I think is salutary, "I'm not here to further other people's agenda, I'm a poet." It's a real act of determination.'

The controversy over the Northern Ireland Office's use of Heaney's image to celebrate the centenary of the Northern state – or as many nationalists saw it, '100 years of partition' – was in Meehan's view, a recognition of the poet's deep-rooted influence and significance. The artist and creator of the image, Tai-Shan Schierenberg, made a similar point in his response to the controversy when he said in *Belfast Live* that Heaney does not belong to any government or the 'grubby reality' of politics, but 'wanted to speak for, and to us all'.

Meehan said, 'I thought that's interesting that they're now, even unbeknownst to themselves, sending out a message of pride in the cattle dealer's son. Who can claim him? Sure, isn't that the whole marvellous reality of his poetry? That is his great achievement, he belongs to all of us.'

In Meehan's view, many of the talented artists in Ireland, across all the disciplines, largely managed to see the arts as a borderless zone during the relentless decades of conflict. Cultural institutions such as Aosdána, although funded by the government in the South, has included and celebrated and continues to elect many artists from the North, while the arts councils in both jurisdictions have promoted and encouraged her work, and those of other writers and poets, seamlessly.

> There isn't a border in the arts. We would have comings and goings for work – for readings, for workshops, for residencies – and we would have the craic at festivals, and we'd be looking at what everyone was doing as the work came out. Artists from the North were included as 'Irish artists' and they were entitled to be members of Aosdána like the rest of us. The cultural institutions of the South kept a genuinely open hearted welcome and a genuine invitation to practitioners to connect or be involved. Certainly, in poetry and literature, and with the stellar reputations of poets including Heaney, festival programmers and curators down here couldn't but include Northern Irish writers.

There were tensions, Meehan said, which arose from the conflict, and sometimes while teaching in communities or other settings in the North, her unique and distinctive Dublin working-class accent was not always welcome. Like other performers from the South, Meehan also recalled the fear on occasions while travelling in darkness through rural parts close to the border:

> I mean, I never had any trouble from the poets because you just fight your corner: each one of us is steeped in our own language and we carry our cultural baggage. The engagements tended to be fierce and intense. The only time I ever felt threatened was when I was on tour and going down remote boreens with a group of traditional musicians. It was just before the 1994 ceasefire and people were dressing up in the uniforms of the opponent, whoever they thought their opponent was. There was a great deal of random sectarian violence.
>
> It was just so dark literally; November. If you were stopped at a roadblock or something, you just wouldn't let them hear a woman's accent from the South because you just didn't know who they were really. They might be wearing army uniforms but that meant nothing.

Meehan collaborated with the late Ciaran Carson, a poet and traditional musician who worked for the Arts Council of Northern Ireland and who regularly invited her to perform in the North. He encouraged her to let her poems speak for themselves:

> Ciaran was an immensely cultured man. He translated *The Táin*, and Dante from the Italian, he translated from French, a really gifted poet. He was a traditional musician as well. He used to say to me, 'Listen, Paula, keep it low on the introductions – just get straight into the poems.' Like many poets, myself included, he

believed that poetry is complex enough to carry the complexities and paradoxes, whereas if you start to explain yourself or justify yourself, you're giving the audience excuses to disagree with you.

Meehan believes that a united Ireland is inevitable but that it should be an organic process, just as she sees the island as a bio-region.

> My own feeling about a united Ireland, which I think is inevitable, is that it will be fought intellectually, culturally and socially on the grounds of loving the island as a bio-region. I don't carry 800 years of oppression around with me. I just carry the common or garden local oppression of the life I've led or seen. …
>
> It's going to be fought on the basis of the bio-regional approach to the island as a whole. Concern for the very ground of our being. Concern for the water quality, the watersheds, our beautiful rivers and lakes. The rivers don't turn back at the border, the creatures don't fly backwards at the border. The key is to have an integrated and healed Ireland. There's so much potential there. Producing the best of food for example. The models are there for sustainable care of the island and if we all started taking care of the actual island itself instead of crucifying ourselves on theoretical and ideological crosses, I think we'd all be a lot happier. And healthier.
>
> It's about the health of the people, which is determined by the health of the land. When I see a united Ireland it's along those lines of seeing it as an island, a bio-region that may even have fraternal federations with other islands in the vicinity, on an equal footing.
>
> If we had a more holistic lens on the island, then some of those things would work out. It seems crazy to me in a very small area of this planet to have two completely different health systems, two completely different educational policies. That's where I see space, especially in the arts, which by their very nature are in the business

of exploring our *common* humanity, to reveal to the community how much we share.

Integrated is a good word because it also has the subliminal of 'integrity'. I have great hope. I think the lesson of the pandemic has been that we are actually so totally interconnected. It's a terrible way to learn that lesson, but it is true.

Meehan insisted that artists can change society for the better 'by just individuals doing their work, by groups putting on their plays, by bands coming together and putting their work out there'. She said:

> I think there is a movement to jettison a lot of rancour, but that doesn't mean we can't sing rebel songs. As songs. Just as we have a tradition of worker's songs, protest songs, love songs. There are these artefacts like the *aislings* that belong to all of us. If at certain times the *aisling*, the dream vision, is prefigured as the muse, is determined to be Mother Ireland or the young *spéar-bhean* for a revolutionary cause, for the cause of the Republic, well that's a phase of its own tradition. I don't get riled up by someone singing 'The Sash'. I just think it is a little peculiar.

Meehan's poetry is admired for the deep, and beautifully lyrical, insight she provides into the life of women in working-class Dublin and the challenges they faced in a theocratic and deeply unequal society. Her poems are rooted in that experience, just as poets who grew up during years of conflict in the North reflect their surroundings in their work. She said:

> Look at Heaney, look at Mahon, at Longley, at Carson. They are part of a generation that have come under enormous scrutiny, under a journalistic lens called *Northern Irish Poetry*.
>
> But it's not like the women poets in the North have been embraced: they've had to put up a huge struggle to get anything

near approaching parity of esteem. Through that experience there would be strong bonds and understanding forged with their contemporaries in the South.

When my second book was reviewed [as late as 1986], the reviewer said that, until recently, a book by a women poet was as rare as a white blackbird! Not in fact true – it was just that there was deafness and blindness when it came to the lived truths of women artists.

The Northern poet, Medbh McGuckian, by anybody's measure, is an outstanding literary artist, an absolutely dazzlingly brilliant poet. Her mysterious dreamscapes are the perfect embodiment of the psyche of people who were trying to negotiate their way through the Troubles. And the expression of the fractures and tensions in work that is artistically powerful and integrated is itself an offering of wholeness.

Then there is the phenomenal poet Joan Newmann, also from the North, who is seriously underestimated in my opinion; a terrific community builder, an encourager and facilitator of others' work.

There has been so much to admire, not just in the excellence of the work itself, but in the refusal of the poets to descend into agenda-ridden tribalism. I believe as artists we are after artistic power, not political power, and in the failed entity that is the partitioned island, we have offered, and continue to offer to our communities, truths that uncover what we have in common rather than what divides us. The mysteries of the human heart.

As poets in the North wrote of their experiences of war and sectarian conflict, Meehan and her generation were writing of their experiences in the slow evolution from a state influenced by an overpowering Catholic hierarchy. Poetry in both states, she said, captured the ebbs and flows of society in place and time. Now she sees both states in a wider European context:

> There are poets of the Republic who were inheriting this totally dysfunctional theocracy at the same time as the Troubles were fermenting up North. ...
>
> It happened with Eastern European poetry at a particular moment. A lot of those poets had to go into an internal exile or get out. It's happened in South American poetry. There are moments when poetry by its very nature, because of the truths it tells, can suddenly have this huge energy that then gets a lot of attention, which then generates more energy. And there are times when it is dangerous to be a truthteller.

As Meehan said, over the decades, poetry has often reflected the popular emotion and anger in response to an event or outrage, even though its authors may remain distant from the fray. 'The significance of poetry tends to resurface when there's outrage, like with Thomas Kinsella's 'Butcher's Dozen' or as happened in a feminist mode when young Ann Lovett died. These insults to the dignity of a community, these traumas, just demand some kind of expression.' she said.

Ann Lovett was a 15-year-old schoolgirl from Granard, County Longford who died with her infant son after she had given birth beside a grotto on 31 January 1984. Meehan recalled when her poem on the lonely death of the pregnant teenager was used by a Presbyterian minister to attack the Catholic Church and 'Rome rule' in the South:

> They used my poem about Ann Lovett's tragic death as a stick to beat the Catholics. The clergyman got up and read bits of the poem with this big anti-Catholic rant which I thought was bizarre. 'Even the poets of the Republic can see through that idolatrous church!' he shouted. Oh irony!

Christy Moore has been singing songs about Irish freedom and rebellion since he was a child. A political activist for many years, he has used his powerful singing and musical talent to bring the Irish and global struggle against political oppression to a huge audience. Over the decades, Moore's performances and recordings as part of Planxty and Moving Hearts, and with other musicians, have helped to raise awareness of historic and contemporary injustice that have moved audiences across the world. His honesty and humour have earned him a deep respect as Ireland's most popular traditional and folk artist. Moore has sung and recorded songs that go to the heart of the political conflict in the North which have, at times, attracted criticism and the unwanted attention of the forces of the state, on both sides of the border. He has played benefits for many progressive causes over the years from the Dunnes Stores workers in support of their protest against apartheid in the 1980s to those who lost their jobs when Clery's, the iconic Dublin store, closed suddenly in 2015. Moore has performed for the people of Palestine, for those affected by addiction and poverty and in support of the victims and survivors of the Stardust fire in 1981, among many others. He supported the hunger strikers and other political prisoners in the 1980s and in more recent years, signed the petitions gathered by Ireland's Future calling for a citizens' assembly and referendum on Irish unity.

Moore became more aware of the causes of the conflict in the North during time he spent as folk singer in the early 1970s while learning songs that reflected universal struggle against oppression and injustice.

> In the late '60s in England, I was living a very nomadic life, meeting political activists with very diverse views. I encountered Communists, volunteers from the Spanish Civil War, ex-British Army soldiers, English and Scottish policemen, but I did not have any political philosophy. I listened and tried to learn.

On his return to Ireland, he formed Planxty with his childhood friend Donal Lunny, uilleann piper Liam Óg O'Flynn and Andy Irvine. Together they began a new movement in the development of Irish traditional music. Christy popularised songs such as 'Follow Me Up To Carlow' and 'Only Our Rivers Run Free' while gigging across the island in the early '70s.

After leaving Planxty, Moore continued to perform both as a solo singer and with a band that featured Jimmy Faulkner, Declan McNelis and Kevin Burke. He was central to the organisation of the first anti-nuclear festival at Carnsore Point in Wexford in August 1978 at which more than 20,000 protestors occupied the site where the Electricity Supply Board (ESB) planned to construct two nuclear power plants beside the sea on the south-east tip of Wexford. Moore organised and played many benefit gigs across the country to raise funds for the free three-day festival at which many of the top names in Irish traditional music – including The Bothy Band, Clannad, Mary Black and Mick Hanly – came to perform. Local farmers and residents, opposed to a nuclear power station in their midst, gave access to land, electricity and water. Anti-nuclear activists organised food supplies, a Córas Iompair Éireann (CIÉ) train from Dublin, sanitation, camping areas, erected marquees, education workshops, a creche, a stage and a sound system.

The event was a model of mass democracy with a coalition of environmentalists, left-wing activists, doctors, academics and trade unionists combining into a new movement, energised and led by young people, against nuclear power. It was a formative experience for those involved, many of whom went on to become household names in politics, the arts, media, theatre and music. Others went on to oppose attempts to commence uranium mining in Gleann Nimhe (Poisoned Glen) in County Donegal and to assist the survivors of the Chernobyl disaster.

Moore's first overt political engagement with the republican movement came with an invitation to visit the H-Blocks in the mid-

1970s. He was invited to engage with the 'blanket' protestors and to meet the prisoners seeking political status. He recalled:

> I made my first visit to the H-Blocks in 1976. I subsequently met Brendan McFarlane, who was commanding officer of the republican POWs. They were seeking to highlight their jail protest throughout the 26 counties.
>
> I agreed to join them in their efforts. I spent some time with Kieran Nugent, the first blanket man who commenced his protest in 1976. I also met both Fra McCann and Ned Behan upon their release from Long Kesh. After spending time with them, hearing about their experiences, I wrote and recorded '90 Miles to Dublin'. Subsequently, I recorded the *H Block* album, which was well received in certain quarters. The album launch at The Brazen Head, Dublin was raided by the Special Branch, which confiscated the albums. Others who contributed to the album included Stephen Rea, who read two poems by Bobby Sands, Matt Molloy, Mick Hanly, Anne and Francie Brolly, Tony MacMahon, Noel Hill and Tony Linnane. [Moore performed songs from a remastered version of the album which was launched at a private event in the Felon's Club in west Belfast in November 2021 to mark 40 years since the hunger strike. It was attended by former hunger strikers and republican prisoners and their families.]

Along with Lunny, Moore gathered a number of well-known musicians to form Moving Hearts. 'Moving Hearts was conceived with Donal Lunny's interest in developing new music and in new lyrics. The first one to join us was Declan Sinnott, then came Keith Donald. We were the most politically motivated members of Moving Hearts,' Christy recalled.

They were joined by Eoghan O'Neill, Davy Spillane and Brian Calnan. Their mix of contemporary, electric and traditional sound, with lyrics that reflected the burning political issues of the day, won a large and enthusiastic audience after they emerged in 1981. In an atmosphere of censorship and repression, it took courage to perform some of the songs made popular by Moving Hearts. 'No Time for Love' became an anthem for many people in those troubled times. Moore, however, is modest:

> I don't know if I'd view it as courageous. We found it vital and exciting for our music to be relevant and real. Emotions were high around the music of Moving Hearts. Forty years on I still encounter people who express gratitude that we stood with them in their time of need.

As the seemingly endless conflict and war continued, Moore said he became angry and disillusioned at some of the actions of the IRA and other republican organisations:

> Enniskillen and Warrington; Patsy Gillespie strapped into a van loaded with explosives; Tom Oliver in the Cooley Mountains. It became impossible to support such attacks upon civilian non-combatants. I continued to sing the Bobby Sands songs. In 1984, I recorded an album called *The Spirit of Freedom*. This project was to raise funds towards transport for families visiting the H-Blocks.

With Lunny, Moore wrote 'On The Bridge', about the torture of women prisoners in Armagh jail, and 'The Time has Come', which described the grief of the families of hunger strikers who had died. Along the way, there were death threats as well as late-night encounters with the RUC and UDR in rural areas of the North. He said:

> I remember a night in 1972. Planxty were touring the North with the late John Martyn. We were stopped late one night by drunken uniformed men who were intimidating and very scary. Subsequently, there were death threats.

Another night, after an H-Block concert in Derry, I was singled out and held at an RUC/UDR roadblock. Heavily armed and aggressive, they knew the hotel where I was staying, even the room number. It was a time when H-Block activists were being murdered. I did not return to the Everglades Hotel but drove straight back to Sligo instead.

Over the past 30 years, Moore has continued to perform in venues around Ireland, the UK and Europe. Speaking to this author in July 2021 about 'North and South of the River', a song he wrote with members of U2, he reflected: 'With regard to a united Ireland, what strikes me today are yesterday's Twelfth of July bonfires, with the Irish tricolour in flames. Some people maintain that to be part of their culture. Can I reach out to those people? They appear to hate us and hate all belonging to us,' he said.

He has little doubt that the British government will desert the unionists when they no longer want or need them. 'I believe the Brits will pull out,' he said. 'That's when the shit will hit. Where will extreme loyalism turn when that day comes? There seems to be a shrinkage within the angry red-hot centre of those opposed to a united Ireland. Perhaps some hope can be gleaned from that.'

For Moore, it will be the younger generation who will design the future Ireland. They already have in the successful campaigns for marriage equality and women's rights of recent years, as they did with the anti-nuclear protests and various political campaigns of previous years. He is hopeful for the future for the people of the island:

> I would like to see a new, inclusive island free of poverty, oppression and injustice. But I'm 76. My music means a lot to me, to the people around me, to my own age group and there are increasing numbers of younger listeners coming to hear the songs. It is not for me to say what young people should do. Seems like many are

doing very well. Their minds are more open than ours back in youthful times. Our grandchildren have a keen awareness of world affairs, of the environment. They think and talk more freely now. Our young minds were chain fettered.

19

BUILDING THE ALL-ISLAND ECONOMY

T he debate over energy has continued long since the nuclear option was rejected in Ireland in the early 1980s. Massive protests were staged across Ireland, Europe and the US, there were a series of fatal accidents and leaks, and the industry was unable to find a way to safely dispose of its radioactive waste. Forty years later, concerned and angry young people in Ireland and across the world are now protesting about the threat posed by climate change to the future of humanity and are demanding that governments meet the targets required to reduce global temperatures in the race to save the planet.

As wildfires raged across Greece, Siberia and the west coast of the US in mid-August 2021, and life-threatening heatwaves, heavy rainfall and droughts continued across the continents, the Intergovernmental Panel on Climate Change (IPCC) issued a report warning that 'human interference in the climate system is affecting both the frequency and severity of such events'. The report, issued just months ahead of COP26, a planned, global climate summit in Glasgow, Scotland in November 2021, stated that 'All greenhouse gases matter if we are to limit human-induced climate warming … it is only by reducing emissions to net zero by mid-century and subsequent net negative emissions that warming will likely be kept below 2C.'

In its 2021 National Climate Action Plan, the Irish government acknowledged the existential crisis facing humanity and aimed for a climate neutral economy by 2050. For many concerned about the future of the planet, however, it was not visionary enough to deal with the challenges of the present, never mind the future. Promoting onshore and offshore wind farming, investing in more public bus and train travel and cycle lanes, pedestrianising city centres and banning short haul flights where possible, were proposed by climate change activists as further measures. Moving away from intensive beef and dairy farming, revitalising small farms and coastal communities, and encouraging biodiversity and recycling were also among the myriad of ideas environmental activists in Ireland put forward, much to the discomfort of the big agri-food lobbies and their government allies.

By 2020, wind energy provided over 30 per cent of the total energy supply for the island and 85 per cent of Ireland's renewable electricity. Huge state-supported investment is required to utilise the potential of offshore wind power facilities and the connection of renewable energy production with other countries in the EU. The NI protocol provided for the uninterrupted functioning of the Single Electricity Market to ensure the continuation of energy supply across the island, including that provided by renewables. However, according to industry sources, a single island economy and administration will avert future jurisdictional challenges to the development of onshore and offshore wind farming.

Other measures to mitigate climate change and to enhance all-island co-operation include the commitment to improving rail links between North and South. Among the proposals included in the 2020 Programme for Government was a review of high-speed rail links between Belfast and Dublin and on to Cork and Limerick at a potential cost of €15 billion. The New Decade, New Approach agreement contained a similar commitment. In July 2021, engineering consultancy Arup was appointed to conduct the All-Island Strategic Rail Review on behalf of both transport ministers, Eamon Ryan in Dublin and Nichola Mallon in Belfast.

David McWilliams advocated for the development of an all-island infrastructure for rail, broadband and housing to prepare for unification. He is confident that lower interest rates, which are expected to continue across the EU for several years to come, will permit governments to borrow to invest in major reconstruction programmes, just as the Biden administration has commenced in the US. In an article for the *Irish Times* on 5 December 2020, McWilliams wrote:

> Looking ahead 50 years, the reunification of the country makes the Dublin–Belfast corridor by far the most populous part of the country. More than half of the whole island will live in that parcel of coastal land, extending 30 km inland from the sea and stretching south to north from Bray to Ballymena. ...
>
> To combat the economic supremacy of this highly-urban, densely-populated eastern seaboard of the new-island economy, the rest of the country must be opened up all the way down the west, from Derry to Cork. This will take planning, significant infrastructure investment and a transport system that links all nodes of the country.
>
> All-island infrastructure has not been considered for 100 years. Today, we must start building and not stop building until this island has an integrated public transport system that cuts rail time between Belfast and Cork (a distance of 420km) to less than one-and-a-half hours. ...
>
> A combination of global warming demanding more efficient modes of public transport and a new attractive system will coax people to change their habits. A new transport system will change our personal mental maps of the island.

McWilliams also promoted the idea of moving Dublin Port to a new site at Bremore or somewhere closer to Drogheda, in order to free up land for the development of high-density housing and a new city on the sea front. In the midst of a major housing crisis, deepened by a pandemic that further delayed the provision of new homes across the country, accessing state land for affordable and social housing is now a priority. In June 2021, the ESRI called on the government to immediately double its annual capital investment on housing to €4 billion in order to build 18,000 homes, still well below the required demand for more than 30,000 homes in a year. It also called on the government to then use the current low cost of borrowing to run an annual budget deficit of €4–7 billion or 1.5 per cent of GDP, to build up to 28,000 houses each year to resolve the housing crisis. Kieran McQuinn, the author of the ESRI report said that 'while there are many pressing demands for additional state capital investment, without significant investment in residential construction, we risk experiencing another decade of inadequate housing supply and resulting upward pressure on residential prices and rents'.

In September, the government unveiled its 'Housing for All' plan involving the construction of over 300,000 social, affordable and private housing within 10 years. Critics of the plan claimed that there was no clear roadmap as to how the targets would be met and that there was a danger that, once again, public lands, which should be exclusively used to deliver affordable public housing, would be gifted to the private sector. Meanwhile, the rental crisis worsened and house prices escalated as the supply of new homes failed to meet the growing demand. In the North, house prices were a fraction of the cost south of the border, although a failure to build social and affordable homes for lower income groups in recent decades had contributed to a growing rental and housing crisis for young working people and families.

Earlier in 2021, McWilliams hosted the launch of a major study carried out by researchers from Ulster University and Dublin City University on the development of the Dublin–Belfast economic corridor in a project supported by eight local authorities from both sides of the border. The report found that the region had a population in excess of two million people and was younger and more diverse than any other part of the country, with 15 per cent born outside of Ireland. It also had the best educated workforce, with 34 per cent of the population holding third-level qualifications.

Speaking at the online launch of the report, Tánaiste Leo Varadkar said that partition had divided the region, and with two million people living along the corridor, there was now an opportunity to work together rather than apart:

> It's not just about Dublin, Belfast; it's everything in between. To a certain extent, because of the events of 100 years ago, these two major urban centres, this major economic corridor, was split and turned their backs on each other in a way. I would like that to turn around.

Finance minister at Stormont, Conor Murphy, then said that:

> local authorities had been trying to improve the synergy between the two cities since partition and that the pooling of assets would be very beneficial.
>
> There is a huge opportunity to market the areas as one, to recognise the potential of the growth of the population there and the diversity and the economic strength of both cities. We should be looking at a real strong connection between Derry, through Belfast to Dublin and Cork.

The development of the all-island economy and the eastern corridor were also promoted by the Irish Business and Employers Confederation (Ibec) in its detailed submission to the mid-term review of the government's 10-year National Development Plan. It called for a ten-fold increase in the €500 million that the Taoiseach, Micheál Martin, had committed to the Shared Island fund over the remaining years of the plan.

The trade union movement also moved to acknowledge the growing debate on constitutional change arising from Brexit and the NI protocol. The Irish Congress of Trade Unions (ICTU or Congress) – with 800,000 members across the island, including in unionist and loyalist communities of the North – maintained its cohesion through the worst years of the conflict and during the divisive referendum on Brexit. It argued that it was in the interests of workers across Ireland to remain in the EU and subsequently lobbied against a hard Brexit that could damage the interest of its members, particularly in the agri-food and other industries exporting to the UK. Its representatives (along with those from Ibec) attended the regular dialogues of the Shared Island Unit.

In a June 2021 video interview organised by IF and hosted by this writer, ICTU General Secretary Patricia King outlined the importance of building the all-island economy in the interests of all workers across the country. A motion reaffirming the support of Congress for the Good Friday Agreement, to develop policy on a unity referendum, and the need to strengthen the all-island economy was prepared for the biennial conference of the union in Belfast in October 2021.

Meanwhile, in the early summer of 2021, Trade Unionists for a United Ireland (TUNUI) – formed in 2019 by members of different unions on both sides of the border – published its *Vision for a New and United Ireland*. In his foreword, the chair, Gerry Murphy – a SF member who was also serving as president of the ICTU and writing in a personal capacity – said that 'the interests of working people, their families and society are best served by the ending of partition and the creation of new all-Ireland economic and social models' and that the TUNUI proposals, 'such as an all-Ireland National Health Service, a Just Transition to tackle climate change and collective bargaining rights are in line with the proposals made by the ICTU in its "No Going Back" document released in May 2020'.

In 'No Going Back', the ICTU's May 2020 policy paper, the organisation warned government and employers that the lessons of the Covid-19 crisis must be learned. In the future, it demanded, vulnerable workers on the front line in healthcare, transport, retail and meat processing must be protected and their collective bargaining and other rights enhanced. Poor, unsafe working conditions, low pay and the absence of sick leave provisions for workers in meat factories, which remained open through the lockdowns, led to a wave of infections among the, largely migrant, workforce. The paper set out a vision for workers' rights, including the legal right to collective bargaining and an end to conditions of low pay and precarious work in which almost 25 per cent of workers across the island are trapped. Published in response to the Covid-19 pandemic, and dysfunctional housing and childcare provision, No Going Back set out the ICTU's plans for a universal public healthcare system free at the point of use, a massive public investment programme in public housing construction on public lands and a high-quality public service for early years care and education. It also sought increased education spending at all levels to tackle the lowest levels of per-pupil spending and the highest pupil–teacher ratio levels in primary schools across the EU, as well as the consistently high number of children from disadvantaged communities leaving secondary school early.

In early September 2021, the British government announced that it was going to further extend the grace period before the full implementation of the protocol for another three months and beyond its expiry in October, in a unilateral move that was, nevertheless, anticipated by the EU. Announcing the decision, David Frost said that it allowed for more time for further discussions with the EU to mitigate the damaging impact of the protocol on trade between the UK and NI. In response, the EU noted that the decision was in breach of the Withdrawal Agreement, but it did not propose any retaliatory sanction. It confirmed that there would be no renegotiation of the Brexit deal or the protocol, but postponed any showdown with the UK government and took the wind out of unionist plans to intensify its campaign against the Irish Sea border.

Secretary of State Brandon Lewis, however, managed to upset both unionists and nationalists, and UN human rights advocates with his proposals to proceed with legislation that would grant an amnesty for all conflict-related killings in the North carried out before 1998, and to halt coroner inquests and other investigations into them. Human rights activists in the North claimed that the scheme was intended to protect the security forces and their agents inside loyalist paramilitary organisations from exposure and to prevent a detailed examination of how the secret state prolonged the conflict. Up to 1,000 cases – brought by relatives of people killed and survivors of armed attacks in which British police, soldiers and agents were culpable – were in legal process; cases that were based on evidence collected by Relatives for Justice and other groups over decades. IRA and loyalist paramilitaries would also be covered by the amnesty.

Fabián Salvioli, UN special rapporteur on the promotion of truth, justice, reparation and guarantees of non-recurrence, and Morris Tidball-Binz, special rapporteur on extra-judicial, summary or arbitrary executions also condemned the amnesty proposal. In an August 2021 *Irish Times* article they said that the planned amnesty, 'forecloses the pursuit of justice and accountability for the serious human rights violations committed during the Troubles and thwarts victims' rights to truth and to an effective remedy for the harm suffered, placing the United Kingdom in flagrant violation of its international obligations.'

Notwithstanding the protection it purported to offer IRA volunteers, senior Sinn Féin adviser Stephen McGlade said that republicans rejected the plan and insisted that the small number of former IRA members who might benefit from an amnesty, did not support it either. 'The majority, if not all, of the republicans that I know from that generation have served time and lengthy prison sentences. I don't think there are many republicans from that era who see any benefit from it,' he said.

It was no coincidence, he added, that the proposed new laws came after the families of those killed in 1971 by the Parachute Regiment in Ballymurphy, Belfast, finally learned the truth of what had happened to their loved ones through a coroner's inquest. In an interview with this author, McGlade argued:

> What the British Tories are proposing will deny families access to the truth through inquests. They are basically seeking a blackout of the entire judicial process. When you think about the relationship between the state and citizens, what does this say? It's a matter of truth and justice. The Ballymurphy families for instance secured a coroner's inquest to get the truth. The British government now wants to shut down all judicial processes which would ordinarily be open to any citizen in a modern state because they don't want the truth revealed about their role in the conflict.

He pointed to the lawyers, academics and human rights activists from the nationalist community who are leading the campaign for truth and justice, and are committed to exposing the role of the British state:

> There is an educated professional class of nationalists whose parents endured the conflict and who are now practising lawyers and academics. They have been able to identify the routes and avenues to successfully access the truth and they're committed to exposing the role of the British state in the communities from which their parents came by expertly advocating for clients in our courts of law. They represent ordinary civilians whose families have been grossly, brutally and unjustly trespassed upon by the state.
>
> The British are taking these measures to shut down judicial processes and access to justice. This is all about exploiting their power and control. At the moment, the British state has jurisdictional control in the North and they are putting the stains

of history to bed while they can and before a negotiation opens up on the constitutional future.

McGlade explained how, through a series of negotiations over the decades since the GFA, republicans, other parties and campaigning groups have forced concessions on a range of issues, including the demand for an Irish language act from the British government. These are central to the achievement of parity of esteem for the wider nationalist and non-unionist people in the North, he argued. The Dublin government, he said, including minister Simon Coveney and his officials, have also recognised that Irish citizens in the North are as passionate about their identity, heritage and culture as people in the rest of the country.

Achieving Acht na Gaeilge is a key issue for SF and the wider nationalist community because of the guarantees they received in the negotiations for the GFA. McGlade said:

> The issue is hugely symbolic but it's also a practical expression of the compromise within the agreement which on one hand was about parity of esteem for nationalists and the principal of consent to satisfy the unionists. For the last two decades, the principal of consent issue has been very much maintained but the issue of parity of esteem wasn't. People who would consider themselves moderate nationalists felt very much that things weren't moving at a quick enough pace in terms of parity of esteem. When Paul Givan, the DUP minister, scrapped the bursary for children to learn Irish in Donegal, that was the tipping point for even moderate nationalists.

It took a new secretary of state, Julian Smith, to force the DUP back into the power-sharing government after it lost the balance of power it enjoyed at Westminster and the support of the Brexiteers in the Tory party. Smith, one of the few Remain voters in the Boris Johnson administration, had, as McGlade put it, a 'more educated understanding' of the issues in the North than many of his predecessors or his successor and current secretary of state, Brandon Lewis.

Smith publicly met with Irish language campaigners and civic society groups and apparently did not disguise his impatience with the DUP, with whom he had dealt previously during its confidence and supply agreement under Theresa May. He frequently met with SF and other parties without any Northern Ireland Office (NIO) officials present. McGlade said:

> Julian Smith came to the job with a more educated understanding and was willing to politically engage. He was prepared to meet with any amount of people including the Irish language activists. He had a different approach to his predecessor, Karen Bradley, and was not wholly dependent on the NIO officials and their agenda.
>
> Previously, he had dealt with the DUP during the whole confidence and supply period, and the impression we got was that he had tolerated the arrogance of the DUP at Westminster and he wasn't going to entertain the same behaviour or attitudes while he was in Belfast.

According to a number of people who have spoken to him, Smith has expressed privately his view that the days of British rule in the North are numbered. During his time as secretary of state, he spent a lot of time in Dublin, where his wife worked with state broadcaster RTÉ. In contrast, McGlade said, Brandon Lewis has a narrow English nationalist agenda and has been a dishonest broker since he took over as secretary of state:

> Lewis has been dishonest with the public since he took on the role. He walked away from commitments made by his government on dealing with the legacy of the past through legislating for the key elements of the Stormont House Agreement and flouted his duty as regards 'rigorous impartiality' as a co-guarantor of the GFA.

He said publicly that the protocol did not represent a border in the Irish Sea and there would be no checks, when evidently there are. Like Boris Johnson, he will do and say anything to get through a week, and a week is a long time in politics. Like every British Secretary of State before him, he has political ambitions elsewhere and his main function is to soothe the Brexit protocol challenges.

Over the years of stop-start government in the North, SF and the other parties have achieved some significant changes to the structure and operation of the civil service, including the manner of appointments to senior positions. Through at least seven series of negotiations, over more than two decades, the pro-union influence has been weakened in the heart of government in the North. From the time that Stormont was prorogued in 1972, the permanent secretaries in the NIO controlled all aspect of government administration and chose who to run it. New regulations and appointment protocols have transformed that practice. Now, nationalists, or those from a Catholic demographic, have taken up some of the highest positions in the civil service, the judiciary and government administration. McGlade explained:

> When the new state of Northern Ireland and partition were imposed in the early '20s, the British officials didn't leave Dublin Castle and go back to London. They went to Belfast and established the Northern state, the old Stormont regime and the civil service. The different pillars of the state included the 'Protestant parliament for the Protestant people', the judiciary, the civil service, the police and the Orange Order. Over the last number of decades, and with the repeal of the 1920 Government of Ireland Act as part of the Good Friday Agreement, there has been further erosion of the different pillars of the Orange state, including the police and the judiciary.
>
> When the old Stormont collapsed in the '70s and direct rule was introduced, the British set up a system of administration

with permanent secretaries running government departments. That was the status quo for well over 30 years until devolution and power-sharing were established. The British secretary and their ministers of state came over once a week and rubber-stamped things, so those permanent secretaries were the power base running a dysfunctional state. They were also responsible for devising policies of oppression in every shape and form during the conflict.

Despite resistance by these powerful civil servants, much of the administration and running of public services was outsourced to 'arms-length' public bodies. In McGlade's view, many of these senior civil service personnel are not fully signed up to the concept of self-determination envisaged in the GFA and are committed to the union rather than neutral on the constitutional status of NI.

McGlade cited the appointments of solicitor Barra McGrory as Director of Public Prosecutions, John Larkin as Attorney General, and Declan Morgan as Chief Justice and his successor Siobhan Keegan, as examples of people from a Catholic background reaching the top jobs in the administration of justice in the North. Just as the balance of power has changed in the executive and assembly where the unionists have lost their political majority, the senior civil service is also becoming more broadly reflective of the diverse communities in the North.

Under the New Decade, New Approach agreement, which restored the power-sharing executive, SF and the other four main parties made reform of the civil service a key commitment. The DUP did not resist this pressure as it was included as a recommendation in the report by Judge Patrick Coghlin into the Renewable Heating Incentive scandal that had caused serious political damage to the party and its leader, Arlene Foster. But as McGlade said:

The biggest resistance to reform invariably comes from within the civil service itself, rather than politicians. Conor Murphy, as minister for finance and in charge of personnel across the civil service is leading this major project of reform. It will be one of the key tasks for Jayne Brady, the newly appointed Head of the Civil Service.

After years of being accused by political opponents, North and South, of seeking to undermine the power-sharing institutions, SF, said McGlade, is more determined to ensure that they function efficiently and reflect the needs of all communities in the North:

> I don't see any contradiction between being opposed to the British state jurisdiction here, while wanting fully functional democratic, representative political institutions at regional and local government level. The people pay tax and deserve nothing less than locally accountable politicians to deliver on their behalf. The difference between Stormont today and previous iterations is that it is now representative of the entire community and its function is to provide political leadership and deliver public services on an equal basis. The old regime and the civil servants who ran it were developing policies which imposed unfair, unequal treatment on the nationalist population, denying services yet taking taxes from them. Not now, that's done.

This does not conflict, he argued, with the SF strategy of promoting the debate around Irish unity and the working out of the commitment to a referendum contained in the GFA:

> Brexit has been the catalyst for constitutional change. Until this point, SF has been a minority voice but now FG and all the mainstream parties on the island, bar the unionists, share a consensus that it is coming. The *Claire Byrne Show* on RTÉ television [in March 2021] was the public manifestation of that.

Micheál Martin is behind public opinion, but he doesn't care because his priority is to get through his term in office as Taoiseach. He's not interested in a vision for the future or preparing for it.

SF has also been accused of not declaring its hand on what a united Ireland would look like in the event of a vote for unity. Again it comes back to the GFA, McGlade argued:

> The Agreement is not going to disappear. The core elements of it, including equality and human rights protections for minority communities, are of critical importance. It is only a matter of time before the unionists realise that those protections will be to their advantage because they will be the minority community. The guarantees within the GFA are very important and must be sustained so everybody has equal treatment and protection within the island.
>
> The core tenets and the strands are in place, including the equality and human rights protections and the principles of consent and parity of esteem. Now unionists have to deal with their loss of a majority, and we need to get a consensus on the future and that will have to be worked out. I'm certain a referendum will happen during this decade. Clearly, the objective of republicans is to secure a united Ireland, but we can't afford an echo chamber with nationalists and republicans talking to themselves. We need to be listening to those who are opposed.
>
> No unionist party is going to be advocating for Irish unity and I don't think that people of a unionist political outlook are persuadable until a date is set and it's in front of us all. That is 20 per cent of the population of the whole island. It is less than a third of the electorate in the North, and you now have people of a moderate disposition going towards Alliance. They see the DUP moving further to the right and the UUP have become less relevant.

When it comes to a vote on the protocol in 2024, Alliance will have a key influence. During the Brexit negotiations, the EU and British government agreed that the Assembly can decide by a straight, majority vote, if the protocol should continue. It was another blow to unionism, which wanted a cross-community vote which would require their support for the proposal.

The Tories deliberately negotiated that with the EU as a straight vote in the assembly, in favour or against the protocol continuing. The complaint of the unionists is that it should have been by parallel consent and cross-community vote, which excludes Alliance. The democratic consent vote in 2024, in my opinion, is going to end up being like a mini-border poll, a prelude to a referendum.

In campaigning for a unity vote, SF will highlight the need for an all-island national health service, the promise of full and immediate re-entry into the EU for people in the North and a progressive system of education that serves all communities, McGlade said:

The health service needs to be a number one priority. Covid-19 put the NHS under severe pressure and exposed the total under-investment of the health service in the North by the Tories for the best part of a decade. At the same time, citizens can rely on it as a free, universal service. What we need to do is take the good bits of the NHS and combine them with Sláintecare. We need proper investment by the Irish government in a national health service, free at the point of delivery. The immediate entry of a unified Ireland to the EU, with all the rights and privileges that it entitles people to, is another selling point, not least for those of a unionist tradition or a British identity in the North.

He said that SF will should seek to develop a single state education system for all communities, one that provides choice to people who want their ethos, culture, history and language reflected in the school curricula:

> The most divisive factor in the North remains segregation and sectarianism. One of the ways to tackle it and confront it, day to day, is through integrated and shared education models. For instance, in Omagh you have the example of six secondary level schools coming together from different backgrounds in shared education. At the same time, people should not be denied the choice to access another medium of education, whether it is private or Irish language provision. What we can't have is a separate state system of education for different communities.

For businesspeople, the dramatic increase in trade in goods across the border since Brexit and the protocol has highlighted the potential advantages of the all-island economy. Some unionists with whom McGlade works at Stormont have described to him with excitement their experience of holidaying in the South over the past year:

> In the North's business community, more and more people are now investing in, and not just visiting, the South, including in hospitality and manufacturing. People can see the opportunities like never before. We're going through a market adjustment on the island. More people from the unionist community travelled south because of Covid-19 and the restrictions on international travel and people from the South came to the North in big numbers. I am talking to people daily who are telling me about their experiences of visiting parts of the island they had never seen before. I'm a republican from Tyrone and I know my country, and here they are telling me I should visit all these wonderful places down south.
>
> This is happening outside of the institutional prism and is welcome. It is happening through these social and the cultural exchanges. We have two societies on one island. It is the politics

that divides us [but] what unites us is the arts, sports and culture. That is what bonds us – GAA, Irish Rugby, our love for music, and so on.

He said that, in his view, there is likely to be a transition period following a unity vote when many issues such as the national debt, pensions, public finances and social welfare will have to be negotiated between the two sovereign governments:

> For people in the public service, in business and other sectors, another issue of concern is their pensions. That will be part of a negotiation process, like in South Africa after apartheid when they had an interim constitution and a transitional parliament for five years, during which they negotiated the national debt, pensions and public finances.
>
> There has to be a transition period here as well. First of all, we must inform people before a referendum on 'What you're voting for,' and … a period of transition where you fine-tune and integrate the public systems across the island. It is about integration, not the North being absorbed into the South. We are talking about a new state, and I think everybody who has a stake in that has to be involved in negotiating what that looks like.
>
> I also think there is a huge danger, when you get into the transition period, that big corporates and the private sector will be trying to push their interests. It is another a lesson to be learnt from South Africa in terms of the loans they took from the IMF [International Monetary Fund] and all the difficulties they got themselves into with the oil barons and other corporate interests. They were trying to determine their economic policies and that is something that has to be done with eyes wide open. They were focused on the politics and the economic interests came in sideways. The ANC [African National Congress] made a flawed

error by bringing in certain economists to work as part of the transitional government. They sold themselves short and were left with a massive sovereign debt for years. It was the poor and weakest who paid the price.

It is another reason, McGlade argued, that preparation for a united Ireland should begin in an organised, systemic way involving a Green and White Paper by the government in Dublin. The Green Paper would set out the constitutional, political, social and economic vision, which would be followed by a citizens' assembly to discuss its contents. He envisaged a White Paper establishing the agreed specifics on policy, constitutional and legislative changes leading to a constitutional convention involving civic society and political parties across the island. The biggest civic organisation on the island is the trade union movement and as a member of a union, he can see the vital contribution it can make.

In McGlade's view, FF and FG were taken by surprise by the rapidly changing political situation, particularly since Brexit, while SF has been preparing for it:

> I think that the establishment and the main parties, FF and FG who helped to negotiate and support the GFA and the principle of consent, did not fathom how things would change so dramatically in 25 years. I don't think they had thought that unionists down the line would be a minority community within a quarter of a century. They didn't foresee that coming so quickly and they now realise that we are ahead of them in relation to the change that is coming down the tracks.

McGlade cited the Convention on the Constitution that was established by the Irish government and that met between 2012 and 2014. It included representatives of the parties in the North, although unionist representatives did not attend, and it led to the subsequent referendums that introduced marriage equality and abortion rights in the South:

The constitutional convention was all-Ireland. The nationalists and Alliance party took part and the unionist parties refused. SF has debated this and arrived at the conclusion an all-island citizens' assembly should consult and respond to the government Green Paper setting out options and ideas. The government should then prepare a White Paper which would set out the proposals for a new Ireland, having had the input from all quarters concerned.

An electoral commission has to put out the facts and the information for citizens to know what they are voting about in the referendum. Preparation and planning could take at least three years before you have the referendum. You're also talking about a new constitutional framework to govern the affairs of the state, and to also safeguard citizens' rights in law.

Nobody will focus until the date for a referendum is set. For instance, the 30th anniversary of the GFA in 2028, which might be a date. We've learned from the shambles of the Tory Brexit process that preparation and planning in advance of the referendum is key. The period afterwards is also critical to negotiate issues like public finances, economic models, investment, services and to get the public administration established.

The EU will have a central role in any negotiation. They bring the pivotal experience from German reunification, integration and accession of member states. I think everybody needs to come to the table with their priorities. No party, including SF, is going to determine every issue. It is going to be a transition process and all these things have to be dealt with thematically, as part of the negotiations.

Both an open-mind and an open-hand by the main political and civic leaders and the people who share this island themselves is what will count. There can be no victories. Then the process of reconciliation and nation-building begins for us all.

20

AN END TO HISTORY

Brian Keenan is best known for enduring over four years as a hostage of the Islamic Jihad, linked to Hezbollah, in Lebanon before his release in 1990. Keenan was raised among the Protestant working class of east Belfast. He lived close to singer Van Morrison, who grew up in an identical terraced house a few streets way, on Cyprus Avenue, and not far from where the Reverend Ian Paisley lived with his family in a Bible belt of evangelical missions.

After completing his A levels at Orangefield, a liberal secondary school, Keenan chose to study literature at the University of Ulster in Coleraine and to discover a different Ireland than the one he was born into in loyalist east Belfast:

> I went to Coleraine because it was away from home and because it offered you a range of subjects within the literature department that Queen's didn't offer, where I could read the American writers. I studied philosophy, history, folklore and I even took a course in the European neo-realist cinema which explored the ethics of the post war world so imaginatively different from my own.
>
> The majority of my friends were all Catholic. Before then, I didn't know about Gaelic literature, about Irish music, but I got to

know it, because I liked the people. In a sense you found what you didn't know was stolen from you.

He discovered a sense of belonging to a community, a culture that was different to the one he had grown up with – an Irish culture:

> At school, I was taught the birth dates and the death dates of a long line of English kings and queens, and I don't remember any of them. My geography lessons were all about the shoe industry in Nottingham or wherever. I had to learn all the rivers that flowed down through England. But what I found at university was something that wasn't being taught to me but was being offered to me in a sense. It was all there: music, culture, talk. You could sit down with a complete stranger and talk about something really meaningful in terms of books and writers.

After leaving college and working in temporary jobs in London and Brussels, Keenan went to teach English in the Basque country:

> By that time, the Troubles were very hot and heavy in the mid-'70s. I came home and decided there was no point in going back. I don't know why. I'm not politically motivated in that sense. Maybe to be witness to the catastrophe is better than being part of it. I decided to stay in Belfast, and I went back to teach in Orangefield.
>
> The boys I was teaching for O levels had no more interest in WB Yeats than I had in a rubber bicycle tyre. They were able to talk about the politics of the streets. The atmosphere had changed totally in the school because of the atmosphere in the streets. I even remember some kid being pulled into the then headmasters office because he brought a gun into school, this boy of 14. I stayed there for the year and then I just thought, 'What's the point? There's nobody interested here.'

On completing a post-graduate course in community development in Aberdeen, Scotland, Keenan returned to Belfast. He worked as a community worker for three years in his home turf of east Belfast and then on the Shankill Road in Protestant west and north Belfast. Soon after he started work on the Shankill, the chair of one community group asked him whether he was a Catholic due to his surname:

> The man, who would have been in his 60s, he took me aside and he said, 'Excuse me, Brian, can I ask you a question? Are you a Catholic?' because of the name Keenan. And I said, 'No, I'm not.' 'I just needed to clear that up,' he said.
>
> The problems that I encountered as a community worker on the Shankill Road were kind of no different than they were on the Falls. Probably worse on the Shankill Road, actually, because, apart from Jackie Redpath [a prominent community worker and now chair of the Shankill Road Partnership], they didn't have an articulate voice. There was huge unemployment. The housing should have been knocked down. There was a great sense of community, but it was rapidly undermined by an insidious sectarianism. If the nationalist areas got something, then the loyalists had to get something in return. Such attitudes only reinforced a 'them and us' division.

Some of those in leadership were members of the loyalist UDA and UVF, but efforts to improve their communities met with a wall of inaction at City Hall, where the city had been controlled for decades by the main unionist parties:

> The members of the UVF (or UDA) wouldn't tell you they were members, but I knew because everybody knew. These were their streets. You would kind of talk to them and if this is what they wanted to do, we could discuss, 'How do you want to go about doing it?' The problem was, when you got groups in these areas

to be able to articulate whatever it was they wanted, they went to a council in the City Hall, which was just divided by sectarianism. The main attitude in the council was, 'We're not giving that to them because they're Catholics.'

Community work definitely wasn't getting anywhere, but the city also wasn't going anywhere. It was almost as if it had blown up any kind of impetus for meaningful structural change. Any that was there was soon knocked on the head by those that didn't want it. It was a city that was going nowhere, and I just wanted out. You were supposed to be doing this work and devising these programmes, but nobody really wanted them.

In the early 1980s, Keenan took a job teaching English in Beirut. The Lebanese capital was also struggling with a legacy of colonial rule, civil and religious conflict and recurrent invasions by Israeli forces along their border and into the sprawling Palestinian refugee camps in the city. In 1986, he was kidnapped. 'I went from the frying pan into the fire,' he said.

Keenan travelled on his Irish passport to Lebanon, and his family and friends found a more willing ear in Dublin during their four-year campaign to free him from captivity than they received from the British government. Although reluctant at first, the Department of Foreign Affairs was more active in seeking Keenan's release through various diplomatic channels and by promoting his Irish citizenship.

Following his return in 1990, Keenan wrote of his hellish experience in the beautifully written and extraordinary book *An Evil Cradling*, which recounts the mistreatment and torture he and English journalist John McCarthy endured at the hands of their captors. Keenan settled in Dublin, where he has since lived with his wife, Audrey, and two children. A regular visitor to Belfast and to his sisters and their families, Keenan noted the continuing failure to improve the educational and living standards for young people in east Belfast and other working-class loyalist communities despite the various peace agreements over the decades since he left. 'The people in these poor communities really never got anything,' he said. 'Some leaders in whatever paramilitary organisation were bought off to become community organisers and they got jobs set up for them, which was fair enough. But it didn't work.'

There is, in his view, a deeper cultural malaise that affects many Protestant people in the communities he left behind all those years ago. It also confirms for him the imperative of creating a new society on the island, which reflects its diversity and can realise its vast potential, not least for those who constantly fear that their identity is being threatened.

In the Protestant community and the Protestant people – what I know of them anyway – there is this inherent sense of precarious belonging. They know they belong there, but they don't know why, or they don't know how. They don't know where their roots are, so they're not too sure; they just know they come from Ulster or whatever. But this sense of precarious belonging is always subliminal. When you ask would-be Protestant loyalists who they are, they define who they are in the negative. They say 'I'm not a Republican,' or I'm not this, but they're not positive about who they are and if they try to say where they want to be or where they're going it's not very far.

There's the same politicians kicking around Ulster now that were there when I left it and that says an awful lot about progression being stopped, or someone throwing a cloak over things and calling it British, or calling it whatever they want without examining it. It's that sense of defining yourself in the negative which I think is a big burden.

If there's going to be … well I don't call it a 'united Ireland' any more, I call it an 'integrated Ireland', it is one where everybody belongs. One where everybody has a feeling and emotional attachment and also has some sort of vested interest in its future. I talk to loyalists now who have all retired from the game, or whatever, and they have a very real sense of being misled, of not getting their emotional inheritance to belong.

Maybe that's got to do with the very poor education system, things I was never taught I now know an awful lot about; the things that were withheld from me for certain reasons, I decided to reclaim. My needs to be a whole person were very urgent. The only person who could fill up the emptiness was yourself. So, apart from travelling geographically a lot, I travelled in mind and I experienced a lot because I felt I needed to.

It wasn't until I was in my 40s and 50s that I realised that there were some very, very good Protestant writers and there always have been. But most of them that I know of became writers because of a sense of disenchantment.

The idea that a British identity covers the experience of being a Protestant person from the North does not explain the sense of precarious belonging to which Keenan relates:

I'm not very sure about this thing, British. When I was working in London – it was one of these temporary jobs – it was myself, there was a guy who was Caribbean and another guy who was a kind of proto-Scots nationalist. The two of them said they were British, and I said, 'He's from the Caribbean and you're a rampant rebel from the Highlands.' I think it's just a term of convenience, covering something. It's like a conjurer's cape, it's thrown over things to cover them and you don't know what's happening underneath but you'd be able to pull a rabbit out of the hat when you take it away.

Keenan's view is that young people across the island, including those he meets on his visits to Ulster University in Coleraine, where he is a lifelong and honorary president of the Student's Union, want to see a new society of equals, a bill of rights, a continuation of the progressive social changes of recent years. They are also concerned with finding a decent job and home, and too often still look to the UK or further away for their future. Keenan said that there is already a significant integration between North and South, with over 70 million border crossings each year and a growing all-island economy. He asked:

> Is this country not already integrated? People are crossing the border because they want to, to an extent that it doesn't exist. I kind of think if people would concentrate on what's happening now, not what was ... What was, we can talk about as calamitous, a disaster, a mistake. It was probably relevant in its time, but we are in a time of fast-moving change; the nation state has long since been washed away.
>
> Writers talk about the end of history. I like that term because I think we need to put an end to history. That's not to say cast it into the oblivion, not to say it should be forgotten. The one thing missing in the declaration of human rights is the right to memory, so have your memory, cherish it and it might make you more whole, and empathetic, but I think we need to move on and grasp change. Memory is only meaningful when it is shared and understood. Shared memory is the way of empathy and that is the single most important element in being human.
>
> I think Ireland is on a cusp and it depends on what attitude you bring to it. If you think about change as being something positive, we could create something better, instead of thinking we have to adjust this part of history and we have to balance this with that. We are at the edge; we could be, if we choose to be, a renaissance. It is a new lease of thinking, a new lease of attitude. This united Ireland or integrated Ireland, or new Ireland cannot be a political decision, it has to be a public one. We have to be very careful about the nature of the dissemination of information around this. We need to create a critical mass of questions which can have the

effect of splitting the atom on our understanding and releasing a new world of possibility.

A Buddhist saying hangs on my wall. It reads, 'Yesterday is history and it is gone. Tomorrow is a mystery, yet to be. Today is a gift, receive it.' If we seize the gift of today, looking towards a new horizon, the mystery of tomorrow reveals itself as a prism of infinite possibility.

The first priority in any new configuration of the workings of this island is to put the idea of social justice at the very kernel and pumping heart of a bill of rights. Maybe we could have a convention of international jurors and legislators to advise on and draw a sample constitution that everybody can feel that they are no longer part of nineteenth-century political structures that don't solve twenty-first-century imperatives. The nation state is gone. We are connected to a global world that was never envisaged a century ago, we have a profound responsibility to the future which we never had before, and we should grasp it now.

In many respects I think we are already in an integrated Ireland. We should talk more about it. The conversations have to take place all over Ireland. We have to understand that partition and sectarianism are ghosts of our past who don't know that their time has passed. They should be left in ghost land. Partition needs to give way to pluralism. The vision needs to give way to diversity. And not just the mixing of two different things. Diversity and pluralism is a multiple thing, it's non-binary. We're taking in a lot here. We're already starting to do it in changes in gay laws and marriage equality and all of that.

Keenan insisted that change is both necessary and is coming but that people, North and South, and not just the unionists, are not prepared for it:

I'm not just talking about the North, because down here has to change drastically too, really drastically. If we're in this, we're all in this together and change is what we all participate in. We all drink from the same goblet. I do think things are naturally falling apart but that's where my worry is. There's nothing there to rebuild, there's no vision there, there's no idea, vision doesn't come easily to unionists.

Keenan proposed a major programme of spending, including on big, island-wide projects, with funding sourced from the EU, the US and Britain in the context of its departure from Ireland. These would include the construction of new rail links, such as between Derry and Cork (as proposed by John Hume three decades ago and others more recently), a national park, forestry, waterways and climate change initiatives.

The plans must commence now, Keenan said, and involve civic society making detailed proposals on how a transition to an integrated Ireland could take place. A lot of the fears among unionism have been deliberately instilled, among them the myth that the Republic is about to annex the North against its wishes. It has to be based on a common vision:

> I remember years ago talking to Gerry Adams, and he said to me that he might see a united Ireland in his lifetime, but if it does come about, it won't be the type of united Ireland that traditional nationalism or republicans have always thought about. And he was the first to admit that.
>
> We've a small island. It's uniquely established; it might have all sorts of different people but so what? That's all the better because it fertilises ideas, and we have the capacity, small numbers and land mass. We're unique within Europe that we can affect real meaningful long-term change and start the dominos falling and let the initiative or energy that comes from that happen.

The word 'revolution' to me still has meaning but it's a revolution in thinking I'm talking about, and we can do that. It's really, really possible to do that. You can do it brick by brick, like you're building a new house. I'm quite convinced that the possibilities here are greater than anywhere else. We just have to find the will. There's people who just won't budge and I'm not just talking about the North but people down here too.

I think there's a very rich culture here and it's not tainted by politics or history. We win awards for movies, for scriptwriting, for actors, for music. I don't ask or know who's Catholic or who's Protestant. The talent is very rich here and growing. Look at all these new books coming out of the North, including by young women.

For Keenan, change can hurt but the question is how it is managed to ensure the best outcome for the most people. More imaginative political and representative structures, including an all-island senate, with members chosen for their ability and talent, are required. Recent decades have shown how transformational change can happen when sufficient energies and resources are dedicated to it. The dismantlement of the RUC upset many of its former members and their allies, but it was essential to build a new and acceptable policing service for everyone. For decades, the British government insisted there was nothing wrong with policing in the North and then, following the political settlement in 1998, conceded 'that the RUC was rotten'.

During our discussion, Keenan concluded:

I'm not so sure about time healing. What it does is it leaves a scar. Those scars don't go away. Let people have their right to memory, I have no objections to that. But I do think, for example, if Chris Patten can come into the RUC and restructure the whole thing in a short time surely any change is possible?

Choice is the crown of life. Not to activate choice, and thus change, is not to be alive. It is the antithesis of life. We are born with eyes in the front of our heads so that we can always move forward. If we make some mistakes, so what? That is how we learn to make things better.

Following the Scottish election of May 2021, the SNP returned to power and as a result, many nationalists, including prime minister Nicola Sturgeon, now feel confident about the outcome of another independence referendum. Eddi Reader, one of Scotland's most popular performers, voted for the SNP in the election and has publicly supported the efforts by the Scottish people to gain independence from England.

Coming from a working-class family in Glasgow, Reader, like her father before her, had been a Labour voter. In an interview with this author in September 2021, she said:

> I was a Labour voter, my family worked in the shipyards and I went to all the Christmas parties organised by the trade unions. That's our background. None of us knew anybody who was anything other than that. ... Later, I was asked, Do you want an independent Scotland? Yes or no was the answer. It was only then I realised I was paying the same tax, living the same life, contributing the same but we had no influence over the decisions made for Scotland. I realised it wouldn't have mattered a fig what I voted for in Scotland – even if Scotland as a whole had voted for Labour – if England didn't want it.

In 2014 she campaigned for Scottish independence in a vote that was narrowly defeated by those supporting the union. Many of those who campaigned were convinced that a late, and carefully orchestrated, intervention by the Queen, who was staying at her Scottish estate in Balmoral just before the referendum, halted the nationalist tide. Reader recalled:

When we had the chance for independence, for me it felt like getting the keys to a new home: you've just stepped away from your father's house and for the first time you have to rely on your own ingenuity, your own creativity, your own money, your own pitfalls, and you had to go and experience it. On the day of the referendum, everyone felt buoyant. The Yes movement felt friendly and loving, peaceful. There was no grievance in it. The next day the unionists in England got their way. They managed to get the Queen to whisper at the church gates: 'Well I hope people will think very carefully about the future.' She's not supposed to get involved but she did.

Reader was in Glasgow the next day when gangs of mainly men waving the Union Jack harassed and assaulted Yes supporters on the streets. 'The day after the vote,' she said, 'I saw the rain, and I saw the aggro, and I thought, that's what the union does. This unfair, unequal, archaic, pre-democracy structure has given all of us this sense that there's a war rather than peace between us all. Across the UK, the prospect of change has forced many working-class communities to turn to the Tories, in what she described as the politics of fear:

They're very frightened and anything done with fear needs therapy, everything that is unlike fear is a loving direction, but all that fear has to come out and it has to be understood. It doesn't have to be a bad thing that you are not a magnificent conqueror, it can be all right to like your Queen that smells of roses and is a nice woman. It can be alright that you celebrate a thing which means you won a war sometime; that's okay, you can love it all. You're not dismissing one by being respectful of the other. That's what has to be taught. The young will get it before we get it, they have the opportunity to get it. As Leonard Cohen says, the crack is in their soul, the light will get in.

Some years ago, Reader discovered that her great uncle Seamus, a trade unionist and socialist from Glasgow, had delivered detonators and other weapons to James Connolly in Liberty Hall, Dublin in advance of the 1916 Rising. She has collected his extensive writings and is planning to publish a book on her uncle's activities, which eventually forced his exile to Dublin, where he died in 1969.

> I went through all my uncle Seamus's stuff which recounted how he was involved in the 1916 Rising. He was born Episcopalian in 1898 and had no Irish background. After the authorities found out what he and his comrades in Scotland were doing to help Connolly, they were in trouble on both counts. They were in trouble with the Free Staters after 1922, as well as with the British government. My uncle had to hide in Dublin from then until his death in 1969.

> It was never acknowledged that all those workers in Glasgow had filled their lunchboxes with detonators to send to James Connolly. It has not been accepted by Ireland or by Scotland. Seamus always stood up for the independence of small nations and obviously for a free Ireland. Nobody questioned it in 1916. It was just Ireland, there wasn't any north or south, it was just Ireland in entirety. It's kind of interesting we're still talking about it 100 years later.

> The same people who made the totally disastrous partitions in Pakistan and India and all over the world were responsible then. Even now with Scottish independence, a lot of the unionist mouthpieces will use the words 'partition of the UK' to describe what they think Scottish independence would be. It's a total distortion of what's going on.

The majority of English people are not responsible for the narrow-minded nationalism that has surfaced in recent years and led to the self-destructive Brexit vote, she said: 'The majority of English people don't have that feeling of superiority. It's a small minority that are very loud. The voice of the decent English person is very quiet.'

After independence, Reader said, the Scottish people will decide what type of society they want and, in her view, it will be one where no one is left behind:

> All we need is a key to the door and that's what the SNP will give us. I think if you guys in Ireland get your referendum, you get the key to the door. You can choose to be in love with any god or royalty or lordship or elitism that you want, but it will give people the chance of making that choice.
>
> We need safety nets in society because we can tell everybody; 'We love the fact that you're here and we're going to look after you from the cradle to the grave. No one is better than you and no one's worse than you.' When you say that to a child, that child will provide for you; that child will go to the ends of the earth loving you back and that's what you do with society. You nurture it that way. At the same time, human beings grow with challenge. I have faith in that at least.

21

CONTROVERSY AND PRAYER

In response to the continuing and unsettling effects of the protocol, the calls for a referendum and the instability within political unionism, a string of initiatives were unveiled to combat the perceived threat of a unity vote: Uniting UK, a pro-union lobby group, was formed by UUP councillor Philip Smith and others; another group, We Make NI, brought civic unionists together in a campaign to make the case for the North remaining within the UK; and former DUP leader Arlene Foster took on the role of chairperson of the Castlereagh Foundation, a British government-funded body agreed in the New Decade, New Approach deal which was aimed at creating 'a civic voice for those of us who are British', as reported in the *Belfast Telegraph* of 23 September 2020. Foster also joined arch-Brexiteer Nigel Farage as host of a show on the GB News television channel in order, as reported in the *Metro* in July 2021, 'to bring Northern Ireland politics into the mainstream'.

In the *Irish Times*, civil rights activist and commentator Emma DeSouza questioned the claim by the Taoiseach and others that discussion on Irish unity was premature and divisive given the preparations by unionism to defend the North's constitutional status:

Voicing support for the preservation of the United Kingdom is not condemned as 'divisive' or 'unhelpful' by political leaders, it is accepted as a legitimate position embedded into political discourse across these islands. So too should support for Irish unification be considered equivalently legitimate. There exists, at many levels, a real need to normalise the holding of and vocalising of such a position. The call to silence such views under the veil of 'not now' is no more than an attempt to undermine and delegitimise a key principle of the Belfast Agreement that confirms and recognises divergent political aspirations.

The 'others' or 'middle ground' in the North so often left out of the conversation are now set to be the kingmakers in any vote, and unionism knows it. While political leaders hold the line that a border poll is not imminent, unionism is clearly subscribed to the age-old adage of 'fail to prepare, prepare to fail' and by any measure, they are ahead of the curve. (*Irish Times*, 20 July 2021)

As the summer of 2021 came to a close, a fresh surge of infections from the Delta variant of Covid-19 generated 2,000 cases a day in the South and 1,500 in the North. Only the extensive roll out of vaccinations across the population averted a new wave of hospitalisations and ICU admissions in the South but a similarly successful programme in the North did not prevent serious pressure on hospital emergency facilities. Almost a year to the week of its traumatic Golfgate experience in August 2020, when a minister, other politicians, a senior judge and an EU commissioner were among 81 guests at a golf dinner in Galway, in breach of public health restrictions, the government fell victim to a similar Covid-19 related debacle. Tánaiste Leo Varadkar and other notables attended a function in the Merrion Hotel in Dublin hosted by former minister Katherine Zappone; more than 50 people were in attendance, in apparent breach of Covid-19 guidelines. A week after the event, Minister for Foreign Affairs Simon Coveney nominated Zappone for the position of special envoy on 'freedom of expression' at the United Nations. Unfortunately for Coveney, he had not informed the Taoiseach of the planned appointment of his former cabinet colleague (Zappone was the former minister for children in the previous FG led government). In the controversy that followed, embarrassing information surrounding the event in the Merrion Hotel emerged. With memories of the Galway golf dinner still fresh, the government sought to assure the public that the gathering at the exclusive hotel across the road from Leinster House was permitted under the health guidelines, which, it said, allowed up to 200 people to attend outdoor functions. The Attorney General was consulted and confirmed this position, even though much of the hospitality industry across the country was under the impression that the guidelines prevented such large outdoor parties or celebrations.

Fine Gael was further damaged when it transpired that one of its ministers had alerted the media of the cabinet discussion on the matter and that the Taoiseach had expressed his concern about Coveney's failure to inform him of the appointment in advance. Following the uproar, Zappone said she would not accept the job, Varadkar said he regretted his attendance at the hotel event and Coveney accepted that the Taoiseach should have been informed in advance that he was bringing the proposal to cabinet. The controversy refused to go to bed and for weeks fresh details emerged which undermined Coveney's explanation to an Oireachtas committee of the background to Zappone's job offer and the manner in which it had been apparently fast tracked through the highest levels of the Department of Foreign Affairs. Some of the shine surrounding her Dublin Bay South by-election victory wore off new Labour Party TD, Ivana Bacik, when she confirmed that she had attended the event. However, her party supported a motion of no confidence in Coveney, which was tabled by Sinn Féin for the day the Dáil resumed following the summer break in mid-September.

The inquiry into the cabinet leak that, as party leader, Varadkar was obliged to carry out, only served to remind the public about another scandal: that Varadkar was still under investigation by the Garda for a possible breach of the Official Secrets Act and the Criminal Law (Corruption Offences) Act 2018. In November 2020, *Village* magazine revealed that in April 2019, the then Taoiseach had given his friend, Dr Maitiú (Matt) Ó Tuathail, access to a confidential document relating to government negotiations for a GP contract with the Irish Medical Organisation. Ó Tuathail was president of the National Association of GPs, a rival organisation of doctors. A Garda investigation began within weeks of the *Village* piece, but by September 2021, the investigation was still ongoing and there were questions raised by opposition parties as to whether there were 'political' factors influencing the delay.

The government and the long-promised Sláintecare project suffered a blow when two leaders of the project unexpectedly resigned in early September. Executive Director Laura Magahy and adviser Dr Thomas Keane, left their positions amid allegations that senior department officials and the government had obstructed the programme, including the key proposal to decentralise health services to six regional and autonomous agencies and the failure to address the waiting list crisis.

They also complained that a key recommendation – that Sláintecare be directed by the Department of the Taoiseach and removed from the remit of the health department and the HSE – was never adopted. Their resignations raised questions over the commitment at the highest levels of government to the ambitious plan endorsed by all parties in the Dáil. The Sláintecare committee of health professionals added its voice to the claim that Minister for Health Stephen Donnelly had supported the delay in the funding and implementation of key targets for the health reform project, apparently due to the competing demands arising from the Covid-19 crisis. The government meanwhile denied claims from Social Democrat TD Róisín Shortall and Independent TD Catherine Connolly that there was institutional resistance to implementing Sláintecare within the health department and HSE.

A further resignation in protest at the delay in radical health reform came when Professor Geraldine McCarthy of University College Cork stepped down as chair of the South/Southwest Hospital Group. In her letter of resignation to Donnelly, published in the *Irish Examiner*, she said:

> Despite the excellent care delivered at the frontline by committed staff, it is regrettable that much of the needed reform of the health service has not been delivered.
>
> This includes the establishment of regional health authorities with autonomy over decisions, budgets and capital spend. It also includes free GP services for all and elective hospitals to address waiting lists and ensure rapid and equitable access to services. I have waited for a long time for developments led by successive ministers for health, and government. However, recent information and my own experiences tell me we are no nearer to the required reform than we were six years ago.

There were also calls for a public inquiry into the state's handling of the Covid-19 crisis, and for those with any responsibility for the more than 5,000 deaths to be held to account. Details of significant overspending and wastage by the HSE in its acquisition of PPE, masks and other emergency medical supplies at the outset of the public health crisis were also revealed at the Oireachtas health committee.

Another unexpected controversy erupted when President Michael D. Higgins declined an invitation to attend a religious service organised by the main Christian churches to mark the centenary of partition and the formation of Northern Ireland that was due to take place in Armagh in late October. President Higgins said that he had alerted the organisers several months earlier to his concern that the event would commemorate partition and suggested that they might alter the title. As President of Ireland, it was not appropriate, in his view, to grace an occasion that marked the tragic division of the country with his presence.

The church leaders, including Catholic Archbishop Dr Eamon Martin, claimed that they had only recently learned of the president's decision to decline the invitation, notwithstanding the insistence from Áras an Uachtaráin that its concerns had been notified to the organisers months previously. The dispute escalated when former Taoiseach John Bruton complained that the president had not complied with his obligations under the Constitution to consult the government in relation to such an invitation. When it emerged that there were extensive communications between the Áras and the Department of Foreign Affairs on the matter, Bruton withdrew his more serious claim but insisted that the president was wrong not to attend and, along with other commentators, said it was an insult to unionists and those of a British identity.

Peter Sheridan, chief executive of Co-operation North, of which Bruton was vice-chair, joined in the chorus of those who were upset by the president's decision to decline the invitation. In contrast, many ordinary members of the public, North and South, agreed that it was inappropriate for the head of state to engage in any commemoration of partition, however well-intentioned or spiritual. The row provided an opportunity for Jeffrey Donaldson to accuse the Irish government of influencing the president, a claim that was rejected. That Higgins was on a visit to the Vatican to meet Pope Francis when the controversy erupted added a certain irony to the affair and an amount of discomfort for the Catholic archbishop. The *Irish Times* reported on 17 September that during the audience in the Vatican, Pope Francis praised the Irish president as 'a wise man of the people'.

In a defence of the President in the same newspaper, Diarmaid Ferriter, a member of the expert advisory group on commemorations, explained that its role was to try 'to ensure that significant events are commemorated accurately, proportionately and appropriately in tone', but 'there should be no attempt to contrive an ahistorical or retrospective consensus about the contemporary impact and legacy of divisive events'. He added that, in its commemoration of the years leading up to partition, the formation of Northern Ireland and civil war, 'the state cannot be expected to be neutral about the events that led to its formation'. Ferriter said:

Historian Brian Hanley has rightly raised the problem of 'shared history leading to commemorative trade-offs that ignore questions such as imperialism, power and inequality'. Soft-centred aspirations to please everybody are not conducive to honest confrontation with difficult historical legacies. Discussion about these questions needs to be vigorous and uncomfortable, and in making his decision, the President has acknowledged that, and continues to engage in historical deliberation. Perhaps we should see this controversy as a vindication of an independent presidency, a reminder of the limitations of 'shared history' and a measure of the divisions, historic and contemporary, that we still must confront with debate rather than prayer.

Other questions remained unanswered, including why the NIO in Belfast and the Department of Foreign Affairs in Dublin appeared to assume that President Higgins would eventually agree to participate in the event and did not engage with him from March, when he first expressed his reservations, until the row erupted in the autumn. There was no discussion over whether Queen Elizabeth was invited in her role as head of the Church of England as well as monarch. Given the friendship she had developed with the President and her often-stated commitment to a lasting peace in Ireland, the fact that no other royal family member was asked to go in her place when ill health forced the queen to cancel may not be altogether surprising.

As the debate over the cancelled Armagh visit subsided, Brendan O'Leary suggested that unionists should recognise the 'significant opportunities' they would have in a united Ireland where they would represent a sixth or seventh of the population on the island. He was speaking at a forum organised by the UCD Institute for British–Irish Studies in late September, where he revealed findings from the latest in the series of consultations about Irish unity that he and his colleagues had carried out with groups of citizens across the island. In April 2021, they convened a participatory forum with a 'cross section of 50 citizens of the Republic, broadly representative of the wider population'. This found that:

> a super-majority of participants strongly favoured Northern Ireland uniting with Ireland rather than staying in the United Kingdom. Given the choice between two feasible models of Irish unification most preferred an integrated model in which Northern Ireland would be dissolved to a model in which Northern Ireland becomes a devolved entity within a united Ireland.
>
> Our participants favour broader, inclusive, and all-island conversations on Irish unification. There is overwhelming support for North–South co-operation. Reconciliation in the North is similarly backed. Both are combined strongly with support for starting 'detailed preparation for a possible referendum on Irish unity which may be held by 2030'.

Addressing the online forum, O'Leary said the model of the integrated Ireland that was put to participants in the forum 'was clearly not a majoritarian one because the electoral system used for both chambers would be proportional representation. … It would be overwhelmingly unlikely that a single-party government would be formed. Therefore, unionists would have significant opportunities to play a role in voluntary coalitions.'

22

RISING TEMPERATURES

I n late September 2021, the four main unionist parties issued a joint declaration against the protocol, claiming that it damaged the economic and constitutional status of the North within the UK. Jeffrey Donaldson and Doug Beattie were joined by TUV leader and MP Jim Allister, and Billy Hutchinson of the PUP, a councillor in Belfast City Council.

'The Irish Sea border must go. … It undermines the union and is costing Northern Ireland £850 million a year,' Donaldson said at Stormont, where the four leaders appeared in a video message that accompanied the statement. UUP leader Doug Beattie asserted that the protocol 'undermines the Belfast/Good Friday Agreement' while Allister said that removing the protocol is the imperative for anyone 'who wishes to oppose the all-Ireland that the protocol is seeking to design'. According to *Belfast Live*, Hutchinson claimed that the 'British government tore up the Act of Union and also the Belfast Agreement. In doing this they diluted our Britishness'.

Although the protocol was the pretext for the display of unionist unity, it was clear that the impending Assembly elections of May 2022, and the prospect of a Sinn Féin first minister at Stormont, were also exercising the party leaders. It was also inevitable that the joint declaration would revive tensions over the protocol among some loyalists, prompting concerns among nationalists and within the Irish government about the prospect of renewed street violence.

In a detailed analysis of the protocol in the *Irish Times* a day earlier, Donaldson and Allister insisted that it had 'ripped up' all the guarantees contained in the Belfast Agreement. They wrote:

> A central pillar of the agreement is that it would be wrong to make *any* change in the status of Northern Ireland, save with the consent of the majority of its people. This consent principle was central to assuring both unionists and nationalists that the future direction of Northern Ireland would be decided democratically and not by force or coercion. However, the protocol has introduced seismic changes in the constitutional position of Northern Ireland.

The two leaders claimed that the UK government has admitted in court that the passing of the European Withdrawal Act, and in particular the protocol section of that act, 'impliedly repealed' article six of the Act of Union 1800 and removed the principal benefit of the union: namely the guarantee of unimpeded trade between the countries that make up the UK.

Donaldson and Allister asserted that, as a result of the protocol:

> 60 per cent of the laws governing our economy will be made in Brussels not in Belfast or London. They must be implemented without any discussion let alone possibility of amendment by either the Assembly or the Westminster parliament.
>
> If they are not implemented and applied in Northern Ireland then the European Court of Justice [ECJ] is empowered to punish the UK and impose whatever sanctions it decides, making the ECJ a supreme court for Northern Ireland.

They referred to the UK government's command paper, *Northern Ireland Protocol: the way forward*, which was presented to Westminster in July 2021 and that recognised the need to replace the protocol. The two party leaders continued:

> time is running out on the October 1st deadline when the full force of EU barriers to trade between Britain and Northern Ireland are due to be put into force. Time is also running out politically.
>
> In light of this, unionists cannot continue to operate structures set up to provide for co-operation between Northern Ireland and the Republic when the more vital relationship with the rest of our own country is being smashed. We believe we would be failing in our duty to the people of Northern Ireland if we were to continue to operate the North/South bodies set up under the Belfast Agreement while our links to the UK are being ripped apart.

They also claimed that their efforts to remove the protocol had helped to restrain more extreme elements of unionism:

> The reason why the unrest has not spilled over into greater disorder is due to the work which we, our parties and community workers, have been doing to prevent it. We have no desire to see rioting in our streets, young people getting criminal records and damaging headlines across the world resulting in a flight of investment from our already-damaged economy.

Both politicians had opposed the GFA: it had prompted Donaldson to leave the UUP in 2004 and Allister to depart the DUP in 2007 over its agreement to share power with Sinn Féin. Speaking at the Balmoral Agricultural Show days before the joint declaration, Allister said that he would prefer a return to direct rule from Westminster than living with a Sinn Féin first minister in the Assembly at Stormont.

The perception of a pan-unionist offensive in the face of the protocol was dented when UUP leader Doug Beattie made it clear that his support for the initiative did not imply a potential pact in any future election. Indeed, Beattie had previously informed some of his closest supporters that his appearance with the other unionist leaders at the bonfire in north Belfast in July was to deflect any suggestion by the other parties that he was less than enthusiastic about the protocol protests. For the same reason, they suggested, he signed the joint declaration. However, Beattie did make a clear distinction between positive and negative unionism when he clarified his position on the election pact issue in the *Belfast Telegraph* on 25 September 2021, in advance of the Stormont launch of the anti-protocol alliance:

> As a political party we are confident in our pro-Union message. It is for others to ask if they wish to vote for positive unionism or negative unionism, to vote for a vision for the people of Northern Ireland focused on the future or a backward protectionist, power-driven vision focused on self-preservation. If it is the former, then the vote will be for the Ulster Unionist Party and a Northern Ireland confident with its place within the United Kingdom.

Notwithstanding the nuances of the inter-unionist relationships, David Frost ensured that the heat was maintained under the protocol issue when he declared, almost on a weekly basis, that the British government was close to triggering Article 16 of the NI protocol, which would lead to a renegotiation of its terms with the EU. He also echoed the unionist insistence that the ECJ should have no part to play in the administration of the law in the North, even though it is the ultimate arbiter of any trade dispute within the EU common trade area.

In early October, Frost said he intended to send new legal texts to the EU to support his proposed changes to the protocol, which would eliminate the majority of checks and certification requirements on goods made in the UK coming into the North and remove the enforcement role of the ECJ.

The Labour Party MP and shadow NI secretary of state, Louise Haigh, accused Frost of inflaming tensions by discrediting a deal he had himself negotiated. 'Tory Ministers should show some responsibility,' she said, 'and do what businesses across Northern Ireland have been telling them for months – get round the table and negotiate a veterinary agreement to help lower the barriers they created down the Irish Sea.'

Meanwhile, Maroš Šefčovič and his officials had assiduously engaged with business, farming and community interests in the North to establish the precise nature of their objections to the protocol in a move which led to a complete overhaul of its provisions.

In mid-October, Šefčovič surprised both the objectors within unionism and the UK government by eliminating 80 per cent of the checks on food and other items and some 50 per cent of customs requirements on goods entering the North and associated with the protocol. 'We have completely turned our rules upside down and inside out,' Šefčovič was quoted in the *Irish Times* as saying. 'If I'm talking about 80 per cent reduction in checks, about half of the customs formalities to be reduced, about express lanes, about all really bespoke solutions, I think that it's quite obvious that we are really doing our utmost. And I hope that this will be reciprocated by our UK partners.'

The proposals included a change to EU law to allow medicines to continue to be distributed from British hubs, special exceptions to allow fresh meat goods deemed to be important to 'national identity', and formal structures to involve stakeholders and authorities in the North in overseeing the arrangements.

The solution offered by the EU effectively ended most checks on goods moving from the UK to supermarkets shelves in the North, while half of previous customs formalities were abandoned. The solution was welcomed by the Irish government and non-unionist parties, but Donaldson described them, on Mydup.com, as unsustainable 'short-term fixes'. He said, 'Short-term fixes that reduce checks and potentially give the appearance of easements compared to the current time will not of themselves solve the problem of divergence within the United Kingdom.'

The ECJ also remained an issue for Donaldson, even though the UK government and unionists had accepted its jurisdiction when the protocol was first agreed.

For many observers, including in the Irish government, both the DUP and Frost appeared determined to maintain the tensions surrounding the protocol and to encourage the small but vocal street protests by some loyalist groups in east Belfast, Newtownabbey and other parts of the North. By threatening to collapse the executive if the protocol was not removed in its present form, and warning of the dangers of unrest, Donaldson was also placing himself in a potentially compromised position if, and when, Boris Johnson altered course.

As Alex Kane wrote of Donaldson in the *Irish Times* in October 2021:

> He is the third DUP leader this year and opinion polls have his party at its lowest level of support in almost 30 years. He needs to take control of the unionist agenda if he is to survive, and that has meant provoking a showdown with Johnson and threatening possible collapse and lengthy instability. His problem, of course, is that Johnson has let down (although party representatives prefer the term 'betrayed') the DUP twice since he became prime minister. The protocol is primarily his doing: pushed through to 'get <u>Brexit</u> done'.
>
> But triggering Article 16 of the protocol – which is what Donaldson wants him to do – would bring nothing but a huge confrontation with the EU, which is the very last thing Johnson wants right now, not least because vast swathes of the regenerated English nationalism which delivered election victory for him two years ago don't actually give a stuff about Northern Ireland.

Noting that the appearance by unionist leaders at fringe events of the recent Conservative Party conference did not appear to excite middle England, and that the protocol went unmentioned in Johnson's speech, Kane concluded:

> I think the feeling in UK government circles is there is no real appetite across unionism for a fight with the government, especially one it has no guarantee of winning. Yes, there are clearly elements of unionism and loyalism very unhappy with the protocol, but it's very unlikely they have the numbers or the strategy for a long period of protest. Johnson, I reckon, believes unionism will finally learn to live with the protocol, albeit with a few changes to help businesses.

Community worker Tommy Winstone felt there was little appetite among working-class unionists for street protests against the protocol. Those taking place were small, and any violence that erupted was largely unorganised, although he maintained that social media was used to bring young people on to the streets, as happened in Lanark Way at Easter:

> Honestly, social media, Facebook, that's what done it. This year was pretty quiet, a couple of incidents have happened around Lanark Way, and at the end of the day there was a bus burnt. But sure, there's been thousands of buses burnt here over the years.
>
> There was no organisation behind it, for want of a better explanation. Those people who were connected to organisations were on the street trying to quell some of it. The tabloids were asking, 'Why are the people of influence not doing something?' Well, they all were. They don't want it; people don't want it. Is there some people behind it? Probably.

Jamie Bryson had shared platforms with Jim Allister at the more recent public rallies against the protocol and was involved several years ago in demonstrations over restrictions on the flying of the Union Jack. Bryson has been identified in the media as a key loyalist organiser of the protests. Winstone said:

> I think Jamie is his own worst enemy sometimes. Jamie is a capable guy if he could be stuck to doing one thing. He's a bright kid but I think the problem with Jamie, is he wants the finger in a whole lot of different pies and people would use him.

According to Winstone, among those using the protests for their own benefit are a group of criminals and drug dealers calling themselves the East Belfast UVF but who are not affiliated with the paramilitary group:

> I think there's a lot of people that were once connected to the UVF [but] are now involved in criminality … [in] criminal gangs. People [previously] within the UVF have told the police that. The police say, 'Well, why don't you do something about it?' Well, what would the UVF do about it? Go and shoot them? And then what? It's up to the powers that be to take them out. Like, everybody knows who they are … but they're still doing it. You have it in your own place with the Kinahans and the Hutches. Everybody knows who they are, but they're still doing it.

Winstone said many people suspect that the PSNI does not interfere with some of these criminals as they are 'touts', or police informants – but that he is not so sure. 'Touting what?' he said. 'There's no paramilitary activity going on so if they're touting anything, they're touting on each other. That's how the police get their information … but then [the police should] do something about it. Let the people see that you're going to do something about it.'

Winstone has little faith in Jim Allister or the DUP to resolve the problems in the Shankill community where his Northern Ireland

Alternatives office is located. He was not impressed by the image of the TUV and other unionist leaders standing with his former UVF colleague, Billy Hutchinson, at Stormont to launch their joint declaration against the protocol. Neither did he accept a statement by his former co-accused, Hutchinson, that the killing of two young Catholic workers, for which they were both jailed in the early 1970s, helped to prevent a united Ireland and that he had no regrets.

> It's bullshit. I have regrets. Sometimes, you have to understand that people play to a crowd; people play to the lowest common denominator all the time because they think they have to. I'm me. My past is 50 years ago. I don't want to keep living there. I want to look forward. I want to give opportunities to young people to look forward and move forward. Hence the work that we do across the divide. I went to prison nearly 50 years ago and the Falls Road was there, and the Shankill Road was there, and it's still the same. Same people living there, maybe some have moved on, but it's the same communities. I'd say 50 years from now it won't be the same communities.

He also has little confidence in the LCC, purportedly the voice of the loyalist paramilitaries that are no longer active, and even less in its chair David Campbell. 'Some of them [the LCC] are doing it genuinely wanting to make things better,' said Winstone. 'I think they've backed the wrong horse, if I'm being honest, with David Campbell. If they're doing things, they should be doing things off their own back.'

In November 2021, Campbell, a dairy farmer in county Antrim, was appointed by agriculture minister Edwin Poots to the board of the Agri-food & Biosciences Institute (Afbi). SDLP MLA Patsy McGlone told the *Irish News* that the appointment was 'baffling' and that he was 'incredulous' that Campbell had not declared his political activity, as required by guidelines for those taking up such posts.

Winstone was even more dismissive of the unionist politicians of the DUP and TUV who come to collect the votes of people in his community but do nothing for them. On top of that, the DUP were, in his view, sucked into supporting the protocol without realising that it led to a watered-down version of the UK. He said:

> The DUP gets sucked into something and I think they were left short. They believed all that Boris was telling them and we all know that Boris can tell lies and prove it. He's absolutely fantastic at it. But I know this from whatever shade you're coming from, unionism will never accept this protocol and will do all in their power to get rid of it. People in unionist communities were really pissed off with the DUP and I think they're in for a good awakening. People tend to knee-jerk react here. We don't vote for the party of our choice, we vote to keep people out here. But I think that's starting to maybe change a little bit.
>
> I am very critical of the DUP. They accused the Ulster Unionists of being big-house unionists – the fur-coat brigade basically – and [that] they were a working-class party coming up, but now they've turned that completely. They are now the fur-coat brigade; they don't get down and dirty; they don't engage with 'loyalists' for want of a better term, they pay lip service a lot of the time.
>
> They are frightened that working-class loyalist communities are doing things for themselves because they think that it's maybe a movement to take over from them. Talking to many people that are in this type of work, they're sick with the politics, they're interested in community and helping with development of community. I think certain individuals within the DUP see well-meaning loyalist community workers as a threat to their livelihoods.

Now Donaldson and Allister are seeking cover from former loyalist activists like Hutchinson and the PUP to join with them in the battle against the protocol. 'They all met up in the Shankill so many years ago,' Winstone said, 'and Allister wouldn't sit at the table with some people because they were ex-prisoners or whatever. I think it still bothers him. He's a politician, you know what I mean? He can stomach it when it suits him.'

Asked about claims by some Sinn Féin councillors that they're seeing an increase in the members of the loyalist working-class community coming to their clinics to deal with fundamental issues like housing and poverty, Winstone is not surprised:

> Yeah, I know people who've done it. It's practical stuff and I think people do it for their own reasons obviously. Maybe they're not getting any help from their own local councillors. Most Sinn Féin councillors, and now probably MLAs, have come up through the street politics. Most of our politicians are career politicians, they've come from universities. They haven't really got down and dirty; they haven't got into the street politics. With the odd exception of the odd councillor here and there but they're few and far between.

Yet despite the work NIA and its counterparts across the North are doing, there are still groups of young people taking to the streets to riot. On 1 November 2021, just after the end of October deadline set by Donaldson and others for the removal of the protocol, a bus was hijacked in a loyalist area of Newtownards, County Down. Then, on 3 November, street violence erupted on the two nights following a loyalist protest against the protocol in the Shankill Road, close to Winstone's office. Some of the loyalist protestors sought to engage in fighting with nationalist youths at a community interface on the Springfield Road in west Belfast. This followed reports by community leaders in the nationalist community that loyalists, over previous weeks, were entering the area and seeking to provoke young people into a row. On 7 November, a bus was set alight after four men jumped on board and ordered passengers off near the loyalist Rathcoole estate in Newtownabbey, north of Belfast.

The protests, however, were minor compared to earlier in the year. As the end of the first year of the protocol approached, it became apparent that many in the wider unionist business community recognised the longer-term benefits of remaining in the EU customs and trade area. Political unionism, and the DUP in particular, was also seeking a way to retreat with dignity from their campaign against the protocol when they saw that a compromise between the British government and the EU was a more likely outcome. Going to war over a trade dispute was not an option.

23

LIES AND CONSENT

As the antagonism over the protocol simmered among unionists in the North, and between the UK government and EU, various elements of civil society were deepening their engagement in discussions for a unity referendum and its possible consequences.

In October 2021, the ICTU, at its biennial conference in Belfast, unanimously supported a motion put forward by the Waterford Council of Trade Unions (WCTU) regarding the debate surrounding the timing and potential outcome of the referendums envisaged in the Belfast/GFA Agreement. As outlined in the agenda and list of motions for the event:

> Conference is mindful of the unity of the trade union movement and the necessity of ensuring that the pursuit and maintenance of the rights, interests and concerns of workers are part of any such debate. In this context, conference mandates the Executive Council of Congress as the steering body of the largest civic body across the island, in liaison with affiliate unions and trade councils to identify the priorities of working people and their communities across the island of Ireland and to develop a policy on the referendums, consistent with the 'No Going Back' objectives.

The ICTU also passed a motion rejecting the plans of the British government to introduce a statute of limitations 'that would not only stop current and future criminal prosecutions, for all troubles related crimes committed before the Good Friday Agreement but would also bar the police and Police Ombudsman from investigating them'. This would lead to the 'ending of all other judicial activity and inquiry in relation to the legacy of the conflict, including civil cases and inquests'.

Seconding the motion by her union, Unison, Patricia McKeown was quoted in the *Irish Times* as saying that the plan was 'about one thing and one thing only: impunity for the British government. They want impunity for their actions past, present and yet to come in relation to the conflict.'

The biennial conference, representing over 45 trade unions across the island, also passed a motion calling for the harmonisation of an all-island health service, free at the point of delivery, and for the two governments to fund a new university in Derry.

The women's movement, which played such a central role in the successful campaigns for marriage equality and abortion rights, has also engaged with the growing debate on a unity referendum. In July 2021, the National Women's Council (NWC) – which represents over 190 women's organisations across the island – set up an all-island women's forum. Funded partially by the Shared Island Unit, the forum invited women from communities on both sides of the border to join in discussion on the role of women in forging a new Ireland.

Orla O'Connor, Director of the NWC, explained that the forum is an organised effort to bring together women from both sides of the border to address the under-representation of women in North–South discussions on the future of the island and to further develop women's role in peace building and civic society.

> We thought the best place to start was to bring together women from the North and South to come together and identify the

issues they want to talk about. It came from NWCI members highlighting in the course of consultations on our new strategic plan, 'No Woman Left Behind', the need for women to be part of the conversation about the future of Ireland and asking – where are women in those conversations and where are marginalised women? There was a real concern, for example, that so much of the discussion about the impact of Brexit was a very male discussion. Also, women are looking back to the Women's Coalition and thinking there needs to be a similar focus on women now.

She said that the work on the Repeal the Eighth campaign, the solidarity shown by women in the North and the absence of women's reproductive rights in the North brought women's organisations closer together. In addition, the conversations on Brexit raised serious concerns on what will happen to women's rights in the North and the impact of losing the protections of EU agreements and laws: 'For example, there are implications for the future protection of women under the European Convention on Human Rights, which women felt could be lost for women in the North.'

O'Connor said those women at the forefront of campaigns for workers' rights and in organisations confronting violence against women, or poverty in border areas, or for an all-Ireland health service, are among those influencing the debate within the NWC: 'There is that sense of there's all these conversations happening, North and South, but we are predominately hearing men on the media. It's quite a male debate.'

The forum has met monthly since it was announced in July 2021. It has also held public webinars on topics including peace building, the experience of the Northern Ireland Women's Coalition – a cross-community, all-female political party which ran from 1996 to 2006 – and its key role in the negotiation of the GFA, the impact of Covid-19 on women and the social media abuse directed at some women active in loyalist communities in the North.

Emma DeSouza, NWC Leadership Co-ordinator, and Ailbhe Smyth who, with O'Connor, played a key role in the successful campaign to repeal the eighth amendment on abortion, have important organising roles in the forum. Eileen Weir of the Shankill Women's Council and Dr Joanna McMinn of Ulster University are also members, along with a range of other activists across the island. A key demand is for the inclusion of civic society in the debate on the future of Ireland, said O'Connor.

> I think a citizens' assembly is a really good idea. It has the potential to be an important space to both engage people and to have thorough and informed discussion on the future of the island. Our learning from our work is that we need to engage people in a discussion that advances equality and rights in the formation of a new Ireland. The Shared Island Unit has created an important space to facilitate conversations and there is a need now to take it to the next stage on how to address the issues that concern people North and South such as poverty, public services, equality and a new approach to peace building that includes civil society at its core.
>
> Women's and community organisations in the North have raised the extent of poverty for women in the North, the inadequate social protections and how the impact of Covid has made the economic situation worse for women and families. In the North, there was less protection for people from the impact of the pandemic as there were no wage subsidy payments. Poverty among women is continually raised as a core issue for women in the North.
>
> Another challenge is for women who are dealing with all of the long-term impact of conflict and trauma within families, communities and society. It's women who are and have been dealing with that and there needs to be more appropriate supports.

In addition, issues of migration, racism and discrimination are key issues of concern and the inclusion of marginalised women, including disabled women and Traveller women are regularly addressed in the forum discussions.

O'Connor described how many NWC members are concerned about the continuing role of the Church in education and healthcare, which is so important in discussions on a future Ireland. 'There is definitely a huge concern and push in terms of separation of church and state,' she said, 'where NWC members want to see religion as being a private matter and not having a role in our public services, particularly our education and health systems.'

O'Connor argued that there is not enough talk about workers' rights and women's rights in the debate on the national question and suggested that the recent citizens assembly in the South on gender equality provided a useful roadmap on these issues:

> If you look at what the citizens' assembly on gender equality did, it gives a very clear roadmap for what you would do and a lot of that is about the need to invest and advance our public services. It's about public childcare, universal healthcare, public housing and a really decent social protection system. In the North, there was a better infrastructure around public services including childcare than there was in the South. However, economic poverty is deeper in the North now than in the South as a result of austerity in the UK, where basic social welfare rates are lower.

At a public meeting of Ireland's Future in the Mansion House, Dublin in early November 2021, the nature of a united Ireland was addressed by a panel which included FF TD Jim O'Callaghan, FG TD Neale Richmond and SF president Mary Lou McDonald. Also addressing the meeting was DCU professor John Doyle and Shaykh Dr Umar Al-Qadri, a leader of the Muslim community in Dublin and chair of the Irish Muslim Peace

& Integration Council. Chaired by RTÉ journalist Audrey Carville, the meeting was attended by 300 people and watched by thousands more on YouTube as the speakers set out their stalls on the benefits of a future unified Ireland.

For his part, Doyle argued at the meeting that a cross-party Oireachtas committee should be tasked with preparing the ground for a referendum by setting out detailed proposals for what a united Ireland would look like. Similar to the cross-party committee that reached consensus and proposed the Sláintecare model for healthcare in 2017, Doyle proposed that it should hear from representatives of civil society, North and South, and from informed specialists across the range of issues, including health, education, the economy and constitutional change, before issuing its report.

Accepting that unionist politicians are unlikely to join the debate until, 'after a referendum has passed', Doyle said that it was disrespectful to their position, and to voters across the island, for government and politicians in the South not to advance details on the substance of the proposed new Ireland: 'I think only an Oireachtas committee with membership of senior government politicians who can speak for their political parties, who have authority with the media, with the public, is the next big step we need to make in moving this forward,' Doyle said.

During his speech at the event, Dr Umar Al-Qadri said that the Irish Muslim experience in the South 'is one of the best, if not the best, in the whole of Europe. ... In the six counties, however, the narrative is completely different.'

He cited a devastating arson attack on the Belfast Multi-Cultural Association (BMCA) in Belfast in January 2021, which the police described as a deliberate hate crime, as evidence of a deep racism evident among some communities in the North.

BMCA was not just a mosque or an Islamic centre. They ran a soup kitchen, they provided shelter to the homeless, they provided essential supports to the frontline workers and health service, they provided food parcels throughout the pandemic.

Al-Qadri asserted that despite having no historical or familial connection to the constitutional question in Ireland, black people, Muslims and other minority groups living in the North may well decide that partition is not working for them.

> Recent polls have shown the nationalist and unionist split in voting is approximately 45 per cent each. The constitutional question … in all likelihood, will be decided by the 10 per cent who remain undecided. A large proportion of those are people that are new arrivals, migrants or people of colour.

May Lou McDonald in her speech agreed it was likely that 'unionism won't formally engage with this conversation until we have had a referendum', but said it was critical that they are invited to participate:

> I still believe it is critical that we invite that perspective and make it clear that nobody is handing down a new Ireland on tablets of stone. As the leader of Sinn Féin and the republican movement, I'm not doing that. I will lead, and we will lead, those of us who are republicans in delivering our perspective, our ideas and commanding and marshalling all of our energy to make this process succeed. But we are very, very well aware that it will take all of us to make this right. They say that it takes the village to raise the child. It takes the nation in all of our parts, in all of our diversity, whether we had grannies in the GPO, whether we had relatives in the H-Blocks, whether that's not part of our experience and our people served and fought in the First or Second World War, all of that is in the mix but it's not really the point. The point is that Ireland must advance and the question for us is what does that look like and what contribution do we make.

In McDonald's view, the conversation should start with the health service:

> We have the Bengoa process in the North, we have Sláintecare in the South: two platforms for radical change. The smart money would join those up; the smart money would work together for a single-tier, universal [health service] for all of our people across the island. ...
>
> The healthcare system should be absolutely free at the point of entry and whatever about there being a role for private health, what we really need to knuckle down on is what the state will sponsor.

McDonald argued that the challenges facing the health service in the North are replicated south of the border, including over-reliance on agency workers, in diagnostics and with capacity. For McDonald, the first priority is workforce planning:

> However technically we will assemble our new health system, the one thing we know is we are not doing it without doctors, nurses, therapists, care workers, and the truth is, North and South, we are running up short. The conversation around healthcare has to include third-level institutions of education and we need to figure out how do we produce enough GPs to ensure we don't endure the shortage we're living with now; and how do we hold on to our nurses and midwives. I'm all for travel and broadening the mind, but we need to say to those workers, we need you here at home because we need to build this system. Let's make room for the next generation to deliver the thing that we dream of.

McDonald agreed with the proposal for an all-party Oireachtas committee but also called for a citizens' assembly in order to democratise the discussion on the nature of a united Ireland. She said there needs to be a government in place to prepare for change and drive preparation. She called on the British government to make clear what threshold is required for it to call a unity referendum.

During his talk, Jim O'Callaghan insisted that it is perfectly legitimate to pursue Irish reunification but also to oppose it. The real question to ask, he said, is 'what is the benefit of Irish reunification?' He argued:

> The reason to vote for Irish reunification is because it would transform the island and it would create a new country in which there would be greater opportunities for people living in both jurisdictions. It would create a stronger country that would have much more influence throughout the world. It would create a country with a much bigger economy that would increase the standard of living for everybody on the island. It would create a country with a much more diverse population.

Brexit, he continued, was the reason the debate has moved up 'a number of gears' in the past five years:

> I used to think Brexit was a political event that took place in 2016. It's not, Brexit is a political ideology that demands constantly that there is tension between the British government and the European Union. At some stage it's the protocol on Northern Ireland, at another stage it's going to be fisheries policies, but this is going to continue endlessly. We need to recognise that the opportunity for everyone on this island lies on us ourselves developing and agreeing our own future.

He also agreed with other speakers that a citizens' assembly was a potentially important tool in progressing the debate on the nature of the new Ireland, although he submitted that it would be premature to convene one immediately. He agreed that preparatory work should commence on constitutional change but that it was only one strand:

We also need a body of work done in terms of what the economy of a new Ireland would look like, what would the health service look like, what would the legal system look like, how would we approach climate change and also a recognition that just because we vote in favour of a united Ireland it doesn't mean the irreconcilable differences and the grievances that exist in Northern Ireland are going to fade away immediately. We need a process of reconciliation to deal with that issue too.

Neale Richmond, in his speech, described his unionist background and how Brexit had reinforced his view that a united Ireland was not only essential but a way of healing divisions of the past:

The vast majority of my family living in Northern Ireland are unionists. I didn't have a great-granny at the Easter Rising. I did have a couple of family members but I'm fairly sure they were shooting into the GPO rather than shooting out. But that doesn't take away from my fundamental belief that an independent Irish state with a full membership of the European Union is something that we can and simply need to achieve. We need to achieve it, not just to fulfil historical aspirations but for our future generations to show a united and independent Ireland can and simply will be a better place than the two jurisdictions that we know on this island. When we look to build a united Ireland, we're looking to build a new Ireland. A confident, mature state that can throw behind the divisions that separated so many of us in the past.

The Fine Gael TD said that the new Ireland should be:

a warm place, it's a generous place, it's not going to be a state that will all be about 'Brits out' ... I fundamentally believe it is going to be a state that's about Brits in: the 300,000 British citizens who live in this jurisdiction, and the near one million British citizens who live in the North. I don't want anyone, of a unionist persuasion or other, to feel that they have to leave a united Ireland. Not just because it would make the dinner table at my family Christmas a lot smaller if they all left, but I want them to stay because this is their country as much as it is our country.

The ability to call a border poll is not in the gift of any of us, but the ability to state what the process will be, is. And that is the challenge for all of us who hold political office and everyone else to say this is what the process will be, this is how it will be inclusive and this is how we can achieve a better Ireland.

Neale stressed the urgency of preparation as what he described as this 'untrustworthy' British government could call a referendum at any time.

Later in the month, IF held another significant event in Belfast when they invited businesspeople from across the North to a lunch in the Crowne Plaza Hotel to listen to David McWilliams outline his views on developing the all-island economy. Among those in the audience from a unionist background was prominent hotelier, Bill Wolsey OBE, while Tina McKenzie, board member of the Federation of Small Business, Seamus Leheny of Logistic UK and Conal Henry chair of broadband provider, Fibrus, also attended. The CEO of Retail NI, Glynn Roberts, and CEO of Hospitality Ulster, Colin Neill, were present, along with politicians, journalists and sporting figures from North and South.

In mid-November 2021, as a round of negotiations over the protocol began between the EU and the British government – represented by Maroš Šefčovič and David Frost respectively – foreign minister, Simon Coveney, ruled out any compromise on the status of the ECJ in the discussions:

It is a black and white issue. Basically, what the EU is saying is that the European Court of Justice has to be the final arbiter on EU law and regulations.

Elements of the protocol rely on the implementation of EU law. I do not see how the EU can outsource the arbitration on EU rules and regulation to a court outside of the EU.

As he prepared to enter the talks, Šefčovič told the BBC's *Andrew Marr Show* that the EU was doing everything possible to avoid the triggering of Article 16. 'We are doing everything possible to avoid it because, of course,' he said, 'it will have serious consequences, first and foremost for the people in Northern Ireland, but also for the EU–UK relations.'

Days earlier, on 18 November, Coveney and Šefčovič participated in a discussion for the Brexit Institute at Dublin City University (DCU) where they outlined in detail the background to the protocol row and their objectives in the negotiations. Also participating was Brendan O'Leary whose paper for the discussion, 'Three Great Lies amid the Perfidy over the Protocol', was considerably less diplomatic than the approach of the two politicians. In the paper, O'Leary asserted that the 65 former colonies that celebrate independence from Great Britain know that 'treaty breaking, threatening to break treaties and making treaties insincerely, are not novel British activities peculiar to Lord Frost, Brandon Lewis and Boris Johnson.' He wrote:

> The official UK lie, hardly a noble lie, is that Her Majesty's government negotiated and intended to implement the protocol in good faith, and would have done so but for the EU's 'legal purism' in its roll out. This ill-considered phrasing unintentionally implies that the UK specialises in legal impurity.

O'Leary recalled how, in 2020, British Tory MPs, including Steve Baker and Michael Gove, suggested voting for the Withdrawal Agreement 'without reading it' and on the basis that 'we could change it later'. He continued:

This October [2021], Philip Rycroft, former Permanent Secretary at the Department for Exiting the EU (2017–2019), told the BBC's *World at One* that, 'The government knew absolutely what it was signing up to when it signed up to the Protocol.' The government means the cabinet, its ministers, its senior civil service advisors, and its prime minister.

Turning to the role of the DUP, O'Leary suggested that by defeating Theresa May's attempt to achieve a softer exit from the UK, the unionist party was seeking 'to recreate a hard border on the island of Ireland'. He wrote:

> They sought to make the EU's future border with the UK coincident with the historic partition line. No other explanation makes sense of their conduct. They had a cover-story: tall and ever-changing tales of 'alternative technologies' with near-miraculous regulatory, customs, and VAT-assignment and collection capacities.

The DUP, he said, then supported the ousting of May by Boris Johnson who went on to:

> use and abuse their switch of allegiance by agreeing the protocol with the then Taoiseach, Leo Varadkar, and with the EU … as the fastest route to accomplishing his allegedly 'oven-ready' Brexit. …
>
> The DUP's biggest lie has become the claim that the protocol violates the principle of consent embedded in the Good Friday Agreement of 1998 (which they never endorsed).

O'Leary recounted how, in October 2019, then DUP MP Nigel Dodds claimed that the protocol 'drives a coach and horses through the Belfast Agreement by altering the cross-community consent mechanism,' and that, 'In a garbled reply, Johnson concluded, correctly, that the protocol "is fully compatible with the Good Friday Agreement," but did not indicate how.' O'Leary continued:

The law on these matters is clear. The consent principle in the Good Friday Agreement applies solely to the transfer of sovereignty over Northern Ireland. Whether Northern Ireland re-unifies with Ireland, or remains in the UK, is to be decided by the people of Northern Ireland in a referendum. A simple majority will suffice, as stated three times in the Good Friday Agreement.

If the protocol modified Northern Ireland's constitutional status as part of the United Kingdom, then unionists would have a point. ... The protocol does not put Northern Ireland outside the UK. Rather the UK's sovereign parliament has decided to take Great Britain, not Northern Ireland, out of the EU's single market, and out of its customs union, while leaving Northern Ireland within the single market's regulations, and subject to the EU's customs code for imports from Great Britain. The enacting legislation comes from Westminster. ...

No constitutional, legal, or even conventional requirement of cross-community consent is required for the matters related to the protocol. That is because the functions addressed in the protocol – mostly customs, EU single market regulation, and VAT – are not Northern Assembly or Executive functions, under the GFA, or the Northern Ireland Act (1998), or the treaty annexed to the GFA. They are Westminster functions. ...

The way the big lie about consent works rhetorically is simple. Unionist leaders assert that the 1998 arrangements give unionists a veto on *any* change in Northern Ireland's political arrangements. Loyalists choose to believe this falsehood, judging by posters, wall-slogans, and the burning of buses.

Unionists do not even have a veto over Irish reunification. That veto rests with the people of Northern Ireland who are not identical with unionists, though that is the premise of much unionist and loyalist political rhetoric.

25

THE ISOLATION OF UNIONISM

The negotiations over the protocol continued into December with little or no progress until Maroš Šefčovič announced a unilateral decision by the EU to change its rules in order to guarantee the supply of medicines to the North from the UK. The move prompted the British government to drop its demand for the removal of the ECJ from any role in the implementation of the protocol.

This progress followed weeks of intensive discussions between Šefčovič and Frost that culminated in an acceptance by British government officials that their EU Commission counterparts had no mandate from the member states to renegotiate the protocol. It was agreed that their negotiations should concentrate on the practical difficulties, including the further reduction of customs checks and procedures, arising from the implementation of the protocol arrangements. Frost's objection to the ECJ's ultimate legal responsibility for the operation of the customs and trade agreement through the NI protocol was now removed, allowing for a resumption of talks in the new year.

In late November, Frost conceded that his frequent threats to trigger Article 16 would not 'affect the standing of the Protocol as a whole'. In a response to a question by former UUP MP Reg Empey, a member of the House of Lords, Frost said, 'Article 16 is a safeguard provision for addressing serious economic, societal and environmental difficulties. It is part of the Northern Ireland Protocol. Triggering it does not affect the standing of the Protocol as a whole'.

It also emerged that the UK government's advisers had confirmed that it could face legal action by the EU if it did not clarify what aspects of the protocol it intended to suspend, and why, in order to adhere to the rules surrounding any decision to trigger Article 16.

If Article 16 was triggered, the UK would be able to suspend only some parts of the protocol, temporarily, and in very limited circumstances. It would still be legally obliged to implement the rest of the protocol. Following months of upheaval and tension, it was now apparent that the threat to use Article 16 was more useful as a political bargaining tool than as an actual weapon.

This did not prevent Jeffrey Donaldson warning Boris Johnson that his party would collapse the 'political institutions' if the Irish Sea border was not removed. Donaldson was particularly annoyed when the British prime minister said that he believed that the protocol could be worked differently but that the EU had to be convinced of this. With Frost retreating on the wider issue of the ECJ, the DUP leader was now struggling to find willing allies in the British government for his battle against the protocol, and he was quoted in the *Irish Times* on 12 December as saying,

> I have given space for talks. I have been reasonable, but Brussels is being unreasonable. These talks cannot go on for years. The prime minister must realise that if there is no progress then, as I said, on September 9th, our continued participation in political institutions that are being used to impose the protocol is not sustainable.

With his party refusing to operate other elements of the GFA and boycotting meetings of the North South Ministerial Council, Donaldson was subjected to criticism from all parties in Belfast over his threat to bring down the power-sharing government at a time when it was grappling with another, highly infectious variant of Covid-19 that threatened to overwhelm the already struggling health service. The recently created unionist alliance against the protocol was ruptured when UUP leader Doug Beattie asserted, as reported in the *Irish Times*, that bringing down the executive and assembly at Stormont 'would be bad for the people of Northern Ireland and for unionism. It will do nothing to address the protocol'.

There was no breach in the collective approach across EU member states on the dispute, and the UK government was clearly reluctant to escalate matters to a potentially self-destructive trade war. After he was elected as German chancellor in early December 2021, Olaf Scholz and his coalition partners, in an explicit criticism of Westminster, confirmed their support for the terms of the GFA and the protocol in their programme for government. Johnson was also subjected to continuing criticism from Emmanuel Macron over post-Brexit fishing rights; in addition, there were differences over the hazardous movement of illegal migrants across the English Channel. In late November 2021, 27 people died attempting to make the 33-kilometre crossing from France to England when their small boat capsized.

Johnson and his colleagues also found it increasingly difficult to persuade the British public that their project for a new, independent and prosperous UK, released from the shackles of Brussels, was about to attract trade deals across the world. However, the apparent change of strategy and tone over the protocol in London was arguably more influenced by the decision of the US government to maintain tariffs on the import of steel from Britain while suspending those imposed on the EU.

According to a report in the *Financial Times*, the decision by the Biden administration to retain tariffs on steel and aluminium imports from the UK was directly influenced by the British threat to undermine the NI protocol. The newspaper quoted a communication by a US Department of Commerce official who said that the British threats to trigger Article 16 of the protocol had obstructed talks on easing metal tariffs imposed during Donald Trump's presidency. The UK government downplayed any link between the tariff talks and the protocol, but informed sources in Washington told the newspaper that pressure from powerful figures in the US Congress prevented them from moving ahead.

During a visit to Washington and New York in early December, Mary Lou McDonald met with influential Irish American congressmen and senators, who confirmed that the tariffs had become embroiled in the protocol standoff. Her message to them was to continue to defend the GFA and to encourage the Irish and British governments to prepare for referendums on Irish unity in the next five to ten years.

Ciarán Quinn, the Sinn Féin organiser in the USA, said that 'no one blinked' when McDonald informed politicians across the aisle and in the administration that the logical extension to the GFA and Brexit was a united Ireland. On her visit, during which she also addressed the New York Bar Association, the Sinn Féin leader told US politicians and the media that the task was to 'start preparation now for an orderly, democratic and peaceful transition from a partitioned Ireland to a united Ireland'.

In an interview with the author, Quinn said:

> Brexit, the rise of Sinn Féin in the South, and the ending of the perpetual unionist majority in the North has changed the conversation ... Previously the discussion on Irish unity had been deemed as aspirational at best and dangerous at worst. This time no one blinked. There was an acceptance that things have moved on. The discussion was on the shape of the next five to ten years, how to manage change, and the constitutional question.
>
> The Good Friday Agreement is a US foreign policy success. Those we spoke to in Congress and the administration are keen to ensure that the peaceful and democratic principles of the Agreement

remain the only way forward. It was also clear to them how Brexit has changed the relationship between Britain and the EU concerning Irish unity. Before Brexit, the border was a dispute between two member states. Post Brexit it is a border dispute between the EU and a third country. Irish unity is now in the interest of the European project. Now, the US has to find a balance in its strategic interests with the EU and Britain. The rule of thumb is that the economic and geographic advantage rests with the EU.

The financial cost of Irish unity was the subject of much discussion following an opinion poll for the *Irish Times* that showed that 62 per cent of people in the South were in favour of unity, but 79 per cent would not accept higher taxes or poorer public services to pay for it. The opinion poll, carried out by Ipsos/MRBI in early December 2021, also showed considerable resistance to the idea of a new flag (77 per cent against) or a new national anthem (72 per cent opposed). The preferred timeline for a referendum, chosen by 42 per cent of respondents, was 'in the next ten years'.

According to Seamus McGuinness of the ESRI, asking whether people are prepared to pay higher taxes or accept poorer public services to achieve a united Ireland is highly premature given that the appropriate modelling has not been carried out to establish what cost, if any, would be involved. McGuinness is one of the authors of an ESRI project to develop, with their counterparts in the UK, a suite of macroeconomics models that would allow for accurate comparisons to be made on an all-island basis.

In collaboration with the employer group Ibec and the National Institute of Economic and Social Research (NIESR) in the UK, the three-year research project will aim to produce economic forecasts and a framework to analyse the impact of a range of public policies that will affect business over the coming years. While the workplan for the new model has yet to be established, it will likely examine the impact of Brexit on cross-border trade on the island, provide more detailed knowledge of the economy in the North and lead to evidence-based policies that can improve and protect competitiveness in the all-island economy.

McGuinness said that the question posed in the opinion poll for the *Irish Times*'is pre-supposing that there will be a higher cost to unification'. He told the author in an interview:

> That is not necessarily true. The need for subvention or additional taxation really rests on the assumption that unification would take place without addressing the low productivity issues that create the need for a subvention in the first place. The whole point of unification would be that it would improve welfare levels for people in the North and for the people in the South, that would provide a framework other than partition and that would allow the North's economy to meet its full potential. It is clearly under-performing at the moment. If you had a planned pathway that allows you to do that, not only could you reach a scenario where there is no cost to taxpayers in the Republic but there could be net benefits in terms of increased growth in the Republic as well as in the North.

The macro modelling project, led by the ESRI, will allow for accurate comparisons to be made between the two economies, North and South. By 2024, when the continuation of the protocol is due to be debated in the Northern Ireland Assembly, politicians, businesspeople, academics and wider civic society will have a tool that could measure its benefits or otherwise to the all-island economy. It could also help to put numbers around the protocol and what would have happened in its absence, McGuinness said.

> In reality, most of the work will be done in the ESRI. We will be doing most of the model building. We'll look at the mechanisms by which our existing model and the new model can talk to each other so that they can be within a common framework. If there is an

increase in foreign direct investment (FDI) or export orientation or an increase in educational participation or achievements in the North, we can examine the implications not only for productivity and income levels in the North, but also for the Republic.

In the UK, NIESR will assist with building the common modelling framework on which real comparisons can be made and, ultimately, the impacts of economic policies analysed on an all-island basis, which will help inform any transition to unification.

Structural macroeconomic models, such as the one being developed by the ESRI and NIESR, would allow you to actually do the analysis and put numbers on that and plan for different sorts of scenarios in terms of how you best achieve the ultimate gains for citizens, North and South, including any transition to unification. That type of analysis needs to be done before a border poll as part of the planning process.

The first year of the protocol saw a significant diversion of trade in just a few months, with exports from the North to the South increasing rapidly while those to Britain declined, McGuinness said.

That diversion of trade happened at a pace in the space of a few months that hasn't been seen over years. It's likely to continue on that trajectory because under Tory administration what you will find will be increased divergence away from EU rules and standards which will place an onus on the EU to put further restrictions on any sort of imports from Britain. That will incentivise operators in the North to reorientate supply chains away from Britain and towards EU suppliers. With increased divergence from EU standards by Britain as they pursue trade deals with other countries, there will be increased integration by NI operators with both the Republic and the EU.

Almost a year into Brexit, there was also a significant shift in companies in the South switching their supply lines from Britain to Northern Ireland under the protocol, while there was a sharp decline in trade with Britain.

Researchers in the ESRI and the Department of Finance in Dublin said that an examination of detailed product data showed a sharp decline in trade between the Republic and Britain, while trade with the North 'has increased considerably'.

CSO figures in late December 2021 showed that firms in the North exported an extra £1 billion of goods to the Republic in the first 10 months of 2021. The ESRI said that the reorientation of supply lines post-Brexit had resulted in the share of Irish imports originating in Northern Ireland rising from six per cent in 2015 to over 40 per cent in 2021, mainly driven by the food and beverage sector.

An unfortunate consequence of Brexit was the new immigration laws introduced by the UK that will force non-Irish EU citizens to apply for pre-travel clearance before crossing the border to the North. The Nationality and Borders Bill will, if enacted, require them to apply online for an Electronic Travel Authorisation (ETA) before entering the UK.

Attempts by MPs from the Alliance Party, the SDLP, Labour and the Liberal Democrats at Westminster to exempt travel on the island of Ireland from the ETA requirement were unsuccessful and the Bill was passed in the House of Commons in early December 2021. Once agreed in the House of Lords, it will come into effect in 2025, adding extra layers of bureaucracy and creating 'legal risk and jeopardy for people crossing on land journeys into Northern Ireland', according to Alliance MP Stephen Farry.

The fear of migration into Britain, which was a key motivation for Brexit, will delay and obstruct the movement of EU citizens on the island, particularly those living in border counties and crossing into the North for work, often on a daily basis.

26

THE POLITICS OF FEAR

*N*oli timere – don't be afraid; the last words of Seamus Heaney in a text to his wife, Marie, before the poet's death in 2013, could be prescribed for the people of Ireland as the debate on unity progresses. Fear of change, of possible loyalist violence, of continuing political instability, of more taxes and fewer public services, of a different flag and anthem have all been put forward as reasons for the people of the South to retain the status quo.

For Protestants and unionists in the North, fear of losing their British identity, political influence and their loyalist culture, the free National Health Service, the annual subvention from the UK, the monarchy and the BBC have been cited as reasons to hold on to the union.

In his report for the Oireachtas Committee on the Implementation of the Good Friday Agreement in 2017, Senator Mark Daly said that rural unionists expressed the fear of losing their land along with their identity in a future united Ireland. Former members of the RUC, the British Army and the Prison Service feared that a triumphalist nationalist community would punish them in retribution for past deeds. Loyalists said they would not be able to parade, fly the Union flag or make bonfires on the Twelfth of July (Daly, *Unionist Concerns and Fears of a United Ireland*, 2017).

Many of these fears were addressed by the GFA, which promised that all citizens would be entitled to the full protection of their rights, identity and citizenship if and when people voted to change the constitutional arrangement and decided by a majority in the North and South, concurrently, for unity.

In early December 2021 the power-sharing executive's Commission on Flags, Identity, Culture and Tradition (FICT) published a detailed report that sought to address the concerns of people across the North on a range of sensitive matters.

Chaired by Professor Dominic Bryan, the 15 commission members, 14 of whom were men, were unable to forge a consensus, despite five years of work and consultation and a cost of almost £800,000 (€938,000) since it had been established in 2014. The report called for a ban on the display of paramilitary flags and murals and said bonfires should only be permitted where they are compliant with the law.

However, no action plan to implement the proposals was agreed and the Alliance leader and justice minister, Naomi Long, said that the report merely kicked the can of dealing with contentious issues down the road. The DUP blamed Sinn Féin for weaponising culture and identity and criticised the party for refusing to commemorate the centenary of the Northern Ireland state, among other insults.

'Sinn Féin in 2021 denied unionist MLAs the opportunity to mark Northern Ireland's centenary by laying a simple stone or planting a rose bush in Stormont,' DUP MLA Christopher Stalford was quoted in the *Belfast Telegraph* as saying. 'Sinn Féin snub the royal family. Unable to even mark the Duke of Edinburgh's passing in the same way as other countries. Such cultural and identity weaponisation will make solutions very difficult to come by as some want cultural domination rather than respect.'

Sinn Féin MLA Gerry Kelly replied that the DUP 'doesn't do equality' and was 'unwilling to confront sectarianism' associated with flying flags at hospitals, schools, places of worship, interfaces and mixed housing developments.

'It has chosen to support those engaged in intimidation and anti-social behaviour at bonfires which have no regard for the protection of people, property or the environment,' Kelly said. 'Progress in tackling sectarianism in this society will be made in spite of the DUP's efforts to deny rights and equality'.

The DUP was also accused of blocking the introduction of a Bill of Rights, and of delaying urgently required protections against climate change.

Under the New Decade, New Approach (NDNA) agreement that restored the executive in early 2020, an ad hoc committee was formed in the Assembly with the task of examining the implications of a Bill of Rights, proposed under the GFA. When the committee sought to appoint human rights advocate Professor Colin Harvey to an advisory group, the appointment was blocked by the DUP, leading to the suspension of the work of the committee at Stormont.

According to Patrick Corrigan, the director of Amnesty International in Belfast, the failure to appoint the panel was a breach of the NDNA agreement. 'It is even more concerning if the failure to agree this five-member panel is because of a refusal to appoint someone of the standing of Professor Colin Harvey, a leading authority on constitutional and human rights law on these islands and one of the most distinguished researchers and writers on the Bill of Rights for Northern Ireland,' he said in the *Irish News* in November 2021.

Harvey was quoted in the *Belfast Telegraph* as saying that he believed that his work with Ireland's Future led to the refusal by DUP to agree his appointment. 'I am saddened to hear these reports about the expert panel and it is disappointing to see what appears to be a further political blockage to the Bill of Rights process,' he said.

The episode confirmed for many the deep hostility within the DUP to the human rights and climate change agenda pursued by Harvey and other activists before and since the GFA. For Harvey, the unity project provides a unique opportunity to embed human rights protections in the constitution and polity of a 'new Ireland'.

'The Good Friday Agreement prompted significant human rights and equality reforms, North and South, but it is well known that this agenda has not gone as far as anticipated. The expected Bill of Rights was never enacted and there is no Charter of Rights for the island of Ireland. Commitments in the Agreement on rights will flow into planning for reunification. The chance to advance more extensive protections for everyone on the island should not be missed,' Harvey said in an interview with this author.

> A new and united Ireland must include enhanced guarantees for social and economic rights, in areas such as housing and health-care. An appropriate rights-based mechanism must be found to respect existing Agreement guarantees on parity of esteem in these new circumstances, including more extensive recognition of minority rights. Better domestic equality protections – inclusively defined in terms of groups and scope – will be essential. If the preparations incorporate ideas for a new constitution, this conversation is likely to broaden considerably.

The 'innovative thinking on what a modern Bill of Rights might contain, and the extent of the practical engagement with comparative and international experience' can assist any forum established before or after the unity referendums, Harvey said.

On climate change, DUP Agriculture Minister Edwin Poots placed a bill before the Assembly which does not include the globally accepted target, largely agreed at COP 26 (held in Glasgow in November), of decarbonisation by 2050.

John Sweeney, Emeritus Professor of Geography at Maynooth University, said that the Poots bill contrasts with another put forward by

Green Party MLA Claire Bailey, which endorses the 2050 decarbonisation target and is accepted by all other parties except the DUP, which has a fair number of climate deniers in its ranks. 'Poots has a record of fundamentalism and creationism. He hasn't touted that publicly as a reason for not having an adequate response to climate change, but he is using the same arguments as the Irish Farmers' Association, for example, are using in the South to limit the effectiveness of any bill,' Sweeney said in an interview with this author. In his view, only a co-ordinated all-island approach can meet the existential challenge from global warming.

'The only way I can see that there would be homogeneity in an all-Ireland situation would be if the North was in the EU and therefore subject to EU legislation. Otherwise, we're going to have this ongoing discrepancy between the legal systems in both jurisdictions,' said Sweeney, who attended the two-week COP 26 gathering.

> It certainly would be easier to have one jurisdiction and one set of international rules to abide by. That really is what was coming out of COP as well, commitments to reduce [carbon emissions] by 50 per cent by 2030 internationally. We've got that in the Republic but we haven't got it in the North officially yet.
>
> There were some positive bits that came out of COP 26 in terms of finance, in terms of Ireland's role in particular this time around, which was much more progressive than previously.

Sweeney also cited as significant the international agreements on deforestation and reducing methane gas emissions. However, he was sceptical about whether some key countries will implement the targets on deforestation.

Ireland signing up to the Beyond Oil and Gas Alliance was something that wouldn't have happened 10 years ago, he suggested, although the Irish government has been less than convincing on its commitment to drastically reduce methane gas emissions. In the long term, a united

Ireland would be ideally placed to maximise the benefits from wind power, including offshore electricity generation.

> The offshore wind resources in both jurisdictions are phenomenal. I don't see any problem reaching 70 or 80 per cent of our electricity demand from wind. There will be an issue with the integrity of the marine environment being protected, but I don't see it as being a major one. Ireland will be potentially an exporter of energy for wind in the future. Therefore, we will be able to get the security of energy supply from interconnections that will be important for the times when we don't have wind or solar power.

Many young people from the North who travel abroad to university or for work do not return due to the sectarian divisions and political instability there and, in recent years, due to the unwillingness of some parties to deliver rights that are accepted as normal in most other modern democracies. This trend was confirmed in a recent survey of 300 young people who left the North to study or work abroad. Only 12 per cent planned to return to the North after graduation, while older professionals made a similar response. The survey was carried out by Belfast think tank Pivotal in 2019.

Emma Campbell is among those who returned to the North. She spent 13 years studying and working in Wales and England. A member of the Array collective of artists in Belfast, Campbell said that the struggle for human rights, including abortion, LGBT and language rights, and climate action are the biggest challenges facing young people in the North. Array, which consists of 11 artists, won the prestigious Turner Prize in the UK in December 2021 for an installation they built involving a shebeen, or illegal pub, containing artwork depicting and imagining a wake for the partition of Ireland. When I spoke with Campbell, she said:

> The shebeen is just the holder for the artwork itself which is a film that we made of the Druithaib's Ball (Druids' Ball). We had

performers and activists and all sorts of people and we celebrated a wake for the centenary of the partition for Ireland. That's the main feature for the work we submitted for the Turner Prize, which is obviously really significant if you're thinking about a united Ireland.

I think it was really important to us that we consciously didn't include any flags in our work. We included rainbow flags or created other flags and banners but we purposely didn't include any national flags in the work. It was the year of commemoration and celebration of partition and we felt like we wanted to take this really particular and controversial and potentially explosive moment in time and talk about it differently and from the perspective of queer people, of gaelgeoir, of artists, of feminists, and make sure that those voices and the experience of life in Northern Ireland for us was also included.

The collective, with a majority of women members, works in a shared studio space in Belfast and came together from their involvement in a range of social and political campaigns over recent years.

After returning to Belfast, Campbell became involved in the Abortion Rights Campaign, advocating for women's reproductive rights through creative and direct action, North and South. From a cultural Protestant background in east Belfast, Campbell attended art college at Ulster University before completing her studies in Wales.

The art college in Belfast at that time was way more of a hotbed of student political activity than it is now because it had a really strong students' union and it had a big open café where everybody used to go and meet. I was the welfare officer for a year, mostly giving out free condoms, I'll be honest with you. I went to Wales for three years and then went to London where I was mostly working in the photography industry in various roles. It was the time of the big anti-Iraq war marches and I was involved in a feminist group in south-east London.

Array includes artists from across the island, as well as one from Italy and another from Manchester, who share a progressive and radical left political outlook. Campbell continues:

> I was fairly lucky in that my parents weren't hard-line unionists. I have mixed grandparents and one is religious, so I suppose that's quite unusual. I also went to a fairly mild church, a Methodist church. I wouldn't say it was a typical Protestant upbringing. My partner is from Waterford and when she asked me 'what about this Orange Order thing?' I said you are asking the wrong person.

During Campbell's primary school years, the Troubles meant bomb scares and bag searches and occasionally the sound of explosions, but she knows it was different for those living in Catholic areas.

> I'm aware the constant scrutiny and the army visibility everywhere was probably less frightening for me than my Catholic neighbours. But we had to go through army turnstiles at the gates. I was working in Castlecourt in Belfast on the day of the Omagh bombing and we had to search the shop for [cassette] tape bombs. I didn't even know what I was looking for.

A teenager when the GFA was signed, Campbell only got to befriend young Catholics when she went to college. Segregation in education is still a key challenge. 'It's still really difficult to get your child into an integrated school. My child has a parent from two different backgrounds essentially and we still couldn't get him into an integrated school because there aren't enough places,' she said.

> We have a problem in the North and I think it's this democratic deficit where quite often people will vote for parties based on

national identity rather than their social policy. It delivers this false mandate so people will be voting for the DUP because they want to be British even though they might support equal marriage or abortion rights. There's plenty of evidence to show that even among the hardline loyalist community there's still a majority of people who support gay rights and abortion rights.

When Campbell and her friends discuss a united Ireland, there are concerns over the loss of the National Health Service, as well as house prices and the cost of living in the South. 'I think the biggest fear around a united Ireland isn't a loss of identity but a loss of a National Health Service. Among the left, there's a fear about the liberal taxation system in the South, the astronomical housing and fuel prices and that kind of thing. We are in a kind of affordable bubble here in the North and there's a bit of a fear of that being risked,' she said.

People are happy to discuss a united Ireland but have deep reservations about who will govern it, particularly given the mess made by the existing parties.

We don't want that, Fine Gael and the DUP running the place. That would be the worst-case scenario. Everybody is incredibly concerned about Brexit especially as the majority of people in the North voted to remain. I think people would be interested in a united Ireland. People are also impatient that the government here for three years, they just didn't sit at all, which is absolutely anti-democratic. Even though the Good Friday Agreement was supposed to enshrine a bill of rights, we still haven't got that over two decades later. There's a lot of frustration that's feeding into this kind of civil unrest. The frustration is twisted and abused by sectarian messages. Trying to campaign for a progressive Ireland would be something that would appeal to my generation and the generation after me because what we see now isn't working,

North or South. A lot of the stuff that Array tend to protest about is because of this frustration. It is coming from a genuine concern for people just having liveable lives.

I also think there's a difficulty for the whole island of Ireland. It's still a really immature democracy and there's an issue with the kind of people who end up in government. In the North, the majority of people who end up in the big parties are there simply because of a strong belief in a particular identity. A lot of the people who end up in the big parties in the South are people who can afford to be or people from wealthier backgrounds, so it's not properly representative.

Many younger and progressive voters in the North have shifted to Alliance and the Green Party in recent elections, although these parties may not be left-wing enough for Campbell's circle of friends and campaigners. She is involved in a 'feminist constitution' project which has examined how the rights of women who have suffered abuses while in care or in institutions like the Magdalene Laundries can obtain redress. Campbell has also worked on a project which examined how women were disproportionately affected by the Covid-19 pandemic.

There are huge issues like the treatment of women in institutions such as the Magdalene Laundries, North and the South, things that are currently quite toxic in the whole island. Let's not get too bogged down in emblems and think a bit harder about housing rights, and how people are expected to survive, what a fair tax system looks like, what a fair education system looks like and what about transport and so forth that serve more than just the big urban centres.

All of these things hugely impact women more than men. There's a women's policy group which I'm also involved with and has written a feminist Covid recovery report. It details quite plainly how all of the issues that were already impacting women more have only been exacerbated by Covid. How do we imagine an Ireland that has universal free childcare, never mind universal free healthcare? That's a problem for the whole island. How it impacts women in terms of employability, in terms of affordability of housing. I think the work that needs to be done from the left is to try and imagine what that fairer Ireland could look like.

Campbell and other artists collaborate with organisations across the island, including those active on migrant rights, with housing groups and trade unions as well as, in her case, Alliance4Choice and the Women's Policy Group in Belfast. They would welcome the type of universal basic income that has been introduced for artists in the South.

It's not necessarily a perfect scheme but the universal basic income for artists, if it works [in the South] then it would be good for that to be expanded. That could be a central facet of a new Ireland. Artists are there to kind of reflect and to allow the nuances in things and maybe just get the chance to be aired in political discussions. I think it's also our duty to reflect the voice of the people that aren't normally heard in those arenas. The work that Array have done for the Turner Prize has been described as a kind of utopia, so we can imagine these utopias and if we can imagine them then how can we make them part of the future of Ireland?

27

TIME AND TIDE

The arrival of the Òmicron variant of Covid-19, first identified in South Africa in November 2021, threatened to overcome the hospital services North and South as the second pandemic Christmas approached. When the infection began to circulate more widely in schools across the country, the shortcomings of the government strategy in the South to deal with Covid-19 became more apparent. Most negligent was the failure to introduce more effective ventilation systems, and the decision to suspend contact tracing, in schools to combat the airborne virus. Despite a successful roll-out of vaccinations across most age groups during the summer and autumn, the new, more transmissible Omicron variant threatened to engulf the country in a massive fourth wave of infection. The new version turned out to be milder, leading to fewer hospitalisations and ICU admissions, but it did have the ability to infect people who were doubly vaccinated and boosted. As the year turned, daily Covid-19 cases were officially exceeding 20,000 in the South, with proportionally higher figures in the North. As the virus spread rapidly through the population, PCR testing facilities were unable to keep up with demand and case numbers were estimated to be three times those reported by the health authorities.

Covid generated another political scandal in the UK when photos emerged of Boris Johnson and his wife, Carrie, celebrating with his staff in the garden of 10 Downing Street during the strict Covid-19 lockdown in May 2020. Claims by ministers that those present were working, while enjoying cheese and wine and eating pizza, were widely rubbished. Days later, in a by-election in North Shropshire, one of their safest seats, the Tories suffered a devastating defeat to the Liberal Democrats. The by-election was called following the departure of former NI minister Owen Patterson in the wake of a lobbying and financial scandal, and the result saw his majority of more than 20,000 overturned.

As the new year dawned, Johnson was fast losing his friends and allies in his cabinet, his party and the establishment media while coming no closer to attaining the dream of the sovereign, global and prosperous Britain he had promised. Among those to jump ship was chief Brexit negotiator David Frost, who resigned over the direction of the government under Johnson and was replaced by Foreign Secretary Liz Truss. For unionism, the declining popularity of Johnson and the sudden departure of Frost made their ambition to get rid of the protocol and the 'border in the Irish sea' all the more unrealistic. An announcement by Jeffrey Donaldson, reported in the *Belfast Telegraph* in early January 2022, to 'pause' his threat to bring down the Stormont institutions and to allow Truss time to resolve the problems created by the protocol in renewed negotiations with the EU was an acknowledgement of these shifting realities. A month later, First Minister Paul Givan resigned as the DUP collapsed the executive.

The soaring support for Sinn Féin in the end-of-year opinion polls in the South, with the party gaining 15 points over both Fianna Fáil and Fine Gael, raised the real prospect that Sinn Féin might, within a few years, lead the government in the South while also being the largest party in the North. An Ipsos/MRBI poll for the *Irish Times* showed the party at 35 per cent (compared to 20 per cent for both Fianna Fáil and Fine Gael) in early December.

Warning unionism to prepare for the inevitable, Alex Kane wrote for the same publication at the end of that month:

> Sinn Féin is now topping opinion polls on both sides of the Border and remains on a continuing upward swing in the south. While nothing is ever inevitable in politics, only a fool would dismiss the possibility of there being a Sinn Féin first minister and Sinn Féin taoiseach in office at the same time in or around early 2025. And if losing their overall majority in the Assembly and possibly even the role of first minister in a few months are clearly psychological blows for unionism, I'm not sure how a first minister/taoiseach tag-team would be described.

Whether as Taoiseach or leader of the opposition in the coming years, Mary Lou McDonald will have a crucial role to play in negotiating the course to a successful unity referendum which, she insisted, can be achieved by the end of the decade.

Asked by the author what preparations she would make if she were in power, McDonald said that the first would be to declare that the government was committed to a strategy to achieve unity 'not just rhetorically but as a matter of contemporary imperative in the here and now'.

> At the same time, London has to decide to act within the spirit of their claim that Britain has 'no selfish or strategic interest in Ireland' and within the spirit of the Good Friday Agreement, which explicitly says that it is for the Irish and the Irish alone acting without impediment to decide our future. The EU has to decide to protect its interest as it now emphatically has skin in the game. The Irish border is now not just our problem, it is now an ongoing European problem. The EU needs to become a vehicle and a persuader for Irish reunification. There is precedent for them taking [such] an approach in the past in Cyprus and Germany.

'The next phase is preparation and that is where a citizens' assembly comes in. It is also where unionism needs to step up and to engage in the first instance. Following that, the modalities of the referendums themselves have to be worked out, the timing of them and the nature of the question,' she said. This involves clarity on the basis of calling a referendum 'whether that is demographics, election results or a combination of those'. This will require detailed engagement between Dublin and London, with the Irish government pressing for clarity on the metrics and measures the British propose to apply, McDonald continued.

She said there should be detailed policy analysis and preparation on an all-island health and education system and on constitutional changes, and that following the referendums there is likely to be a transition period of up to a decade.

> Even with the referendum campaign successfully run and taken over the line, you are then into a phase of transition. So the question arises, not just in terms of duration, what does that look like? That's the core issue. So we can have a policy position around an all-island healthcare system or implementing a new constitution and we can draw from examples internationally as to how others have done that. But what will be unique to us here in Ireland is the question around how quickly, at what pace, what's the dynamic of actually finally delivering that?
>
> My working assumption is that, post-referendum, you will probably have a decade of transitioning. Some of the changes will happen very quickly. The economic, trading dynamic across the island will knit together very quickly. The evidence, post-Brexit, on how all-island trade has spiked gives an indication of that. It will take a longer-term transition to deliver on the models of education, plural, and what they look like. If you have kids and young people somewhere on their educational path and journey,

we can't disrupt that and put very young lives into disarray. We have to be mindful of real people living their real lives, looking after their families in real terms while trying to reach the higher-level transitional objectives.

Based on the political experience of previous campaigns, the Sinn Féin leader has a view on how successful unity referendums can be achieved.

People look to the campaigns around repeal of the eighth and marriage equality and there are elements of that approach that will apply. For the referendums to pass and to translate into a successful transition, civic society outside of the political bubble has to be fully engaged. All of this has to be informed by what people actually want. The political system on its own will not have broad enough shoulders to carry this on its own, so politics will need the expertise and engagement of NGOs, the voluntary sector, business and trade unions. That can have the really positive, knock-on effect of engaging people at the grass roots, ordinary punters who normally would not be part of a big political campaign or a big political transition. We will be forced to make room for people, and I think that's a healthy thing.

Given the scale of the task of preparing for a transformation of political and constitutional structures and of society, she envisages a rolling process of citizens' assemblies. This would ensure a representation of citizens across both jurisdictions reflecting gender, class, region and identity.

'It has to be regarded as a rolling process that is populated and then re-populated and the work for which would be very intense. These would be supplemented by a dedicated Oireachtas committee on a united Ireland following the Green and the White Papers and that more formal political process,' she said. A department for a united Ireland would only be useful if the government 'has declared for unity and [is] making moves'.

Returning to the campaigning during the referendums, McDonald expects that each political party would have its own campaigns.

> Unionists will argue for the union and those who want reunification will argue for that. You will have the persuadables, the immovables and a collection of the indifferent somewhere in the middle. The contours of that campaign are going to be very interesting and very different from anything that we've ever seen before in the North. However, during the big constitutional debates on marriage equality and on reproductive rights there was as big an interest north of the border in those campaigns. Those were essentially all-Ireland campaigns even though it affected the 1937 constitution and only the 26 counties. The impetus for reunification includes Brexit, the shift in demographics and electoral realities. But there is also the generational shift which to me is perceptible all across the island and where I believe younger people and activists will coalesce in ways which would not have happened 20 years ago or even 10 years ago.

McDonald believes that more people will come out to answer the big and 'profound' questions posed by a unity referendum than would normally participate in national elections.

> Once these great questions are asked, a different and a deeper type of sentiment is rallied. You got a snapshot of that with marriage equality, with abortion. Watch this space because it will speak to something very profound. These changes will be fundamental. We have got lots of things wrong on our partitioned island. This is our big chance to get things right. Nobody is saying we have the referendum tomorrow. What we are saying is start deciding and preparing today.

McDonald said that women will be a hugely influential force in this process of change as they were in the recent referendums. 'Women will be essential. Women were at the heart of marriage equality and the change for women's reproductive rights. That is not to discount men at all, but women as an emerging and really strong political force will be key to this. I think we will find common ground in a way that many wouldn't expect and that our young people, in whom I have the most immense confidence, will drive this really hard.'

McDonald does not believe that the question of the flag, anthems and symbols of a new Ireland will be deal breakers in the process of constitutional change. 'The belief that I hold is that the green, white and orange tells the story of a united Ireland. It shows the two anchor traditions of the island in peace. Others will take a different view. Let them bring that case to the table. Similarly with the anthem. As long as it's not "Ireland's Call" people will be happy!' she joked.

> For me, the flag is the tricolour, 'Amhrán na bhFiann' is our anthem. Others will come to the table with a different view, that's fine, let's hear it. But is that going to be the deal breaker? No. For me as a woman, for young people, for people with ambition and drive who want the best chance and opportunity, for people with disabilities, for people who really believe and see how Ireland can do so much better, are they going to be the deal breakers? I don't believe so.

McDonald does not accept the contention that there will inevitably be violent resistance to a transition to unity.

> There is an assumption by some people of an inevitability of violence. I will not accept that. It is very important that people like me in leadership roles and perhaps even more importantly people from the loyalist and unionist tradition agree at the outset in our deciding that this is done peacefully, in an orderly and democratic fashion.

Whatever happened in the past has happened. That is not to discount people's passionately held views and the experiences and the scars that are real and that are still sore. I know all of that, but this conversation ultimately and essentially is about the future. It is about what your life looks like, for your kids, grandchildren. It's about what we can achieve together. It is the ultimate reconciliation programme.

Among the 'immovables' who will never be persuaded by the argument for unity is loyalist activist, Jamie Bryson, who edits and publishes the *Unionist Voice*. Early in the new year, he generated controversy over his claim that nationalists have taken over many professions in the North, including in the public service, and are using their position to promote a united Ireland. His view was supported by Baroness Kate Hoey, a former Labour Party MP in Britain.

'There are very justified concerns that many professional vocations have become dominated by those of a nationalist persuasion, and this positioning of activists is then used to exert influence on those in power,' she said in her foreword to a document entitled 'Vetoing the Protocol' published by *Unionist Voice*.

Bryson went further, accusing nationalists – including legal, business, media and sporting personalities who signed the IF letters to the Taoiseach – of weaponising their professional status.

The actual issue is the weaponisation of the professional class by those of a predominately nationalist political persuasion. I call this an elite nationalist network of influence. I am bemused at the outrage of nationalists who suggest no such network exists, they literally created a 'civic nationalist' movement to try and use the professional status of its members to credential nationalist political ideas.

This was not some clandestine movement. They published multiple letters in a national newspaper with the signatories not identified as merely individuals, but rather by their professional status. They therefore self-identified as nationalist academics, lawyers, journalists, etc.

Commentator and author, Susan McKay, accused Hoey and Jeffrey Donaldson, who welcomed the former MP's remarks, of re-igniting sectarianism against nationalists. Such attitudes, McKay suggested in an *Irish Times* article, contributed to loyalist attacks in the past, including against members of the legal profession and journalists in the North. Hoey's comments were also criticised in a statement by the Belfast branch of the National Union of Journalists (NUJ) who said her remarks represented 'an appallingly blinkered view of professional journalists in Northern Ireland'.

The NUJ is affiliated to the Irish Congress of Trade Unions (ICTU), the largest civic society organisation in the country, representing almost 800,000 workers across the island. The ICTU can play an important role in managing the discussion on unity referendums, particularly across communities in the North, according to its general secretary, Patricia King. Congress includes union members who both support and oppose a united Ireland, she said, and the motion agreed at its BDC in October 2021, supporting the idea of preparing for referendums, is discussed at each monthly meeting of its general purposes committee.

There are a number of people on the Congress executives, both North and South, who have an interest in this and who didn't want to see the motion just going off into the ether. The plan will come together as to how we can integrate the conversation into the debate. We have a membership in Northern Ireland, some of whom would be very actively in favour of a united Ireland. We have some who would not be in favour in the Protestant work force. It's going to be a tricky enough debate but I don't think it is one Congress can or will shy away from.

Speaking personally, King said that the debate on a united Ireland cannot happen without the labour movement being at the forefront. 'We need to get into a place where we identify the social and economic issues that need to be addressed in both jurisdictions and where we can establish beyond doubt that having one economy and one society is better and more pleasing for the population than having a divided economy and a divided society.'

The views of people and the demographics are changing all the time and generational change is key to shaping a new Ireland, King added. While there will be those who will resist any change, she believes that a 'good majority' of people will accept that a single economy and society can work better for everybody and that change can be managed by consensus. 'That is where Congress should be aiming for. We should be shaping our policies to push both jurisdictions to improve the societal and economic benchmarks and to show a better life for a majority of people,' King said.

Employers are already engaged in the discussion on building the all-island economy and Congress regularly meets with their representative organisation, Ibec, at meetings organised through the Shared Island Unit in the Department of the Taoiseach, she said. 'The labour movement has a part to play in the discussion on a united Ireland. We are an all-island body that has managed for decades and decades to traverse both sides of the divide in the North. There is no reason why we can't have the debate respectfully.'

For President Michael D. Higgins, the debate on a new Ireland 'should be preceded by discussion on the matters about which we might be united'. In an interview with this author, President Higgins said that:

If we had a discussion on the matters about which we might be united, you could get an intergenerational agreement on the importance of ecology, you could get an intergenerational agreement on the importance of gender equality and social inclusion, on new forms of institutional arrangements. You could get a general agreement on the separation of Church and state, in terms of integrated education.

For many years and particularly in the British political system, President Higgins suggested, there were too few people who grasped the concept of Irish people solving their own problems. 'They did not get the idea of all of the Irish people, whatever their backgrounds, possessed and dispossessed, Catholic and Protestant, men and women, discussing on an Irish basis a future for the island of Ireland. That is where we are at now,' he said.

The issues of constitutional change and of territory would be best discussed after people find the points on which they agree: President Higgins provided one recent example where there has been a broad unity on the question of the proposed and controversial amnesty for conflict killings by the British government. 'We're already united on something very important. We're united on the immorality of the so-called amnesty. The united Irish view from all sides, from both victims of the IRA or victims of state executions and so forth, is that it is better to acknowledge and transact than to invent a bogus amnesia. We're united on that.'

For his first series of *Machnamh* discussions and reflections, the president invited a range of academics and writers to examine the key components of history that led to the War of Independence and partition, to consider neglected or under-represented issues, including the role of class and gender in the events of the revolutionary period. This will be followed by further inquiries into the civil war and the evolution of the two states, which can, he said, inform the discussions now taking place on a united Ireland.

In his speech at the opening of the Northern Ireland parliament in 1921, President Higgins recalled, King George V clearly assumed that partition was a temporary arrangement. What evolved was, instead, a mould or shell around each state, one that grew harder and less inclusive as each developed in its own form. In both North and South, and not least to do with clerical influence, 'in the 1920s and by the time you come to the '30s it has a shell that is so hard that it is almost impenetrable'.

'Yes, the migration from the southern state was based on economic reasons but it's always implicit that sexual oppression and the monstrous treatment and misogynistic nature in relation to its institutions was an important factor,' President Higgins continued.

'The oppression of the minority nationalist community in housing, employment and basic civil rights formed a different, but no less undemocratic and unequal, society in the North. Neither state had as its primary purpose providing for the wellbeing of all its citizens on an inclusive basis,' he said.

It is possible, he argued, for the welfare state and socialised healthcare models that people enjoyed in the North for decades to be extended in a modern, intelligent and effective way to the whole island. There is also a need to adopt a regional approach across the island to ensure that there is more local democracy in the provision of public services, he said.

> What you need are devolved powers of meaningful and effective regionalism with budgets that are made accountable. If necessary, and to facilitate all of this, change the local government system completely. Get rid of the county system. Reconsider the design of the cities. You could have a whole series of satellite towns with good communications and transport. That is what people are interested in. An active, well-educated, energetic, caring society. We need to redefine the world of work to say that working in the care environment will be as important as working in the financial area. We need agriculture to take account of sustainability. It won't be all volume producers but sustainable production for genuine farmers.

Separating people in relation to education isn't helpful, President Higgins said, and a citizens' assembly might be a way of exploring a new system that improves outcomes for children, with an inclusive curriculum reflecting the needs and aspirations of all.

> There could be a citizens' assembly to discuss the matters upon which we might agree. You could start with work on the curriculum. I'm not talking about a secular curriculum being imposed either but an open curriculum in the sense of the adequate literacy for our times, a moral guide. You do that work first. Then you look at the control of the schools. You also need to have better school buildings, more teachers. For the first time we might say we're not going to abandon parents of children who have special needs.

The future Ireland, for President Higgins, 'isn't a continuity or a simple modification of what happened North or South. What is necessary is a transcendental leap that passes the excesses of both of these great institutional failures. And they are institutional failures. Emigration is the test of it for so many of the decades.'

> We have always been a migrant people. In 1901 there were more people born on the island of Ireland living abroad than living on the island. Now when I visit schools, primary schools in particular, I see people from 50 nationalities being taught by bright young national schoolteachers, working with school management committees which are now mostly lay people.
>
> The future on a shared island is about Irish people solving Irish problems. The role of the state is central to all of this as we have learned from Covid. The recognition suddenly that the person who cleaned the hospital was very, very important. In relation to the new future, the trade union movement should be at the front of the change. Theirs in relation to resisting false divisiveness is the best record in our history.

They include some of the best people to talk about the green economy, the invaluable intersection between housing, education, social policy, ecological change, the value of work and the importance of the shared social space.

President Higgins argued that the discussion on the future of the island has to include consideration of universal basic services to remove the insecurities facing working people, including the curse of low-paid, precarious work.

'The integration of social responsibility and ecological responsibility also offers an opportunity to improve workers' rights while eliminating the tedium of work. The idea of universal basic services is to remove the insecurities and fears associated with food, education and housing,' he said. All of this discussion has to take place from the ground up, including through local and regional discussion, citizens' assemblies and debate among elected politicians.

We need to have discussions and seminars, North and South, on the title 'Of That Upon Which We Might Agree' and that has to precede any simple head counts. Those people who want to call themselves Irish, British or both, or Internationalists, isn't a difficulty. There is no difficulty about multiple identities. We are not locking our versions of the contemporary Other into the ancestor's actions. The character of the new place has to be specified as a space of non-exclusive participation and we must be willing to think about new forms and shapes of institutions.

The future has to be made an attractive one. It is not about accommodating old prejudices, it's a matter of accommodating present realities and future possibilities. We need to be able to live as sensate responsible people, recognising difference. We're not near that at the moment, for example, in relation to most of the gender politics. The discussion has been about moderate recognition of absolute rights or about moving from the minimal recognition of difference in many cases as a tolerance. My view is we have to get to a point where we see the richness and celebration of difference.

President Higgins said he wants to 'encourage the maximum openness of mind in relation to institutional change on the issue of unity'.

I'm simply saying the foundations have to be laid for a discussion that will be adequate and positive and that means that we also need to discuss institutional failures and successes, North and South. We haven't brought our co-operative efforts to where it matters, beyond the handshaking classes. The next stage is where you start into new forms of community exchanges that come from the ground up. The government has a responsibility to encourage patience and understanding. It's not a matter of making demands. I think there is a big difference between what is an aspiration and what is a demand.

We need to achieve a transcendence. This is what happens at a concert when people actually have a moment of transcendence, it happens in good writing. This is possible, by children and people of all ages, in any part of this island and they must be invited to do that. It's the quality of the invitation that matters.

The historic and current expression of unionist identity and culture can be protected, while nationalists in the North have a right to the full equality and parity of esteem promised by the GFA.

The issue isn't in reality the drums or the parades. It is the purpose, the motivation behind it. If it is so important culturally, why would you not do so in the more open spaces rather than go through areas where you have people who have actually struggled with the excesses and the exclusions of your previous regimes. There's a need for a new sophistication in all of this. Equally, I would invite nationalists to see the difference between seeking any mimic of how they were treated as a minority and the emancipatory challenge of how they must now treat a minority.

President Higgins said that he hopes the *Machnamh* series will address the question of institutional change in a way that can facilitate a discussion on 'the issues upon which we are united'.

I do have views on it. I want to encourage the maximum openness of mind in relation to institutional change and a discussion on the issues upon which we're united. We need to recover a form of utopian thinking. People think that utopian thinking is abstract. In fact, it is from the Greek word '*eu-topos*', which means a good or better place. We need to have courage and find that better place.

INDEX

abortion

  in the North 25, 229, 357, 358

  in the South 28, 29, 294, 332, 333, 369

Abortion Rights Campaign 358

Act of Union (1801) 204, 318, 319

Adams, Gerry 108, 136, 204–6, 208, 223, 257, 304

African National Congress (ANC) 293–4

Agri-food & Biosciences Institute (Afbi) 326

agriculture 14, 111, 116, 198

Ahern, Bertie 201, 210

Aiken, Steven 165, 230

Al-Qadri, Umar 226, 334–5

all-island economy 241, 243, 244, 248, 276–95

  climate change and 276–7

  Dublin–Belfast economic corridor 279–80

  education system 291–2

  electricity 277

  health service 291, 337, 339

  housing 279

  IF and 340

  legal system 339

  public transport system 277–9, 304

  trade unions 281–2, 294, 372

  transition period 293–4, 304

All-Island Strategic Rail Review 277–8

Alliance Party 96, 201, 290, 295, 353

  General Election (2019) 30, 73, 190

  NI Executive 31, 175

  NI Protocol vote 291

  travel restrictions, ETA and 351

  young voters and 361

Alliance4Choice 362

Allister, Jim

  DUP, departure from 320

  GFA, views on 202, 226, 320

  NI Protocol, views on 204, 318, 319–20, 324–5, 327–8

  perception of 100, 225, 325–6, 328

  TUV and 198, 232, 318

Amnesty International, Belfast 354

amnesty proposal, NI and 283–4, 373

Analysing and Researching Ireland North and South see ARINS project

Anglo-Irish Agreement (1985) 182, 220

Anglo-Irish Treaty (1922) 81, 103

anti-nuclear protests 271, 276

anti-protocol alliance 321

Aosdána 264

ARINS project 119, 122, 144, 186, 188, 240

Array Collective 357–8, 359, 361, 362

artists, universal basic income 362

Arts Council of Northern Ireland 265

Atlantic Philanthropies (AP) 76, 225

atrocities/killings

  British Army 152, 159, 284

  IRA bombings 97, 262, 273

  LVF and 140

  UVF and 17, 114, 140, 156